RECORDING

RECORDING
Guidelines for Social Workers

SUANNA J. WILSON

THE FREE PRESS
A Division of Macmillan, Inc.
NEW YORK

Maxwell Macmillan Canada
TORONTO

Maxwell Macmillan International
NEW YORK   OXFORD   SINGAPORE   SYDNEY

The Free Press
A Division of Macmillan, Inc.
866 Third Avenue, New York, N.Y. 10022

Maxwell Macmillan Canada, Inc.
1200 Eglinton Avenue East
Suite 200
Don Mills, Ontario M3C 3N1

Macmillan, Inc. is part of the Maxwell Communication
Group of Companies.

Printed in the United States of America

Hardcover printing number

  2 3 4 5 6 7 8 9 10

Paperback printing number

    13 14 15 16 17 18 19 20

Library of Congress Cataloging in Publication Data

Wilson, Suanna J.
   Recording, guidelines for social workers.

   Bibliography: p.
   1. Social case work reporting. I. Title.
HV43.W524 1980   361.3   79-7636
ISBN 0-02-935810-8
ISBN 0-02-935940-6

This book is dedicated to those students, field instructors, social work practitioners, and educators who share my frustration with abstract, vague, and highly intellectualized texts that don't explain how to go about doing the nitty-gritty tasks associated with social work practice.

CONTENTS

PREFACE

A much briefer, preliminary version of this book was available to students in field placement in my agency for several years. Its successful use led to the demand by students that I publish the material so they could purchase their own copies. With much trepidation I arranged to have 500 copies printed privately. The vast international success of that edition encouraged me to produce this greatly enlarged, updated, widely applicable version of what began as a field instruction aid for personal use.

In the initial version I invited readers to supply feedback on how the book could be improved. The resulting suggestions were carefully considered in preparing the current edition. The illustrative examples of diagnostic and process recording have been expanded greatly, since many readers felt they not only helped with recording but also taught them how to interview. Additional outlines for various kinds of summary recording have been provided. Chapter 14 was added in response to field instruction and classroom faculty who asked for self-instructional exercises that could be used to teach recording skills, especially to students who have not yet had their first client contact. There was much interest in the chapters on confidentiality of case records, and these have been expanded greatly to provide more detail and specific guidelines for maintaining confidentiality of various kinds of record material. The material on the purpose and use of recording has been expanded. Most sections have been completely rewritten. An entirely new chapter on specialized recording styles has been added in response to interest in problem-oriented recording, coded, statistical, and computerized recording, and goal-oriented approaches to recording. There have been some revisions to the Analytical Thinking Model, designed to simplify and clarify the various steps in the thinking process. Finally, the list of suggested readings has been overhauled and greatly expanded. Readings are organized by subject area and cover topics such as accountability, audit and peer review, casework/interviewing texts, computerized data, and so on. A special section of readings pertaining to minority concerns has been included, since this book does suggest the importance of a differential approach that takes cultural and ethnic factors into consideration. Classroom faculty who use the book as a primary text in practice skills courses will find the list of readings sufficient to provide up-to-date assignments related to recording and interviewing, ranging from beginning to more advanced concepts.

Finally, I have retained the informal, down-to-earth style of writing of the initial version, while making significant improvements in organization. A few minor changes have been made in punctuation and spelling in the examples of student recordings when felt necessary to avoid confusing the reader. Otherwise, recording examples, altered to preserve confidentiality, appear as written by the recorder.

Those seeking a theoretical text with numerous footnotes and abstract philosophical conceptualizations will be disappointed. Recording can be a dull topic if it is expounded in a dry, uninteresting textbook—and a text is of no value unless someone reads it. This book is written deliberately in an informal style—almost as I would talk. My goal is to capture the ambivalent reader's attention with Chapter 1 and hold his interest through the final page.

It is hoped that this book will prove a useful and relatively painless educational experience for all those concerned with delivery of social work services.

ACKNOWLEDGMENTS

This book would not have been possible without the encouragement and contributions of a number of students and field instructors. It was Pam Elfenbein and Eleanor Grossman, students placed at Jackson Memorial Hospital in Miami, Florida, for training during 1976–1977, whose insistence that this material be published so they could have copies forced me into producing the first, locally printed version. We never imagined that it would undergo three printings and develop into this revised, nationally published edition. Thus, without their initial encouragement and conviction that students needed this material, I would undoubtedly still be telling everyone about my intention to "publish something on recording some day...."

Field instructors, staff, and former students in several social work settings deserve special thanks for their willingness to allow examples of their work to be included. Linda Anderson, Claudia Antuña, Kathy Caldwell, Doug Campbell, Ruth McEwen Canipe, Margie Cento, Bunny Coltune, Karen Drozdowicz, Sandra Goldstein, Jennifer Howells, Susan Kingsbury, Brenda Ledlow, Sammi Maker, Nancy Regis, Islia Rosado, Karen Schmid, Natalie Snyder, Jackie Taylor, and John Walker are among those who contributed invaluable material.

Brian Brodeur of the Coral Gables Printing Service must be thanked for his encouragement, his interest and belief in the original version of the text, and his many helpful suggestions. Finally, the staff of The Free Press, especially my editors, Gladys Topkis and Bob Harrington, must be thanked for their cooperation and assistance in publishing a rather unorthodox text that has posed some complex and uncommon challenges to editorial staff, and those concerned with format and typesetting.

INTRODUCTION

One of the few things on which the majority of social work students and practitioners agree is their almost universal dislike for social work recording. Many people simply don't like to write. Others feel caught in a time-pressure vice ("I only have eight hours each day to give to my clients, and direct contact with people is more important than recording"), so recording goes to the bottom of the priority list. Others have inadequate practice skills, and this lack produces scanty or ineffectual recording. Some settings have rigid, unrealistic recording requirements that are excessively time consuming and not sufficiently goal-oriented to convince staff of the need for recording. Other agencies lack specific guidelines for staff and students. A few supervisors and field instructors use recording as the *sole* means of assessing their supervisees' performance and practice skills, creating an unpleasant game called, "I don't care if I learn how to do social work or not, but I'm sure going to learn how to write to please my supervisor!" All these factors contribute to negative or apathetic attitudes toward recording as a part of social work practice.

Social work recording need not be a negative experience; in fact, it can lead to better provision of services and be a tool for growth for both social worker and client. Social workers' attitudes toward recording *can* be changed from distaste to downright enthusiasm for the process. How does such a miracle occur? Through a better understanding of recording and how it can be used, a deeper appreciation of the importance of the process emerges. When *specific* techniques and guidelines are provided for the social worker to follow, he (or she) no longer needs to avoid recording because he doesn't know how to do it. The result is a willingness to learn, and it is up to the school/agency/supervisor to take it from there. As the student puts into practice what he has learned, he gains a sense of satisfaction from doing recording properly and effectively, and this reinforces the positive attitude. Soon he is trying to convert others to his wonderful new discovery.

Little has been written on social work recording since Gordon Hamilton's classic *Principles of Social Case Recording* in 1946,* except for short and necessarily superficial sections in basic skills textbooks and one or two brief texts with limited distribution. This book is designed primarily to teach students and beginning practitioners the basics of social work recording. Much of it is self-instructional. The section on diagnostic thinking presents an Analytical Thinking Model that will be of interest to the more advanced practitioner as well. It is hoped that the book will also be useful to supervisors, field instructors, and classroom faculty who are responsible for teaching principles of recording and basic skills of interviewing to their supervisees and students.

Many of the recording examples provided in this book contain actual supervisory comments, and several chapters (especially Chapter 5) offer specific suggestions for supervisors, including a checklist to aid in evaluating the quality of interviewing skills as reflected in student process recordings. Supervisors should review carefully the self-instructional exercises in Chapter 14. Agency staff often hesitate to have a beginning-level practitioner or student make entries in official case records when they know nothing about the individual's recording style or abilities. These exercises provide real-life situations for learners to respond to, even if they have not yet experienced direct client contact.† Some of these exercises involve the supervisor as well.

Administrators and program planners may want to use the material in this book to develop appropriate recording guidelines for their settings. Agency personnel with staff-development responsibilities will find that many of their BSW and MSW staff

---

*New York: Columbia University Press.
†The term "client" appears throughout the book. It is a depersonalizing term that I don't particularly like, but I have used it for lack of a better one.

can benefit from this material. Members of such disciplines as nursing, psychology, guidance counseling, and other "helping professions" who maintain records of any kind will find much of the material pertinent to their daily practice.

Finally, this book teaches basic interviewing skills. I had no intention of producing a text on interviewing. However, many readers of the locally printed version reported that they learned a great deal about interviewing through the examples of actual recordings done by students and practitioners included as an integral part of the book. Most students and staff have little opportunity to examine interviews and reports of other social workers beyond those encountered in the records of their own agency. The anxious student needs to see exactly what happens when an interview takes place and to recognize that other students facing their first interviews are also often scared out of their wits. By comparing their own work against the examples provided, students can identify rather quickly their areas of strength and limitation in interviewing skills. The checklist in Chapter 5 can be used to self-assess interviewing and recording skills, and has helped both instructors and students to look more objectively at their skills.

The process-recording examples, with their accompanying supervisory remarks, also help readers attach labels to the skills they may be using intuitively. Supervisory personnel who give the kind of feedback depicted in the examples will be teaching conscious awareness and differential use of basic interviewing/counseling skills as well as recording.*

The ideas in this text are drawn from the author's years of experience in staff development in public welfare and also in the medical social work setting. They are not presented as the *only* way to do social work recording and diagnostic thinking. Rather, they are concepts that I and many others have found useful. Most of the settings where social workers function have their own specific recording requirements as to frequency, style, and outlines to be used. The guidelines presented here are general and are intended to provide an effective background that will help practitioners and students to fulfill the specific recording requirements of their respective schools and agencies.

Most of the examples provided are actual recordings and appear exactly as presented by the student or practitioner, with identifying details omitted or disguised to preserve the confidentiality of both client and interviewer. A few examples were made up for the purposes of this book but are based on typical interview recordings.

Most readers will be quick to notice the seemingly heavy emphasis on process recording. I do recommend process recording *as a teaching tool* but *not* as a form of social work recording to be used in day-to-day practice. Tape recording, one-way mirrors, and videotaping can be much more dynamic ways of teaching students basic social work skills. Unfortunately, however, many settings do not have the necessary facilities or equipment, and others that have rarely use it. A creative approach to process recording seems a desirable alternative. However, success in using any of the techniques presented in this text will depend to some degree upon the knowledge, personality, and instructional approach of the supervisor/field instructor/educator. If these ideas are presented in a manner that provides an interesting challenge and encourages creativity, even the least motivated student will respond with some degree of eagerness.

Many of the examples throughout this book are drawn from the medical setting, since this has been my primary area of practice. Rather than solicit material from friends, administrators, and educators in a variety of other settings, I concluded that a more dynamic and down-to-earth text would result if I used material with which I was personally familiar. However, I have tried to present the material in such a manner that it can be adapted readily to a variety of other social work settings as well as to classroom use.

---

*For a detailed text on techniques of field instruction, see Suanna J. Wilson, *Field Instruction: Techniques for Supervisors* (New York: Free Press, 1980). It provides additional examples of student recordings, with emphasis on techniques for supervisory assessment and feedback. It also contains numerous self-instructional and group discussion exercises for field instructors.

WHAT WOULD IT BE LIKE TO HAVE NO RECORDS?

"I have only eight working hours in a day and the most important thing is seeing clients and their families. I can't afford to waste valuable time writing about what I do—the main thing is that the job gets done." Such was the harried comment of a busy social worker. Ah, Utopia. No records. No paperwork. No supervisors getting after you because you're behind in your recording. All those extra hours that can be spent seeing clients. Let's join the Utopia Hospital's Medical Social Service Department and experience the absence of records.

8–9 A.M. Thirty workers, three supervisors, and one director straggle into the office, followed by one secretary and fifteen social work students. The phone rings. A nurse on East Wing 18 wants to know if the social worker has seen Frank Appleman yet. Since there are no master card files, the secretary calls out, "Who here is working with Frank Appleman?"

Meanwhile, social worker Sally Smith is sitting in her office trying desperately to remember what she was trying to do with the Mary Brown case. She saw Mrs. Brown last week and they had a rather intense discussion, and she's sure there was something she was supposed to follow up this week. Half an hour goes by and she still can't remember.

In strides an important-looking man with a large briefcase who has a paper to give to one of the supervisors. It's a court subpoena. One of the students made an offensive remark to a patient and the patient is suing and holding the supervisor responsible. As the supervisor heads for the director's office for a hasty consultation, she is heard muttering, "But I didn't even know about the incident—how can I be held responsible—I can't know what my student does all the time!"

The director tells the supervisor he can't see her until later because he has an important meeting with a group of doctors. In fact, they come in just as the distraught supervisor exits. What do the six M.D.'s and three head nurses want with the director? Well, it seems that the social worker assigned to their area has been "goofing off," at least as far as they can tell, because few patients are being seen. One doctor shoves across the desk a paper with the figure $192,816.42 written on it. "That," points out Dr. Englebert, "is what Medicare owes this hospital and refuses to pay because there is no social work recording in our charts." He goes on to explain that he has recommended to the hospital administrator that this amount be deducted from the Social Service Department's budget over the next three years to recoup the loss. Meeting adjourned.

In comes the secretary with the morning mail. What have we here? Copies of two letters addressed to the hospital director. They are from two important accrediting agencies. One explains, "Since your Social Service Department has failed to implement its own internal peer-review mechanism, we have set up the following system for you to follow." The other letter contains more cheery news. The Joint Commission on Accreditation is coming to the Social Service Department *tomorrow* and wants to see the following: "departmental procedure manual, minutes of all in-service training activities, departmental statistics for the past fiscal year, and a random sampling of fifty records that document social work involvement."

The director's phone rings. It is Supervisor Hennessy explaining that worker Jones called in sick today. "Do you by any chance know what he was doing with the Horace Williams case? It seems Williams is being discharged, and the doctor wants him placed in a nursing home today."

Meanwhile, Supervisor Young is having problems of her own. She recently hired a new MSW graduate to do counseling and is beginning to suspect that his skills aren't all that great. "How can I be sure about my assessment? How can I find out what areas I need to help him with? I wonder if he will agree with my observations?" Her thoughts are interrupted periodically as the secretary bellows: "Anyone here know anything about Mary Ratz on North Wing 8?" "Who was the last person to see Roberta Mugs?"

Worker High-volume struts into the office to announce that he's seen fifteen patients today—only two fewer than he had seen by this time yesterday. "Yessir, this department really gets things done when we don't have to record!" Everyone knows Mr. High-volume is pushing hard for a special merit increase next month.

At 4 P.M. the director receives a phone call. It is the hospital director's secretary announcing an emergency meeting. It seems that the Social Service Department's budget request for the coming fiscal year is being denied. In fact, the hospital can no longer justify maintaining the department at its present size. Thus, effective in two weeks, staff will be reduced to eight social workers, no more than half of whom shall be M.S.W's. The hospital director makes it quite clear that "We'll hire a couple of M.S.W.'s because the powers-that-be say we have to, but otherwise we're going to go with the B.A.-level person who can do the same job at a much reduced cost."

As the dejected director returns to his office, he is met by Worker Adams, who shoves a subpoena under his nose. It seems that she reported a case of suspected child abuse and there is going to be a hearing to ascertain whether the child should remain with the parents. The court is asking worker Adams to "come and bring with you all records which would substantiate the report of suspected child abuse and your recommendations re: placement of the child." Worker Adams is frantic. "What am I going to do? I just know the parents are beating that child!" The director's advice is brief and to the point: "Don't worry about it, Miss Adams—in two weeks neither of us will be here and it won't matter."*

*See Chapter 14, Exercise 8, for a self-instructional exercise based on the absence of records.

CHAPTER 2

THE PURPOSE OF SOCIAL WORK RECORDING

It would be nice if we could state the purpose of social work recording in one concise sentence. Unfortunately, it's a little more complex than that. Recording is not an isolated part of social work practice. Effective recording goes hand in hand with effective interviewing/casework—it is impossible and undesirable to discuss one without the other. Recording and accountability are also inseparable, and some are even advocating that the client himself record social work interviews as part of the treatment process and to facilitate the professional growth of the social worker.

There are various styles and types of recording, with many different purposes. For example, process recording ("I said, he said") sets down the exact details of an interchange and is used primarily in student teaching (see Chapters 5 and 6). Summary recording is an entirely different style of writing and is preferred for intake, transfer, closing, and other special aspects of official agency records (see Chapters 7 and 8). The diagnostic summary is a special analytical statement that assesses what is known about a client and sets forth a specific treatment plan (see Chapters 10 and 11). Problem-oriented recording is yet another specialized form of documentation used to delineate problems identified and treatment goals in interdisciplinary settings, and modern technology has now introduced coded and computerized recording (see Chapter 9).

Obviously, recording in social work practice has a purpose other than to create busy work for social workers and students. Let's examine a few of the reasons why recording of some kind must be a part of the effective delivery of social work services.

Documentation of social work activity   Case records provide an ongoing picture of the nature of social work involvement with a client, progress in achieving social work goals, and the eventual outcome of the interaction between social worker and client or agency. An agency needs to be able to turn to its case records and say, "This is what we do—these are the people we serve and the kind of services we provide." Such recorded entries can become very important if a setting or a staff member is ever faced with the argument, "If the thing didn't get recorded, then it never got done in the first place."

Continuity of service   When a consumer seeks something from a social work agency, he is actually being serviced by the entire setting—not just an individual worker. Thus if an individual staff member should be out sick, absent on vacation, or should resign unexpectedly, the agency must be able to pick up where he or she left off. This would be close to impossible without some kind of record. Ongoing staff also need to refer back to their own notes periodically to develop and follow through with planning for an individual client over a period of time. Cases may also be transferred from worker to worker or be opened and closed several times. The existence of a record of previous involvement can prevent duplication of effort, save time, and result in more appropriate and effective provision of social work services to an individual consumer.

Payment from third-party payers   Many social service programs are supported fully or in part by special grants or by reimbursement for services through an insurance carrier, such as Medicare or Blue Cross-Blue Shield. These payment sources will not part with funds unless they receive written documentation describing the nature of the social work services provided. They may even require a periodic audit to verify that the services for which they are being billed were actually provided. Thus an individual social worker's failure to record appropriately could cost the agency money through lost revenue from third-party payers.

Quality control   Many settings are implementing mechanisms for determining the quality and quantity of services being provided, often through some form of peer review. Records are selected at random, and a team of staff (and sometimes students) reviews them to see if certain criteria have been met. The reviewers must rely on the written records to present a picture of social work activity. As far as they are concerned, anything that is not recorded simply did not take place. The reviewers usually are aware that some highly effective social workers do poor recording that does not reflect the quality of their work, while others with a facility for writing may be able to conceal inadequate skills and services. But as the reviewers cannot guess which category a given worker fits, they must base their findings and recommendations on what is in the record.

The results of peer reviews are used to identify areas where staff need in-service training to upgrade their skills. Results may be shared with upper-level administrators for overall departmental or agency planning. Peer review is often performed to identify strengths and weaknesses in service delivery systems so that any difficulties can be corrected before a formal review by an outside authority or licensing body takes place. Some forms of peer review and audit are required by law, by third-party payers, or by licensing and regulatory bodies. Thus staff who record inadequately may be giving a misleading and inaccurate impression as to the actual delivery of services and in-service training needs of a setting, resulting in inappropriate or ineffective planning at the administrative level. The individual worker can also become resentful if, because of poor recording that doesn't reflect his skill level, someone requires that he undergo special training he really doesn't need.

Statistical reporting   Most agencies compile statistics on a regular basis to demonstrate the nature of the demands for their services, the types of service provided, and the results. Often these data are kept on special statistical reporting forms, separate from the case records. However, most settings periodically use actual case records as sources of data to justify the agency's activities, to seek or maintain funding, to substantiate the need for additional staff, or to do program planning.

Supervisory review   Review of case records is used by most supervisors as a means of keeping track of social work activity. Supervisors are often called upon, in a supervisee's absence, to service a client or to justify or explain the nature of social work involvement with a client. Record review is also a means of assessing the kind and quality of services being provided by an individual supervisee. This should not be the only means of appraising worker performance, but it can be helpful if used properly.

Supervisors consider a number of factors when they encounter poor recording: is the recording poor because the worker simply does not like to write or has difficulty doing so? Or is it unacceptable because his practice skills are inadequate, resulting in poor recording? Obviously, the latter problem is much more serious, and most supervisors would prefer to believe that their supervisee simply doesn't like to record. However, if the pattern persists, the supervisor will begin to look more deeply at the worker's actual skills in an attempt to analyze the problem. If a worker or student has received training in techniques of recording, has been provided with appropriate written guidelines for complying with agency expectations, and has been counseled repeatedly regarding the need to improve his recording, persistent deficiencies usually are an indication of more serious difficulties in job performance. On the other hand, good recording does not necessarily indicate quality work. Practitioners and students who write well may be able to conceal ineffective skills. Thus, most effective supervisors will not rely solely on recording to evaluate performance.

Organizing the worker's thoughts   Formal recording provides a means for the social worker to organize his thinking. Structured presentation of factual data and observations leads to more in-depth diagnostic assessment and treatment planning. Sloppy recording and disorganized thinking often go hand in hand, and frequently result in, or are an indication of, poor service delivery to clients.

Interdisciplinary communication   It is not unusual for social workers, physicians, psychologists, psychiatrists, and other members of multidisciplinary programs such as hospitals and mental health clinics to record in a single central record. Social work entries in these settings not only document activity but also communicate psychosocial-diagnostic information and recommendations for consideration by other professionals who are directly involved with the client in a team approach to treatment.

Part of an eligibility requirement Recording may be a requirement for obtaining services for the consumer. For example, in the public welfare setting, certain facts must be documented and various forms filled out before the agency can dispense funds or services. Inadequate or sloppy recording can deprive recipients of services to which they are entitled.

Teaching When properly used by supervisors and field instructors, recording can be a mechanism for mutual assessment of practice skills and the teaching of new or refined techniques.

Research Properly maintained records contain a wealth of information for the professional researcher seeking to gather and compare data regarding, for example, certain types of client groups, social work activities, or problems of emotional adjustment. When steps are taken to preserve the confidentiality of the data gathered, such research studies can provide valuable information to an agency wishing to study patterns of service delivery or, on a larger scale, to social work as a profession.

Agency defense in legal actions The existence of proper recording has come to the rescue of many workers and their agencies when they have been required to provide evidence in court to justify diagnostic labels, social work intervention, or recommendations. On the other hand, inappropriate recording can actually precipitate or complicate suits directed against the agency or its staff, or can make it more difficult for the setting to serve the best interests of the agency's clients. For example, a protective service setting may identify child abuse or neglect and petition the court for temporary custody of the children. The court will examine agency records for supporting documentation of observations, impressions, and incidents that would substantiate danger to the children and justify their removal from the home. Students as well as paid staff can become involved in both kinds of situations.*

A therapeutic tool Recording can be used as a therapeutic tool with the client. More and more agencies are sharing their records openly with consumers of social work services, either because of a federal mandate to do so (i.e., the Privacy Act of 1974), a desire to be more open with consumers, or increased pressure from regulatory bodies, including the National Association of Social Workers (NASW). This trend is affecting both the quality and the quantity of social work recording. Some practitioners are eliminating all recording for fear that the client might react adversely upon seeing his record. This is inappropriate and could result in problems similar to those presented in the fantasy in Chapter 1. Instead, social workers need to be more open in telling clients just what it is we do, how we do it, and what treatment process is involved. If we were more open in our relationships with the clients we serve, much of what we now record in secret would be known to the client, and there would be less need for concern about consumer reaction to recorded material. Recording could actually become a therapeutic device—something to be shared with the consumer at an appropriate time to help him respond to treatment. And what would be wrong with having the client participate in writing part of his record along with the social worker?†

The most effective means presently available for achieving these various objectives is through social work recording of some kind. There are specific techniques that can be used to make the process less burdensome and the results more effective. The rest of this text presents these ideas.

Finally, we must accept the idea that good recording is a basic part of good social

---

*See Chapter 13 for suggestions on how to avoid legal complications caused by improper recording.

†This was actually done in an experiment reported by Carolyn H. Warmsun et. al. in a presentation entitled "Client Record Sharing: A Solution to Problems of Confidentiality, Accountability and Protection of Client Rights," at the NASW Fifth Biennial Professional Symposium, San Diego, California, November 19–22, 1977. The results of the experiment were quite favorable to both client and therapist, and the agency continues to use the approach.

work practice—the two are inseparable. Agencies must insist on proper recording and must adjust caseloads so that persons who are seen receive quality services. It is better to see fewer clients and serve them completely than to see a larger number and skimp on recording and other activities that make the difference between quality and superficial social work. Unfortunately, many agencies are not yet willing to commit themselves to this stance.

NOTE TAKING DURING AND AFTER INTERVIEWS

"How will I ever be able to remember everything that takes place during my interviews, especially when I see more than one person per day?" This seems to be the concern of every student and beginning practitioner. Most recording techniques require some degree of recall. But even if a worker had total recall of what happened during his interaction with a client, not everything that can be remembered should be set down in a case record. Rather than try to remember and record *everything* that was said and observed, the experienced worker concentrates on recording only the most significant facts of the interaction—those that he plans to comment on or work with in some manner.*

There are some techniques for recalling interview content that many workers have found helpful:

1.   Keep note taking during interviews to the absolute minimum. It makes the worker lose eye contact with his client, thus breaking any rapport that may have developed. Consumers may also become uneasy about what the worker is writing down. The worker may concentrate so hard on note taking that he fails to pay attention to the meaning of what the individual is communicating, both verbally and nonverbally, as the interview takes place.

2.   Never take notes when an individual is talking about his feelings or discussing matters that are sensitive, emotionally laden, or difficult to express. Note taking will turn off such expression of feelings very quickly. Unfortunately, some workers who are unsure of their skills in dealing with emotional material subconsciously resort to note taking and other inappropriate techniques to cut off the presentation of feelings with which they feel insecure.

3.   It is a good idea to take notes when the client is supplying specific factual data that will be difficult to remember accurately without a reminder. Names of family members, addresses, dates of birth, exact amounts of income (if this is crucial to the interview), and similar data may be written down as told. Try to include the client in the note-taking process if at all possible, to reduce defensiveness and suspicion. A simple "Do you mind if I take a few notes? The facts you're giving me are very important and I want to be sure I get them right" can accomplish this. Most consumers will not object to note taking if they can see that it will help them obtain the best possible service. If the individual appears uneasy, share with him what is being written down or discontinue note taking altogether. If it comes to a choice between taking good notes so as to produce an accurate record and establishing good rapport with the client so as to provide effective service, the latter must take priority. Practitioners and students who dislike recording will be tempted to use this statement to argue, "See, I told you so—services are more important than recording. So I'll devote 100 percent of my time to seeing clients and zero time to recording." I hope that a reading of this book will reveal the fallacy of this view.

4.   Try to allow five or ten minutes between scheduled interviews so that you can jot down a few quick words or phrases regarding the most important facts and feelings the clients expressed and/or you picked up. Try to note things that would be most easily forgotten rather than major impressions, which will remain with you for several

---

*Chapter 13 discusses what should and should not be put into black and white, and should be reviewed for an idea of the kind of thing one needn't worry about remembering in detail.

days. It is amazing how much of an interview can be recalled from a review of such notes several days later.

Rough draft or outline notes taken immediately after an interview often are used for subsequent formal recording or dictation. When the formal recording is completed and/or the dictation is typed, all rough draft notes should be destroyed. They do not belong in the case record or on the worker's desk, creating risk of confidentiality violations.

There are times when clients simply walk in one after the other, without appointments, leaving the worker no chance to collect his thoughts between interviews. Even this situation can be controlled, however. It is fully acceptable to say, as client number four sticks his head in the doorway without knocking, "Would you care to have a seat outside—I'll be with you in just a minute," as a means of structuring a hectic day. When practitioners fail to do this, the result is frequently an impressive volume of persons served, but with poor to marginal quality. The worker who maintains this pace for very long usually goes home emotionally and physically drained, thus reducing his ability to respond to the needs of his clients in the days that follow.

When making home visits, you can easily allow time between interviews to take quick notes. However, don't do this while sitting in your car in front of the client's home after you have finished the interview. He may become quite anxious, wondering what you are doing out there. It is best to drive around the corner and park elsewhere. In inclement weather, many workers do their note taking over a cup of coffee in a diner or restaurant.

CHAPTER 4

THE MECHANICS OF RECORDING AND DICTATING

Once a worker determines what information to put into a social service record, he must decide the mechanical means of getting the data into black and white. There are various methods available, some of which are much more efficient than others.

HANDWRITING

While many agencies require that all or most of their social service records be typewritten, some do allow staff to make legible handwritten entries that are placed directly into the permanent file, or may be replaced later by a typed version. Progress-note entries in medical charts or interdisciplinary records are almost always handwritten. Many settings use standardized forms for recording certain data—face sheets, eligibility application forms, consents for release of information—and the data entered on them is usually handwritten. Referrals to other agencies and major summaries (i.e., intake, closing) are often typed, though some settings permit neatly handwritten versions.

Small social service departments with adequate clerical support often have handwritten copy transcribed by a secretary before it is placed in the formal case record. This assumes, of course, that the worker can present legible copy to type from. Unfortunately, secretaries and workers often disagree over what constitutes legibility and the result can be a typed report quite different from what the worker thought he had submitted. Thus, all typed material should be proofread before being placed in the permanent record.

"YOU-TYPE-IT"

This long-standing tradition should be abolished. The average person can write longhand legibly at a rate of perhaps forty to fifty words per minute. Unless the worker can type faster than he can write, he is wasting valuable time doing clerical work. Furthermore, most people talk at a rate of about one hundred twenty words per minute. Even if the worker is a speed typist, he would still be spending more time typing than he would take to talk into a dictaphone. Thus, in most instances, "you-type-it" is *not* an efficient way of recording. This also raises an interesting question: why do so many workers hide behind their typewriters, spending hours on clerical tasks, when they could be using recording methods that are so much faster? Some suggested reasons:

1. "We don't have enough clerical staff—I *have* to do my own typing." As long as social workers are willing to do clerical work, why should an employer spend additional money to hire sufficient secretarial support? The agency will argue that there's no need for these extra people. If social workers would stop doing unnecessary and inappropriate clerical tasks, the agency would be forced to find the positions and funding to hire more clerical staff.

2. "The secretaries are so slow and incompetent—it's faster to do it myself." This may be true if the worker is a rapid and accurate typist. But unless the worker can achieve a faster net rate, with neatness and accuracy, he cannot compete with the secretary in efficiency. Furthermore, the time he spends typing is time he might otherwise spend in direct client contact—something his secretary cannot do.

3. Social workers who insist on doing their own typing may be hiding behind this time-consuming clerical activity to avoid involvement with more appropriate social

work roles with which they feel uncomfortable. If they appear busy, perhaps the supervisor won't notice how they spend their time and will therefore not push them into more challenging roles. "Old-timers" who are having difficulty keeping pace with changing agency expectations may fall into this trap. Newly hired persons who find they lack skills to meet agency expectations in certain areas can become quite dependent on the typewriter. Students may have real difficulty parting with their typewriters as they struggle to move into a new professional role. When agency reorganization creates new positions or changes the duties of existing personnel, those having difficulty making the adjustment may spend an increased amount of time at the typewriter.

4.   The staff member or student who is having a love affair with his typewriter may simply not have enough to do. Perhaps he is in a setting where heavy work pressures alternate with slow periods and staff must "make work" to appear busy. The alert supervisor will investigate further if a student or worker is consistently typing. Often the employee or student with insufficient tasks to occupy his time will wait passively for the supervisor to discover the problem and come to his rescue.

A word or two must be said in defense of the rare social worker or student who really does type one hundred or more words per minute with high accuracy. There will be times when these individuals have rush jobs that they can type faster than the agency secretary, and almost as fast as they could dictate. A special report, a questionnaire, or a detailed bibliography may be something the secretary doesn't know how to do or that cannot be dictated. This kind of typing should be permitted, as long as it occurs infrequently. Consider also the speed typist with illegible handwriting. He may be typing instead of handwriting and doing his work faster than his colleague who writes legibly at perhaps forty to fifty words per minute. Thus for this individual typing would represent appropriate time spent in recording.

DICTATING EQUIPMENT

The most efficient way of getting recording into black and white, used in most social work settings, is for the worker to speak into a small machine that uses tape, belts, or discs to record the dictation. A secretary then uses a special machine to play back the recording and transcribes it as she listens. Her transcribing unit permits her to adjust the speed of the dictator's voice and stop and start as often as necessary, using a foot pedal. The transcriber may be located in the same office area as the social worker, or the agency may have a contract with an outside private steno pool for transcription. Some huge agencies use a telephone-type system where the dictator talks into a microphone that is actually a telephone receiver. The lines run to a central recorder located elsewhere in the building or even across town, where the material is taped and transcribed.

The normal speaking rate for most people is approximately 120–140 words per minute. Thus very lengthy material can be dictated in surprisingly short periods of time once the technique has been mastered.

A surprising number of social workers do not like to use a dictaphone. It can feel rather peculiar to go off into a corner and talk to yourself with only a machine for an audience. However, with a little practice the strangeness soon wears off. If necessary, *force* yourself to dictate for several hours before abandoning the process entirely.

Some persons just cannot use a dictaphone, and this must be recognized. Workers who must dictate in a language that is not their native tongue often have this problem and may need to work out alternate methods of recording. Unfortunately, persons who really *could* learn to dictate may use the same excuses as those who cannot, and sometimes it can be difficult for the supervisor to ascertain how genuine the problem really is.

Others who resist using the dictaphone may argue that they cannot think without writing out their thoughts first so they know exactly what they want to say. If agencies are too rigid in their requirement that everyone dictate, these people will write out their entire report, then read it into the dictaphone. This is double work and a waste of time for them.

Lack of privacy can be a problem in some settings, and a dictating area may need to be designated and a time schedule developed. However, too rigid a schedule can be incompatible with some working styles and should be avoided if at all possible, or at least be implemented flexibly.

A common problem in dictation is long-windedness. We become enamored with hearing our own voices and reading our words on paper. It's easier to be verbose when talking than when writing or typing, and inexperienced practitioners or students often resort to verbosity as the easy way out—"I'm not certain what's important to record, so I'll just record *everything* I know and hope I include what I'm supposed to." This does not require nearly as much skill as selective recording, which sorts out and excludes inappropriate, irrelevant, or excessively detailed material. Thus, students and relatively inexperienced helping persons can expect to redo some dictated entries, removing the unimportant items, before the technique is mastered.

There is a strong temptation to take dictation home. The dictaphone may be pocket-sized and the worker may think, why not? This practice is a mistake for several reasons. First, there is considerable risk of confidentiality violation; others may unintentionally overhear what the person is dictating. Second, there is an opportunity for damage to or theft of dictaphone equipment, for which reason some settings have rules forbidding taking the machines out of the office. Third, taking dictation home can conceal the need for adjustment in a worker's caseload. Why is it necessary for a person to do this work after hours? Suppose fifteen people in a large agency are taking work home on a regular basis. If they all ceased this activity, administration might discover that there is need for an additional position and workloads could be reduced for everyone. On the other hand, a practitioner may be having difficulty keeping up with tasks during normal working hours because of inefficient use of time or other factors. Supervisors will usually evaluate the reasons underlying a worker's consistent desire to take dictation home, and will try to come up with appropriate remedial action.

Some material should not be dictated because it is difficult to give verbal instructions on how it should be typed. Questionnaires with lines and boxes, material organized in columns, footnotes, bibliographies, detailed statistics, charts, tables, graphs, complex outlines, and similar material should be presented to the typist in written form and arranged in proper format. The average secretary does not know the proper style for footnotes and other specialized material—she will count on you to present it correctly or to teach her how to do it. Highly sensitive material (such as an unsatisfactory performance evaluation, a disciplinary action report, or extremely private or incriminating case record entries) should not be dictated, since the large number of people handling the tapes will make confidentiality extremely difficult to control.

There are some mechanics involved in using a dictaphone, varying with the make and type of machine. If a certain kind of machine is used uniformly throughout the agency, instructions for its use should be made a part of the procedure manual or orientation handbook for new staff and students.

The following suggestions are applicable to all types of dictating equipment. These suggestions should be adhered to if the dictator desires clear dictation that can be speedily and accurately transcribed by the typist:

1. Hold the microphone approximately two to three inches from your mouth. If you hold it too close muffled dictation will result. Avoid moving the dictating machine or microphone back and forth in front of your mouth as you are talking. This will cause your voice to fade in and out on the tape and make it difficult for the transcriber to understand you.

2. Always listen back after dictating the first few sentences to be certain the machine is functioning well.

3. Never chew gum or eat while dictating—the sound effects will be horrendous!

4. Organize your thoughts before you start dictating. You may wish to write out exactly what you want to say or perhaps have an outline or some rough notes prepared. Do not leave the machine in the "record" position while you are thinking of what to say next or looking up something. This causes long pauses on the tape that are annoying and time consuming for the transcriber.

5. If you need to make a correction or change after something has already been dictated:

a. On some types of equipment it is possible to go back to the exact spot you want to change and dictate over it, automatically erasing the previous recording. You will then need to redictate everything you said after the spot where you made the correction because, unless the correction takes the same length of time as the original, it will run over into subsequent material. Therefore, it is advisable to make corrections in this manner only if you need to go back just a few sentences. After gaining some skill with the dictaphone, you will find it possible to make some corrections using the same number of words as the phrase you want to change, or varying the rate of speech in order to squeeze something in.

b. If you discover that you need to change, add to, or delete something you dictated several paragraphs ago, do not inform the transcriber of this halfway through the tape. She would have to retype everything from the point where you want to make the change to the place where you gave her instructions about the correction. Attach a note to the belt explaining exactly where the correction is to go by quoting the sentence just before it and stating what change you want to make. This alerts the transcriber before she begins typing.

c. If you are using the type of equipment that cannot be erased once something has been dictated, you will need to use the techniques described in (b) for all corrections.

6. When you start dictating, always give the transcriber the following information:

a. Your name. If you are newly employed or just starting field placement, spell it the first few times and also give your appropriate title.

b. The date you want to appear on whatever it is you are dictating.

c. What it is you are dictating—a letter, a social service report, a memo, and so on.

d. The number of copies you need.

e. The client's name and identifying number (if the dictation is on a specific case).

f. The approximate length of what you will be dictating—is it several pages or just a few lines?

7. Whenever you give instructions to the transcriber, say "Transcriber" or "Stenographer" before you start to give the directions. This alerts her that you are about to say something that is not to be typed as part of the regular dictation.

8. Always tell the transcriber:

a. When you want a new paragraph.

b. When to make a heading, and the wording and relative importance of the heading. If you ask for a "major heading" it will usually come back typed in all capital letters, centered on the page, and perhaps underlined. A "subheading" will be typed on a separate line, starting at the left-hand margin, in capital and lower-case letters, and usually underlined.

c. If you want special single spacing, outline form, or anything different from the ordinary.

d. Unusual punctuation, such as parentheses, semicolons, or dashes. Some people dictate ordinary punctuation, such as periods and commas, as well. The transcriber listens to the rise and fall of your voice to tell where the end of a sentence is to come. If your voice tends to fall in the middle of sentences, the transcriber is apt to give you periods there, and you may thus need to dictate all punctuation.

e. When you have finished dictating a piece of work and are about to go on to the next item. Also tell her when you have finished dictating everything on the tape.

9. Spell out for the transcriber:

a. All proper nouns—anything that would have a capital letter. Even the most common names can be spelled in several different ways. For example, "Jean," "Gene," and "Jeanne" are all pronounced the same.

b. Unusual words that you think she might have difficulty understanding. For example, a word such as "educable" might come back as "educated" or "educator"; "eclectic" might be typed as "electric." If your setting uses a medical transcribing service, do *not* spell out medical terms. These transcribers have special training to handle these words, and it slows them up if the dictator spells them all out. If your transcriber is *not* part of a medical transcribing service, *always* spell out all medical terms.

10. Enunciate clearly. Avoid leaving off the ends of words. Many times it is difficult for the transcriber to tell if a word ends in an "s" or a "d."

11. Don't talk too rapidly; neither is it necessary to talk at an abnormally slow speed. Transcribing machines have special dials for regulating the speed at which the dictator's voice is played back.

12. When dictating letters, give the full name, title, address, and zip code of the person to whom you are writing.

13. When preparing a dictated cassette or belt to send to a steno pool, always attach a piece of paper indicating:

a. The case name.

b. Your name.

c. The date you are sending it to be typed.

d. What side of the tape or belt you have dictated on.

e. The approximate length of the dictation.

f. The name of your agency or department.

14. Keep copies of all original material until the dictation has been returned from the typist.

15. Always proofread what comes back from the transcriber. There might be creative errors that change the entire meaning of what you intended to say, or annoying typographical mistakes. If such errors occur repeatedly, have the appropriate person in your setting call them to the attention of the steno pool so that they will pay more attention to accuracy in the future—or else inform you that something about your dictating style is making it difficult for them to transcribe the material accurately. Typing full of corrections and blank spaces indicates that the transcriber had difficulty understanding the dictation. Listen to your own recording, review these suggestions, and consult an agency secretary for further guidance.

16. Make certain your tape is erased before it is reused. Some offices merely dump the returned tapes in a box; when someone needs one to dictate something, he just dictates over top of the previous material, thus erasing it. This practice can lead to confidentiality violations, especially if the previous material is something not everyone should have access to, such as a performance evaluation.

TAPE RECORDER

Tape recordings are rarely used to document social work activity or to form a permanent part of a case record. They are used primarily in teaching, to help students and staff improve their skills. The content of a taped interview might be summarized, transcribed, and placed in a record along with an analysis of the interaction. However, the tape itself should be erased as soon as its purpose has been served.

Tape recordings can be used in a number of creative ways in student education and in-service training. Obviously, interviews can be taped and reviewed by a supervisor. However, the worker might be asked first to critique his own interview; then supervisor and worker can compare notes. The tape can be played back during supervisory conference and stopped at various points for discussion and perhaps role play of alternate techniques that might have been used. The learner could be asked to identify instances when reflection, interpretation, and other basic techniques were used, or to identify certain behavior on the part of the client. A student might process record (see Chapter 5) the same interview he has just taped, and later compare the two recordings (an effective way of demonstrating selective recall and eliciting discussion as to why certain things were remembered and others were not).

The worker or student should be allowed to chose which interviews he will tape. Perhaps he could be asked to record several, and then to pick one or two to share with the supervisor.

The tape itself can be used as a therapeutic tool with the client. Consumer and worker could each listen independently and then compare their thoughts and observations about the interview. The worker could go back to certain portions to ask, "How did you feel when I said that?" or "What were you thinking when you said that?" The client might even take the recorder with him to voice his feelings and thoughts between therapy sessions. One mental health worker serving psychotic clients who alternated between lucid and overtly psychotic episodes used the tape recorder in a unique way: the patient dictated to himself, while he was rational, messages that he could go back and listen to during psychotic episodes.*

Taped interviews can be saved and listened to months later by worker or client to observe growth and changes with time and therapy. Students especially might want to keep their very first recorded interview to compare with a final one toward the end of their field placement. All such material should be stored under lock and key in a secure location to prevent confidentiality violations.

Many things can be taped that would be hard to record using other methods. Staff meetings, in-service training sessions, agency board and committee meetings, as well as group therapy sessions, can be taped for later self-assessment or critique. A highly secure worker and supervisor might tape a supervisory session (with both in full agreement) to study effectiveness of communication and other aspects of the conference. Students or new employees might carry a tape recorder around for the first few days to record reactions to their new experience, along with observations and suggestions. This could prove helpful not only to the individual but also to the agency as it plans its orientation and in-service training programs.

Many staff and students resist using the tape recorder because "taping makes me nervous and I can't be natural in the interview." Yes, it may make you anxious the first time you use it, but once the machine is going, both worker and client usually

*Suggested by Diane Lindner.

forget it's even there and the effect on the interview becomes negligible. There are however, some real problems in taping that cannot be ignored.

If a taped interview is an hour long, it will take someone an hour to listen to the tape. It is very difficult to skim taped material as effectively as one can a written record. Not all kinds of interview situations can be effectively taped, and taping is inappropriate with some clients. For example, in play therapy with very young children or in sessions with nonverbal adults, there may be long periods of silence or nonverbal communication. Some clients become uneasy, anxious, or suspicious when they are being taped. Some workers simply cannot operate any kind of machinery, even one as simple as a tape recorder. Taping may involve problems of confidentiality violation, and very strict measures must be followed to preserve confidentiality for both the client and the interviewer. Taping can be threatening to a beginning student or a practitioner who is insecure about his skills, or who feels intimidated by authority figures in relation to performance assessment. Certain techniques must be learned for introducing the client to the idea of having his interview taped. Finally, if a student tapes all or most of his interviews, he may not develop skills of recalling interview content and process, since he depends on the ever-present tape recorder to remember for him.

Fortunately, most of these limitations can be overcome. The following basic guidelines should be observed:

1.   Be prepared to recognize and deal with your own feelings about taping. Anxiety, resistence, or ambivalence should be expressed and discussed with whomever is requesting the taping (i.e., a supervisor). Self-awareness in this area, as in any other area of social work practice, is important.

2.   Always ask the client for permission to tape the interview. Be prepared to explain exactly why you want to tape it, who will hear the tape, and what you plan to do with it. Include this information on the consent form that the client signs.

3.   Never tape an interview with a suspicious or paranoid individual. If this characteristic is known in advance, don't even ask permission to tape—just don't do it. Taping will only increase the suspicious client's anxiety, cause him to become resistant in the interview, and heighten his distrust of you. If a client should become uneasy over the presence of the tape recorder midway through an interview, and express concern over your motives for taping, stop the tape immediately. It might be appropriate to explore the client's feelings and reactions, but shut the machine off first and make certain he sees you do so.

4.   Many persons who have never taped interviews before fear that the client will object. In reality, most do not object to taping. You might explain that you are a student and that taping the interview and going over it afterward with your supervisor will help you learn and be of better service to the client. It will also give the client the benefit of the thinking of your supervisor and perhaps of other professionals with more experience than you have. Further, if you do not need to be concerned with taking written notes you can devote your full attention to the interview itself. The client might be advised that the tape will be available for him to listen to as well, and that you and he can use it in your therapeutic relationship.

5.   The taping might be introduced somewhat experimentally. Tell the client, "We'll try it for five or ten minutes, and if it bothers you, we'll shut it off." Most will agree, and chances are that after a few minutes both you and your client will have forgotten all about the tape recorder.

6.   Always have the machine clearly visible. Never attempt to hide it or the microphone. Place it in plain view on the table, arm of the chair, or floor. It should be close enough for you to reach the controls without having to get up and disrupt the interview. Purchase tapes that will last the length of your interview without having to be changed. This is very important, for the action of stopping the machine and

turning over a cassette halfway through an interview can be extremely distracting and can disrupt rapport between you and your client.

7.   Study the mechanics of the machine *before* you attempt to tape an interview, and become so familiar with it that you can operate it more or less automatically. There should be no fumbling. Always check it on both "record" and "playback" just before the interview to make certain it is working properly.

8.   If the tape is to be used in a classroom or heard by anyone outside the agency, the client's written permission must be obtained. Notice that taping requires both permission to tape the interview and permission to let others hear it.

9.   Store the tape in a secure place where unauthorized persons will not listen to it, and see that it is erased when it is no longer needed. Just as in dictaphone recording, cassette tapes automatically erase when someone records over old material. However, do not recycle a tape back into the pool of those available to be reused by someone else unless it has first been completely erased. Otherwise, the person who tapes new material may hear your interview in the process. Never store tapes in a case record—keep them separate. If a client should reveal incriminating or highly sensitive material during a taped interview, you may want to ask him immediately afterward if he would like that portion erased. If he does, make the erasure in his presence. You may decide later to erase more material that you feel could be harmful to your client if the tape were to be subpoenaed or become involved in any legal action. Tapes are considered a form of record and if the regular case record is subpoenaed, you could be required to produce your tapes as well.

VIDEOTAPING

This is one of the newest methods of recording social work activity. It is often done in a studio where special lights can be set up and camera and sound equipment used to record both verbal and nonverbal communications. However, relatively inexpensive cameras are now available that record picture and sound simultaneously under normal lighting conditions. Many of these cameras can be handheld and used wherever the interview is taking place. The result is then played back on a regular TV set. Tapes can be made in both black and white and color. Those made in a studio are usually of a better technical quality.

Many of the comments pertaining to tape recordings also apply to videotaping. It is used almost exclusively for teaching rather than for documentation of social work activity. It has proved an effective aid in achieving therapeutic goals with clients. Videotaping is obviously much more comprehensive (and can thus be more threatening) than tape recording, since both sound and picture are recorded. However, the camera operator needs to be oriented on what to look for in a social work interview. Most videotapes do not show all parts of both persons participating in an interview. The focus may jump from one face to another, or from nervous hands to tapping feet. Because well-done videotapes are so revealing, maintaining confidentiality is essential, but can be more difficult than with other methods of recording, especially because videotaping requires the presence of a third person—the cameraman. Even in an informal setting (as opposed to a recording studio) his presence may make the client uneasy and affect the interview. The photographer must also be reminded of the confidential nature of what he is filming and advised of proper procedures for preserving the client's privacy.

COMPUTERIZATION

This method of recording is used primarily to store and analyze data for statistical and reference purposes. Complete social work recordings are rarely entered into a computer, though facts and identifying data may be recorded. Unfortunately, abuses in the storage, handling, and use of computerized data have resulted in confidentiality violations, and challenges by social workers and members of related disciplines to the necessity for entering data into computers.*

MICROFILM

Many settings that generate large volumes of records that are inactive but must be retained resort to microfilming as a convenient and permanent storage method. Through a photographic process, entire pages of records are recorded so that a file of several hundred pages can be reduced to only a few inches of tiny film. The microfilm is then viewed on a machine somewhat similar in principle to a slide projector.

*See Suanna J. Wilson, *Confidentiality in Social Work: Issues and Principles* (New York: Free Press, 1978), for more details on the specialized problems of preserving confidentiality of computerized data. Several social workers have even lost their jobs because they refused to feed data into agency-maintained computerized systems that, in their opinion, failed to provide adequate privacy protection for their clients. See also pp. 00 in this text.

CHAPTER 5

PROCESS RECORDING: A TOOL FOR STUDENT EDUCATION

Process (narrative) recording is a specialized and highly detailed form of recording. Everything that takes place in an interview is recorded using an "I said then he said" style. In effect, the social worker writes down everything that would have been heard or observed had a tape recorder and camera been monitoring the interview. Most process recording uses direct quotes:

```
W (worker): How are you?
C (client): I'm fine, how are you?
```

Comments about client behavior or feelings experienced by the social worker are recorded in a separate column, using a self-expressive style—"I felt annoyed because . . ."—or a more summary style—"Mrs. Jones looked like she wasn't feeling very well." There is also a kind of process recording that paraphrases and summarizes what was said rather than record it exactly as it took place: "I asked Mrs. Jones how she was feeling and she said she was fine." The use of direct quotes is preferable.

Process recording used to be the accepted mode for daily social work practice. In the early 1900s there was a feeling that "social investigations" had to be thorough, and the client was often viewed as the least trustworthy source of information. It was considered important to verify and double-check almost everything, and completely detailed records were essential to this process.

The picture has changed dramatically today. Clients are regarded as persons with needs, feelings, and certain basic rights. Consumers of social work services must be treated with dignity and respect, and their views and feelings are solicited and listened to. Recording has changed along with the philosophy of social work practice. It is briefer and more goal-oriented. Unfortunately, the pendulum has swung to an extreme position. Whereas process recording was once used almost exclusively, it is now looked down upon. This is a mistake. Process recording is a very valuable tool for enhancing student learning *if it is properly used*. Abuse of it, combined with present-day distrust of the old philosophy of social work practice, has created a real aversion to process recording.

One might ask why so much space in this text is devoted to a discussion of process recording when there are so many better and more modern ways of teaching. The answer is simple: reality. We all know that tape recording, videotaping, and other techniques can be used creatively, dynamically, and effectively in student teaching. But how many settings actually have this equipment, and how many have tape recorders stored in the dark recesses of some back cupboard and don't even use the technology available to them? In reality, process recording ends up being the only practical method that even comes close to direct observation of what takes place in student interviews. Thus it might as well be used as creatively and dynamically as possible, but with full awareness of its limitations and the cautions that must be observed.

INFORMATION THAT SHOULD GO INTO PROCESS RECORDINGS

Well-done process recordings usually contain the following elements:

1. Identifying information: The name of the worker or student, the date of the interview, and the client's name and/or identifying number. It may be helpful to state the number of the interview (i.e., "fourth contact with Mrs. Smith").

2. A word-for-word description of what happened, as well as the student can re-member. For example:

I told Mr. Garcia, "In order to find out what kind of work you might be able to do, you will be seen by the psychiatrist as well as the physician."
Mr. Garcia said, "Psychiatrist? What do you mean?"

This student has chosen to spell out "I told Mr. Garcia" and "Mr. Garcia said." An abbreviated style is preferred, using "W" for "worker" and "C" for "client." Quotation marks are not necessary.

W: In order to find out what kind of work you might be able to do, you will be seen by the psychiatrist as well as the physician.
C: Psychiatrist? What do you mean?

3. A description of any action or nonverbal activity that occurred. For example:

I invited Mr. Garcia into my office and asked him to sit down. He did so slowly and just sat there staring at the floor.
W: How are you feeling today Mr. Garcia?
It took him a long time to answer but he finally raised his head and looked at me and said,
C: I feel terrible.
Before I had time to say or do anything he rose up out of his chair, started pacing around the room and was shouting that there was nothing wrong with him mentally and that he "didn't need to see no psychiatrist."

4. The student's feelings and reactions to the client and to the interview as it takes place. This requires that the recorder put into writing his unspoken thoughts and reactions as the interview is going on. In the interview with Mr. Garcia, for example, the next few sentences might read:

At this point I began to feel a little uneasy. Mr. Garcia seemed to be getting awfully upset and I didn't know why. I was a little frightened and wondered what he would do next and I didn't know what to say.

5. The social worker's observations and analytical thoughts regarding what has been happening during the interview. Most experienced interviewers think to themselves constantly during an interview—"What should I do next? I wonder how it would affect the client if I said such-and-such? Why is he acting this way? I wonder what he really meant by that statement? That seems to contradict what he told me earlier. He said he felt happy but he certainly didn't look it." In process recording, all these silent thoughts are put into writing. If the example of the contact with Mr. Garcia were continued, the next few lines might read as follows:

I was a little puzzled and wondered what to do next. I didn't know whether I should let him shout and get it out of his system or whether I should try and calm him down. I was curious why he was getting so upset but I didn't dare ask him any questions because I was afraid of getting him even more upset. I finally decided I had better show some empathy since he would probably argue and disagree with most anything I said anyway about the psychiatrist.
W: I can see that something about the idea of going to a psychiatrist is very upsetting to you.
C: (turning and looking straight at me): You bet it is. I've been to those headshrinkers before and I've had it with them.
As soon as Mr. Garcia said that a lot of questions came to my mind about his past history and I knew he had opened the door for me to talk with him about this.

Another example of the worker's analysis and observations during the process record-ing might be as follows:

I asked Mrs. Jones if she had any income other than what she gets from our financial assistance program. She said not. She seemed very nervous though as she told me this. She was sitting very uncomfortably on the edge of her chair; she had a scarf in her hands that she kept winding around her fingers and she couldn't seem to sit still. She seemed so nervous that it made me wonder if she was telling me the truth or not. I asked her again, "Are you sure you don't have any other income?"

6. A "Diagnostic Summary" or paragraph on the "Worker's Impressions" at the end of the process recording. Here the worker should summarize his analytical thinking about the entire interview he has just recorded.

7. "Social Service Plan," "Casework Plan," or "Treatment Plan" immediately following the diagnostic summary statement. It indicates the worker's and client's goals for further social service contacts.

MAKING A PROCESS RECORDING

The most efficient way for the student to write down his process recording is to use legal-sized paper, dividing each page lengthwise into three equal columns.* The page would look something like this:

SUPERVISORY COMMENTS	CONTENT-DIALOGUE	GUT-LEVEL FEELINGS
In this column the supervisor can make remarks right opposite the interaction or gut-level feelings that have been recorded.	Record word for word what happened during the interview, including both verbal and nonverbal communication. Be certain to include third-person participants, interruptions, and other occurrences that were not part of the planned interview.	Right opposite the dialogue, record how you were feeling as the activity or verbal interchange was taking place. Do not use this column to analyze the client's reactions—use it to identify and look at your feelings. Be as open and honest as you can and don't worry about having to use any special professional language—tell it as you feel it.

Some students either have difficulty understanding the purpose of the "gut-level feelings" column or feel so uncomfortable putting their own feelings in writing that they use this third column to comment on the *client's* feelings and reactions (see Chapter 6, Example 3). It is often helpful in this instance to use a *four*-column method, with the fourth column headed "analysis." This forces the recorder to differentiate between his feelings and his analysis, and also encourages his budding diagnostic thinking skills. (See Chapter 6, Example 4, for an illustration of process recording using the four-column method.)

Purposes of Process Recording

Process recording is not practical or desirable as a method of social work recording for daily practice, but it is an effective way of helping students learn interviewing skills. Students must have experience with other types of recording as well—writing summaries, special histories, and diagnostic statements. Otherwise they will graduate with unrealistic, unworkable concepts about social work recording and will be unable to meet the recording expectations of the agencies that hire them.

*The exact titles for the headings of these three columns may vary somewhat or be abbreviated. This is acceptable, as long as each column is used in the manner described here.

Process recording is often used to help supervisors determine how their students are functioning and to identify areas where effective techniques are being utilized as well as areas where guidance is needed. It is especially important for field instructors to determine the student's capabilities in order to develop an educational training plan that will give him the experiences he needs to acquire the desired skills. Similarly, process recording can be used as an evaluative tool for staff. Supervisors may ask newly hired staff to process record a few interviews so that they can get an idea of how the worker operates. While process recording is not so complete or accurate as tape recording or videotaping as a method for achieving direct observation, it is a useful tool that produces less anxiety in the student, since it provides him with greater control over what aspects of verbal and nonverbal communication will be revealed to the supervisor. That process recording allows for some selectivity is not usually seen as a positive factor, but it often works that way for the student. It is not always desirable or necessary for supervisors and field instructors to know everything that takes place in the student's interviews, and the selective factor in process recording can work to their benefit as well.

Detailed recordings can prove threatening for a supervisor. Beginning students will inevitably make mistakes. Few will do outright harm to their clients (consumers are quite tough!), but the interaction between beginning practitioner and client can be expected to be awkward at times. The supervisor can become overwhelmed if *everything* in a beginning student's first interview seems wrong, and and he doesn't know where to begin to teach him.

Process recording provides added security for both the agency and the new worker or student. If the person process records in appropriate detail exactly what has taken place during interviews, the agency is kept informed of his activities. This makes it relatively easy for the supervisor to give appropriate guidance and prevent serious mishandling of cases. It also permits the supervisor to intervene in situations the novice might be unable to handle.

Students often express some anxiety over the possibility that they may harm a client. Through ignorance, it is possible for a student to react inappropriately, assume an improper role, commit himself unwisely to something, or fail to pick up the real meaning of what is happening. But if a supervisor is keeping close track of the student's activities and there is reasonably good communication between student and field instructor, major mishaps can be avoided. Very rarely do students maliciously attack their clients.* Supervisory and field instruction approaches that rely solely on the student's telling the supervisor where guidance is needed are usually ineffective. Some students provide only selective feedback.† More often, learners provide open, honest recordings, knowing that they may elicit a critical response from the supervisor. However, many students sincerely say that they see no problem areas in an interview because they do not yet have enough knowledge of human behavior and treatment skills to be aware that something needs attention desperately.

In process recording, students are asked to write down everything they can remember, as opposed to summary recording (Chapters 7–11), where only the highlights are noted. This means that if a student considers something unimportant, he may not include it in his summary, and the field instructor could be totally unaware of a key dynamic that might affect the entire case situation. If the student is required to write down *everything* he can remember about what took place, he will usually come back with enough to give the supervisor a fairly complete picture.

Example 1 in Chapter 6 illustrates this point rather dramatically. The client was a suspected drug user and the student aggressively pursued this possible presenting problem. At one point he wrote down a statement that indicates the possible existence of a disturbed mother-son relationship. It would be obvious to the experienced

*See Chapter 6, Example 19, for an ineffective but harmless interview by a beginning student, as opposed to Example 20, where the student actually harms his client.

†See Suanna J. Wilson, *Field Instruction: Techniques for Supervisors* (New York: Free Press, 1980), for a detailed discussion of techniques field instructors can use to assess student work. Many additional examples of student process recordings, both with and without supervisory comments, are also provided.

reader that this must be affecting the client deeply in many areas of his life. However, the student failed to pick up the significance of the client's statement. When this was discussed with him, he stated that he included it because in process recording he knew he was required to write down everything, but admitted that if he had been using the summary style he would probably not have considered the patient's statement significant enough to report to his supervisor. This is understandable and "normal" for a beginning student who has had little formal training in the psychodynamics of human behavior. However, the use of process recording enabled the supervisor to provide much-needed direction and a rich learning experience for the student. In this instance, part of the learning revolved around recognition of the student's professional limitations, which required that the case be transferred to an MSW-level individual who could assess and deal with the underlying psychodynamics.

Process reading, if done using the three-column method suggested here, can increase the student's self-awareness and help him differentiate among factual data (what actually took place in the interview), his own gut-level reactions to what was occurring, and an objective analysis of what took place. The act of putting personal feelings into writing is an important step toward achieving self-awareness in the new role of professional helping person, and enables the student to talk more freely about his own feelings and how they can affect service delivery. On a more advanced conceptual level, the process can be invaluable in the identification and examination of transference and countertransference (see Chapter 6, Example 17).

Process recording is used by experienced practitioners in special situations. Occasionally something so unusual will take place that the worker does not want to try to summarize it and apply diagnostic labels. Instead, he may prefer to describe the situation as it occurred and let the reader draw his own conclusions. On the other hand, the worker making a complex diagnostic assessment may include brief excerpts of process recording to illustrate interactions and behaviors that support the analyses. In many settings supervision or consultation is offered to advanced practitioners on an as-needed basis. If the worker is facing or has had an unusually difficult interview, he may process record it deliberately to solicit feedback from peers or supervisory staff. In effect he is using them as a sounding board to test his own reactions and assessments of what took place in the interview. Tape recording is also used for this purpose and is usually preferred by the advanced practitioner.

Students sometimes compare their process recordings in a kind of informal peer consultation. This can be helpful, but it also has a major pitfall. If the student who is acting as the "consultant" also has limited experience and/or training, the consultation can easily become a sharing of ignorance.

There are a few settings (e.g., programs granting financial assistance) where it is important to document in detail who said what, how, and exactly what took place. In a fraud or protective services investigation, for example, the client's exact words in response to certain key questions could be very important. Staff and students functioning in settings that require this modified version of process recording usually receive special instructions.

Process recordings do not become part of the permanent case record but remain the property of the agency. They should be collected by the field instructor when their purpose has been accomplished. It is often advisable for the field instructor to save the first few recordings done by the student at the beginning of field placement and then let him compare them with his work at the end of placement. This can present an effective, and sometimes startling, picture of the student's growth.*

Specialized Uses of Process Recording

Process recording is traditionally used for one-to-one client interviews. However, it can be applied in a variety of other situations as well.

Contacts with members of other disciplines can be process recorded. The student

*See Chapter 6, Examples 7 and 8, for examples of "before" and "after" recording.

having his first discussion with a physician or psychiatrist may find it helpful to process record the encounter (see Chapter 6, Example 24).

The student studying group work can process record group sessions or segments of these meetings. Since such recordings will contain a high percentage of inaccuracies and omissions because of the sheer volume and intensity of group interactions, tape recording is the preferred method. However, if the equipment is not available or if the recording process would interfere with group interactions, process recording can be used instead (see Chapter 6, Examples 21 and 22).

If a student is attending or leading committee meetings or participating in other community organization, administrative, or in-service training sessions, these can be process recorded. The format would be similar to that of a therapeutic group meeting (see Chapter 6, Example 23).

A student may be supervising someone as part of his field placement experience. It is possible to process record the conference between student supervisor and his supervisee. However, this can be anxiety provoking for the student and should be introduced only after he has had several conferences with his supervisee and is beginning to feel comfortable with the process. If process recording is required prematurely, the student can become so preoccupied with it that he will have difficulty relating effectively and naturally with his supervisee. The student must participate in determining his own readiness to process record a supervisory conference. In any case, such conferences should not be process recorded on a regular basis. See Chapter 6, Example 25, for a segment of one such conference.

The very secure student and equally secure field instructor may want to experiment with making separate process recordings of (or even taping) one of their supervisory conferences. Students often think they have succeeded in communicating a desire, a feeling, or a reaction to their field instructor only to find later that they didn't get through. Field instructors may expound at length to a student who sits quietly, appearing to be receptive, but the realities of how differently the same communications are perceived can be surprising. Such use of process recording can help to identify and deal with communication difficulties between field instructor and student. However, the technique should not be abused. If it is required by the field instructor rather than done with the student's full (and not just passive) cooperation, the student will feel threatened and cease all open communication. Furthermore, he may become increasingly defensive and resistant to both process recording and supervision in all areas of his learning. In other words, process recording (and other methods that directly observe student-client interactions) cannot be foisted upon the student as a punitive evaluation device.

The student might also ask his client to make his own process recording of an interview they have just completed, and compare the student's process recording with the client's to note differences in their perceptions of what took place, things remembered, and events that were not mentioned. These could be highly significant and of direct therapeutic benefit if discussed openly by worker and client. The client's "gut-level feelings" in response to the worker's comments could also prove surprising and educational for the worker.

STUDENT AND SUPERVISOR RESPONSIBILITIES IN USE OF PROCESS RECORDING

Process recording can be, as we have tried to demonstrate, a creative and effective teaching technique. However, it does have some real limitations that must be recognized and certain reality factors accepted by both student and supervisor. If students do process recording but do not get meaningful feedback from their field instructor, the purpose is negated. On the other hand, students who are not open and honest in their process recordings are only cheating themselves of the guidance they might otherwise receive. Some guidelines for use are spelled out here so that both students and supervisors can be aware of their responsibilities.

Both students and field instructors must recognize that no one can be expected to have total recall of all verbal and nonverbal communications that take place in an interview. Thus, at best, process recordings will be selective and incomplete. The degree of completeness and accuracy will vary from student to student and from interview to interview. Some students become so intent on producing a good recording that their interview suffers as they think to themselves, "Now how am I going to record this?" as the client is talking. Thus the supervisor may want to remind the student that the interview is of primary importance and that he should concentrate on it while it is taking place, and worry about remembering and recording it after it has ended.

Students need to be as honest as possible in recording what happened. It is tempting to polish up the written record, leave out awkward statements, and change the wording just a little so it sounds better. Often the act of writing down the interview makes the student realize that something could have been handled more effectively. He may feel so guilty that he wishes he didn't have to listen to the supervisory feedback. The experienced field instructor is aware that most students cannot be expected to be totally honest in their process recordings, which at best represent a relative degree of honesty. A student who alters his recordings consistently may graduate with deficits in major skill areas because he never risked himself enough to let them be identified and dealt with. When such an individual seeks employment and is expected to perform at a level consistent with his educational degree, some serious problems could result.

It has been demonstrated that if five different social workers observe the same interview, five different process recordings will be produced. Perceptions and memory vary from one person to another. It is a fascinating experiment to set up a role-playing situation, have several different social workers observe and process record it, and then compare the results. The full impact of the benefits and limitations of process recording can be seen rather dramatically in Examples 5 and 6 of Chapter 6. In the first interview, two students were assigned to the same case and interviewed the client jointly. One took the lead, but both participated and each was asked to do an independent process recording of the joint interview. The two recordings illustrate selective memory for details, differing interpretation of client behavior and verbal responses, and quite different use of the "gut-level feelings" column, reflecting the distinct personalities of the two students.

In the second example, a previously process-recorded interview (see Chapter 6, Example 1) was acted out for four MSWs to observe. Three of their recordings correctly reported that the client was adamantly denying that he was a drug user, while the fourth showed him freely admitting to drug abuse. If this had been true, the supervisor would have directed the student toward ways of working with a person who recognizes his problem. Since this was contrary to reality, the student would have soon found himself in a rather confusing position!

Process recording, to be meaningful, must be done as soon as possible after the interview has occurred. Students who are in field placement on Monday, Wednesday, and Friday should not wait from Monday to Wednesday to do the recording. When classes and other activities intervene between the time of the interview and the recording, many important details and feelings are lost. If possible, process recording should be done the same day as the interview.

Process recording takes a *long* time to do. Students may spend one or two hours writing up a thirty-minute interview.

Supervisors should set a deadline specifying when process recordings are due, i.e., "Within forty-eight hours after the interview takes place" or "At least three days prior to our weekly supervisory conference." The material can then be reviewed and returned to the student in time for him to study the supervisor's comments prior to the next regularly scheduled conference.

Students may occasionally procrastinate in doing their process recordings. However, if a student consistently turns in recordings late, the supervisor should begin to explore underlying reasons for the resistance. Not surprisingly, the resisting student is often fearful of supervisory evaluation and may feel insecure about his skills. He may be aware he is not doing well and try to avoid supervisory assessment. On the other hand, the supervisor's approach may make it difficult for the student to respond positively and securely.

EVALUATING PROCESS RECORDINGS

Supervisory comments should identify positives and strengths as well as areas where the student is having difficulty or needs to grow. Many students, especially those entering social work school with some previous experience, already have beginning skills, but are not *consciously* aware of what they are doing and why it works. They often function largely by instinct, and only when a case "blows up" is there conscious recognition that maybe something wasn't done just right. Part of the social work education process is to help students become conscious of existing techniques as well as to acquire new ones so they can select appropriate techniques for use in various situations. Field instructors need to explain why a given technique or interchange was or was not effective, and should be prepared to suggest alternative approaches that might have been more effective. The supervisory conference time could be used to role-play various techniques.

Students must expect some constructive criticism along with positive feedback. This is necessary for professional growth. Everyone has room for improvement. Granted, such feedback can be anxiety-producing. If it is given in a helping and educational manner, the way the student handles this feedback can be a good indication of his personal maturity and commitment to learning. There are times when anyone would react defensively, but if this is a pattern, the field instructor will be unable to teach the student effectively and progress in field placement will come to a virtual standstill.

Standards in evaluating process recordings may be inconsistent. If three different field instructors review the same process recording, they will make different remarks in the "supervisory comments" column, depending on their knowledge, educational goals, and supervisory style. However, there should be some consistency in determining whether an interview was well or poorly done. Even this seemingly simple task raises a number of subjective questions. Which recordings are well done and why? Which indicate problems in the use of interviewing/counseling skills and why? How might techniques have been improved upon? What is the difference between a recording produced by a beginning interviewer and one who is "skillful"? Regardless of the person's level of training or experience, what things would indicate that the worker is functioning at a beginning or a more advanced level in an interview situation?

One small group of staff who had been receiving training in preparation for field instruction responsibilities studied several process recordings in depth and came up with a list of specific, rather easily measured characteristics of process recordings that distinguish beginning students from those with more advanced skills. The list is reproduced at the end of this chapter to serve as a rough guide in evaluating interviewing skills while reading the various process recording examples supplied in Chapter 6.

It is conceivable that a number of supervisors or students could apply this checklist to most process recording examples in Chapter 6 and arrive at basically similar conclusions regarding the skill level of the interviewer. The checklist can be used in several ways. The simplest would be to read a process recording, then read over the checklist and determine whether the student displays a greater number of skills similar to those described in the left-hand column (beginning level) or the right-hand column (more advanced). A more quantitative assessment method would be to use a rating scale of 1–5 and rate a process recording against every item of the checklist. A score of "1" would represent the most basic, beginning level of skill for each item, and "5" the most advanced. If an item does not apply to a particular process recording, mark it "NA." Be careful, however—the mere absence of an item doesn't necessarily mean it is not applicable. For example, number 11 pertains to the social worker introducing himself to his client. Obviously, if the interview is the third or fourth with the same client, this item would be "NA." However, if the student doesn't introduce himself to the client and it is a first interview, the rating would be "1" because an introduction should have occurred.

When all items have been rated, add them up and divide by the number of items rated to arrive at an overall score. The results may be quite surprising!

This particular checklist was developed so recently that it has not been tested fully. However, my experience thus far indicates it has some validity. For example, a group of six persons in training to be field instructors rated a process recording. Two trainees were second-year MSW students; two had one and one-half years post-MSW experience; and two had six or more years post-MSW experience. All gave the process recording the same rating, with only a .5 range in raw scores. The checklist will undoubtedly undergo revision and refinement, but it does represent a beginning attempt to quantify and objectify assessment of student interviewing skills as reflected in process recordings.

DIFFERENCES BETWEEN BEGINNING AND MORE ADVANCED INTERVIEWERS

BEGINNING INTERVIEWER

1. Student usually sees client or client's family members one at a time rather than jointly. There is no, or very limited, group interaction.

2. The purpose of the interview concerns concrete needs rather than emotional needs. The student focuses on the concrete needs.

3. The gut-level feelings column has comments such as "I felt like I was prying," or "This isn't any of my business," or "I felt uneasy asking these personal questions." The student appears unclear or uncomfortable with the professional role of the social worker. He appears unsure of his purpose for being there and seems unconvinced of the necessity for asking personal questions.

4. The reader gets the feeling the student is not fully comfortable with his client or himself in the interview situation. There are obviously awkward moments when the reader can feel the student's desperate struggle to conduct the interview.

5. There may or may not be a feeling of genuine warmth in the interview. Warmth may appear "contrived" or "put on." I.e., the student knows he is supposed to be warm so he tries to come across that way. The reader may not be

MORE ADVANCED INTERVIEWER

1. Student is assigned cases requiring sessions with family members as a group (i.e., as in family therapy).

2. Student deals with concrete needs but uses various interviewing techniques to elicit and explore feelings associated with the concrete needs.

3. Appropriate questions are asked without apparent hesitancy or discomfort.

4. The reader gets the feeling that the student is basically comfortable with himself, his role as a social worker, and the interview. Awkward moments are brief and rare.

5. The reader can actually feel the warmth the student shows for the client, and it comes through as being genuine. It is evident that this warmth was successfully and sincerely communicated to the client.

certain whether the warmth is genuine or whether the student is trying to be warm because his field instructor says it is a desirable characteristic for social work interviewers to display.

6. The student enters the interview situation with a rather structured and clear idea of the approach he plans to use. He may or may not be able to abandon the preplanned approach if greeted with something unexpected or if client shows strong, overt behaviors or feelings when the student begins the interview (such as finding the client crying or acting out hostilely).

7. The student is generally unable to shift gears, change, or abandon the preplanned interview approach *in the middle of the interview*. He might be able to deviate from the planned approach for isolated responses to the client, but usually reverts almost immediately to the preplanned approach.

8. The student uses direct questioning as the primary interviewing technique. The reader may receive the impression that the student has a checklist of information that he is trying to obtain.

9. When techniques such as interpretation, reflection, confrontation, and empathy are used, it is usually by accident and without conscious awareness of the name of the technique that was used or why.

10. The student may be able to label some techniques retroactively or figure out, after discussion with the supervisor, why a given technique was or was not effective. Usually cannot do this *as the interview is taking place*.

11. In initial interviews, the student fails to introduce himself fully to

6. The student enters the interview with an idea of the purpose and some techniques that he plans to use, but is open to change. He is almost always able to change the planned approach or to abandon it if client's presenting behavior or needs at the beginning of the interview indicate a need for this action.

7. The student is able to shift gears and abandon or alter his preplanned approach *in the middle of the interview* if client's behavior, feelings, or needs necessitate a different approach.

8. The student uses questioning selectively and in combination with other interviewing techniques. The questions flow naturally and with an obvious purpose. There is no feeling that the interviewer is getting answers to a checklist.

9. Techniques of reflection, interpretation, confrontation, empathy, and so on, are used with obvious conscious awareness. Student is able to use the "analysis" column to label the techniques used, and to explain why during supervisory conference.

10. The student is consciously aware of differential and purposeful use of selected techniques *at the time the techniques are being used in the interview*.

11. The student almost always introduces himself to a new client by

the client by giving his name, where he is from, and why he is seeing the person. He often starts asking the client questions without explaining why he is there. If an explanation is forthcoming later during the interview, it is usually in response to a direct question from the client (i.e., "Who are you?" or "Why are you here?" or "Who asked you to see me?").

giving his name, where he is from (i.e., the social service department), and why he is there before asking any questions or getting beyond the preliminary, small-talk phase of the interview.

12. The student uses the same basic introduction with all new clients regardless of their situation or presenting problem. He seems to have a "stock" approach for use in all situations.*

12. Introductions to new clients are varied. The student obviously responds differently to each person, depending on the nature of their situation and the presenting problem.

13. The interviewer jumps from one topic to another without exploring any one area in real depth. There appears to be no overall direction or focus to the interview—"things happen as they happen."

13. The student keeps the interview focused—it flows in a logical pattern and seems to be moving toward some kind of objective or conclusion. The student may allow a digression or a free flow of ideas from the client, but it appears to have been done consciously and purposefully.

14. The student often changes the subject by asking a direct question when the client brings up emotionally sensitive material or makes a statement that indicates the presence of strong feelings. The interviewer may occasionally respond to the feelings, but there is a definite pattern of changing the subject quickly to "safer," more concrete topics.

14. The student is usually able to pick up on client statements that indicate the presence of strong feelings and emotions, and to use appropriate techniques to explore them. The interviewer does not change the subject or appear to avoid responding to client feelings.

15. The interviewer rarely permits periods of silence. If the client fails to respond right away, the student jumps in rather quickly with a direct question.

15. The recording or interview indicates that the interviewer permitted appropriate periods of silence where nothing was said by anyone.

16. The student rarely confronts client with anything. When a situation presents itself that calls for a confrontative response, student usually says nothing (ignores it) or asks an information-seeking question. May occasionally confront

16. The student uses confrontation to bring to client's attention the interviewer's assessment of feelings, responses, and behaviors. This is done consciously with a purpose and usually, though not always, results in the client's dis-

*It may be necessary to review more than one interview in order to rate this item. If the evaluator is familiar with the general pattern of the student's work, the item can be rated. Otherwise, it should be marked "NA."

regarding very simple, concrete services planning.

17. The student makes statements that give false reassurance ("I'm sure it wasn't that bad" or "I know the XYZ Welfare Department can help you with that" or "Don't worry—your check won't get lost" or "Don't worry, the nurses here are really very nice," and so on).

18. The student may share personal life experiences with the client in an attempt to communicate "I do understand what you are going through or feeling." Student is usually able to explain later that this was his motivation for sharing the experience, but is usually unable to discuss, or is unaware of, the other pros and cons involved in using this technique.

19. The student uses advice giving— "I think you should do this . . ." or "What you should do is . . ." or "If I were you, I would. . . ." The reader finds himself wishing that other techniques could have been used instead to explore further the problem or the client's feelings.

20. More often than not, the student moves toward problem resolution without completely exploring all possible ramifications of the problem. Student tends to suggest solutions to the client almost immediately after client tells interviewer he has a problem or a need.

21. When the client mentions a concrete need or problem, the student often offers to resolve it *for* the client (e.g., make a phone call, write a letter, contact the welfare department in his behalf).

cussing feelings and presenting emotional reactions or needs in more detail.

17. The interview is characterized by an almost total absence of falsely reassuring statements. Reflective, interpretive, and empathetic techniques are used instead to explore client feelings or to define a presenting problem.

18. The student may share personal life experiences with the client in an effort to communicate empathy. However, student usually considers the pros and cons of using this approach *while the interview is occurring* and consciously and deliberately chooses the technique after determining that the possible benefits outweigh any negatives in that particular instance. Student is able to describe this thinking process in later discussion with the supervisor.

19. There is an almost total absence of advice-giving comments. Instead, student helps client make his own decision and uses appropriate techniques to help him verbalize and explore alternatives. When advice giving is used, student selects it as a treatment technique of choice *as the interview is taking place* and can explain later why he made this decision.

20. Student almost always shows obvious efforts to explore both concrete and feeling aspects of a problem before discussing solutions.

21. When client presents a concrete need, the student explores the client's ability to take care of the problem himself and encourages him to do so before offering to do it for him.

22. The student presents a plan to the client as "this is what we can do for you" and does not give client an opportunity to express how he feels about the plan. He may ask the client directly if the plan is "okay." This usually elicits a yes or no response, with no further elaboration or discussion with the client.

22. The student elicits client's feelings about all social service plans being developed and determines whether or not client wants to follow through with them.

23. Student often recognizes when something did not go well during the interview and expresses accompanying feelings of discomfort in the "gut-level feelings" column. Student usually does not know exactly what went wrong or why and only sometimes is able retroactively to suggest effective alternate ways of handling the situation. Supervisory guidance and input is usually needed to bring this about.

23. Student is usually able to recognize when something did not go as well as it could have during an interview and is usually, though not always, able *retroactively* to figure out why and suggest alternate ways that it could have been handled more effectively. Such comments often appear in the "gut-level feelings" column before supervisory input or guidance is provided.

24. Student records and documents factually what took place in the interview but includes very little diagnostic or analytical assessment of what was recorded.

24. Student does include some diagnostic assessment of what took place in the interview. This would appear in the "analysis" column or in a special diagnostic statement at the end of the recording.

25. The student may use layman's terms rather than professional terminology to describe client behaviors. This can give the reader the impression that the student is being judgmental.

25. Professional rather than layman's terminology is usually used. Diagnostic rather than judgmental terms are used.

26. Diagnostically significant statements or descriptions of client behaviors may be noted by the student in his process recording. However, the absence of comments in the "analysis" or "gut-level feelings" columns about the recorded factual data indicate that student is not aware of the significance of what has been recorded.

26. Diagnostically significant statements and observed behaviors are recorded and the student makes analytical comments regarding the data in the "analysis" or "gut-level feelings" column. Student may or may not fully understand the significance of what he has recorded, but does respond with recognition of its importance and attempts analysis. The advanced interviewer does his analysis inside his head as the interview is occurring. Moderately advanced students will do their analysis immediately after the conclusion of the interview and before supervisory input occurs.

27. Student is able to make some preliminary analytical statements based on behaviors and statements recorded in the interview only with some supervisory guidance and direction. Student is very limited in his ability to do this while the interview is taking place. Thus the student is not able to implement any ideas generated from his analytical thinking until the next interview.

27. Student analyzes client statements and behaviors *as the interview is taking place* and adjusts his behavior or approach during the interview to accommodate the results of his spontaneous analytical thinking. More in-depth thinking may be accomplished retroactively with supervisory guidance and input.

28. Student deals with or evaluates client statements in the present only—very rarely ties his analyses into goal-setting or projects implications for the future. Student may be able to do some of this retroactively following discussion with supervisor, but rarely does so *as the interview is occurring.*

28. Student makes prognostic statements regarding future problems/consequences/benefits based on assessment of client's behavior—a projection into the future. Student is able to do this *while the interview is occurring.*

29. The student's comments in the "gut-level feelings" column indicate lack of awareness of when countertransference occurs. The student may describe the feelings he experiences in response to a client's statement or behavior, but usually questions whether he was supposed to have these feelings, or what he should have done with his own feelings. Student does not label the interaction as "countertransference occurred here."

29. Student usually, though not always, is aware when countertransference occurs. He is usually able to label it as such, at least retroactively, in the "gut-level feelings" column. Student may need supervisory guidance on how to handle the identified countertransference.

30. The recording contains such comments, usually found in the "gut-level feelings" column, as "I felt good because the client was happy," or "Client was smiling and laughing so everything is better now." The reader gets the feeling that the student believes one is an effective social worker if the interview concludes with the client feeling happy. In other words, the goal of social work is to make clients happy.

30. There may be occasional comments regarding a client's feeling happy, but the reader does not get the feeling that the student believes the primary goal of his interaction is to make his client happy. "Gut-level feelings" column comments indicate awareness that some discomfort may be necessary to bring about increased growth, change, or insight, and that it is not realistic for people with problems to be happy all the time.

31. Only occasionally does the student end his interview in a structured, purposeful manner. The interview concludes when there is nothing more to talk about, or an

31. Worker concludes the interview when the objective or goal of the interview has been accomplished. There is usually a summarization, with the client, of what has taken

interruption makes continuation impossible or undesirable, or the client's behaviors or communications tell the worker clearly that it is time to end the discussion.

place during the interview, and a review of any plans made. There may also be discussion regarding the purpose or agenda of future contacts.

CHAPTER 6

EXAMPLES OF PROCESS RECORDING

It is important that students see exactly what process recording looks like and be given an opportunity to observe what happens when other people conduct interviews. Many students and beginning practitioners are relieved to find that they aren't the only ones who encounter difficulties in an interview. Others have no idea what takes place in a social work interview, and are both curious and encouraged to learn that no miracles are expected and that other students share their anxiety over a first encounter with a real live client.

The introductory remarks to the examples in this chapter and the comments in the "supervisory comments" column are designed to provide some guidance to the student learning to interview, as well as to illustrate how process recording should look. The examples also demonstrate the kind of feedback that students should be getting from their supervisors when detailed recording is submitted for review. The time and effort expended on process recording become virtually meaningless without appropriate and timely supervisory feedback.

The various examples presented here represent a cross-section of typical exchanges and problems encountered in interview situations. There is at least one illustration of a rather rare event (Example 20, the student who harms his client), since many students and beginning practitioners worry about these occurrences and don't have many places to turn for examples. Most examples appear exactly as recorded by the student, except for alterations to protect the identity of both client and interviewer. A few, which illustrate negative or highly sensitive areas that prohibit the use of an actual recording, are fictitious and do not represent an actual interview.

Many of the examples take place in a medical setting. However, the interviewing techniques, interactions, and problems encountered are universal.

EXAMPLE 1 An important dynamic, not recognized by the student, is process recorded

The following process recording was done by a first-quarter undergraduate student with considerable life experience and some social work experience in a concrete services setting. He dutifully recorded everything he could remember that took place in his interview, including one or two sentences that told the supervisor the client probably had a much more serious problem than the student recognized. When they discussed the recording, the field instructor returned it to the student with the comment that it contained a "diagnostic bombshell." Challenged to find it, the student returned several hours later still wondering what his supervisor was talking about! Some specific readings were suggested and a few hints provided. This time the student came back expressing amazement that he could have missed "anything so obvious." After a lengthy discussion, a joint decision was reached to transfer the case to an MSW person, since the presenting dynamics suggested the need for assessment and treatment skills beyond what could be expected in a beginning undergraduate student. This provided an important lesson in "knowing one's limitations" and turned out to be a meaningful learning experience for the student, even though he did not get to continue with his case.

SUPERVISORY COMMENTS	INTERVIEW CONTENT	GUT-LEVEL FEELINGS
Why did you feel as you did—what you said was true. It wasn't a bad way of putting it.	Made second visit to client. He was still sitting and drinking water. He greeted me and offered me a seat. I told him that I might have some difficulty getting him into a boarding home. I said that I had learned that he had used drugs.	This wasn't exactly a lie but I didn't feel too comfortable about this right now.
Good! You didn't get caught in the trap of trying to answer his question of "Who told you that?"	He stopped drinking water and said, "What, who told you that?" I said, "If you are dependent on drugs, a boarding home might not take you." He said, "If I use drugs, I get them from a doctor." I said, "You are telling me that you have never used drugs before?" He said no. I asked what kinds of drugs he had used and he said that when he was sick they had given him a shot of this right here (pointing to the spot).	He is being indirect and evasive, also trying to have me answer my own questions.
Good.	I said, "What do you mean?" He said that's what they call it in the streets. I said, "So you have used drugs before, then?"	
	He kind of paused and said yes, that he has only used it three times including once when he was sick. I said, "You mean to tell me that they gave you such a dangerous drug when you were sick?"	
Be careful that you don't confront him so strongly that he becomes angry and defensive.	He said when he went to the doctor he was shaking so bad and in so much pain that they gave him a shot.	This doesn't sound right to me.
Good exploration.	I said, "Why would they give you that particular drug?" He said that he didn't know.	It is pretty obvious to me at this point that he might use drugs but have no real knowledge about them.
	I said, "Then how do you know that is what you got?"	
	He said, "Because I know how it makes you feel."	
Excellent exploration technique!	I asked how it makes him feel and he said it relaxes his whole body.	

His answer tells you he's used drugs before.

I said there are other drugs that have the same effect as it and asked him to tell me how many times or how much he's used them.

He said twice before.

I said, "Are you saying that you had only used drugs twice before that?" He said yes and stated that he is not an addict.

You are coming on a little too strong here—I'm surprised he didn't get angry or defensive.

I said, "I am not saying you are, but still the fact that you have used drugs has to be dealt with."

He said, "I know, but if I were an addict, I would not be asking to be sent to a boarding home."

I wonder why ability and willingness to take orders is so important to him? I think he's trying to say something—you might have explored further.

He looked at me very straight and asked if I thought an addict would be willing to take orders.

I said, "I don't know." He said that if he is sent to a boarding home that he will be willing and able to follow orders.

He said he is not able to go back to his mother's where he was staying. I asked him why not.

Now he is trying to tell me something very significant.

He said his mother is the reason he is in this shape in the first place.

Good—you're exploring.

I said, "How is that?"

Do you realize what he's saying here?! Let's discuss this! No reaction here tells me a great deal!

He said that she just isn't right, that she had he and his brother fighting, and that "she says things that a man's wife might say."

If you had realized what he was trying to say, I don't think you would have asked him quite this way.

I said, "What kinds of things?"

To this, I got no reply, only that "She isn't right and I never should have gone back there to live." He explained that before he had a job but she asked him to come live with her and his sister tried to discourage him. He said he didn't even have a regular place to sleep and slept on the floor.

Shows his ambivalence and emotional involvement with the situation.

By changing the subject here, you may have prevented him from talking more about the relationship with his mother, which I feel he wanted to discuss. I suspect you didn't know what he had meant by his earlier statement or perhaps didn't catch the significance of it. Maybe you didn't know how to handle it or perhaps repressed its meaning so fast you denied its meaning.

I asked when and where he had worked and he said that a couple of years ago he worked for _____.

I asked what did he do and he said he did janitorial work. I asked if that was the last time that he had worked. He said not, and started naming jobs he had held. I asked about the last regular job he had. He gave me the name of a place he had worked and said this only lasted a few months, that he had not worked steady for about 1/2 to 3/4 of a year.

I need to determine if heavy drug user and how it would be financed. Also, any work experience. He is cooperative but suspicious.

Seems like the breaks were bad ones.

Good question.

I asked how had he been making it up until he got injured.

Why does he feel the need to mention this again?

He said "By catching breaks. I know you think I am a drug addict because someone told you I am."

Was it??

I said that is not true.

A natural gut-level feeling on your part. You might have considered why he put you in this position so you'd feel this way.

He said, "It seems like you believe them but when I tell you I'm not, you don't believe me."

I said, "I will put it to you straight. Are you an addict?"

It might have been better to explore his feelings more instead of asking if he is an addict.

He said no.

I said, "If this is the truth, then I believe you."

He said, "Believe me, this is the truth. All I want is to be able to get back to work and live somewhere else. I will do any kind of light work till I'm able to do heavier work."

I feel a little ashamed and somewhat guilty because I must be making him feel bad by seeming to distrust him and believe what someone else tells me about him.

After going through this confrontation, it would be very difficult for him to ever admit to you later if he really is an addict.

Maybe, but also the situation with his mother is creating intense anxiety which

Then he asked me if I might be able to get him placed in a boarding home. He said he didn't care what it is like, but knows this is what he must accept until able to do better, only he doesn't

This seems a sincere and realistic way of viewing his situation.

36

he wants to avoid, and I see this as being the strongest motivator.	want to be on the street and can't go back to live at his mother's.	
I think you've been playing the authority figure a little in the past few paragraphs.	I said OK.	
	At this point client announced he was hungry and was going to get something to eat and asked how much longer we would be.	
	With this subtle hint, I ended the interview so he could eat. I told him I would see him again soon.	

EXAMPLE 2 A student encounters psychotic paranoia for the first time without realizing what it is

The following recording was done by an undergraduate student in his first field placement. He had no prior social work experience and had not yet received training in the psychodynamics of human behavior or abnormal psychology. It was quite difficult for him to believe that his client was "mentally ill," even though he had observed a classic, textbook form of paranoia. This is typical of the beginning student or practitioner as he struggles to move from a layman's understanding of human behavior to a professional, diagnostic, and treatment-oriented approach.

SUPERVISORY COMMENTS	INTERVIEW CONTENT	GUT-LEVEL FEELINGS
Sometimes this kind of situation makes you feel like commenting to the patient re: his condition and starting your interview with some conversation re: how he's feeling.	I went alone to see Mr. S today. He was lying down in bed with a splint strapped to his arm.	I wondered if his condition had worsened as he didn't look too well.
	He appeared not to be as alert today. I said hello and he said to please sit down. He smiled.	
	He asked me what I had to report.	The way Mr. S talks, I could pretty much tell that he wasn't in pain or discomfort, but that he was just tired. I did in the beginning ask him how he was feeling, and he said he was very hungry but otherwise OK.
	I told him that I had talked with the social worker at his apartment complex and with the post office.	
	I explained to him that the post office said that they would release his check to Ms. X and that she had agreed to pick it up. I told him that I had written a letter to the Postmaster, authorizing the release of his check to Ms. X.	

A nice way of
handling it.

Yes, it was relevant.
He needed to know what
he would be signing.

I thought you said
earlier he didn't
appear as alert
today!?

Did he sign the
letter?

I wonder if this is
paranoia, mistrust of
people—it may seem
insignificant, but
this may or may not be
a clue to his complaint
about lack of friends
in your earlier
interviews.

AHA! I was right!
Classic paranoia!
Let's discuss.
Meanwhile, read on
paranoia in Modern
Clinical Psychiatry
by Noyes and Kolb on
our library shelf.

More was happening
than the patient just
airing his thoughts!
The comments he was
making are very
significant diag-
nostically. You
actually should have
let him continue
describing his sus-
picions so you could
have gotten more
information about how
he perceives what's
happening, and you
could better under-
stand his mental

At this point I showed him the letter,
and he said he couldn't read it, so I
asked if he would like me to read it to
him. He said yes and I read him the
letter. He seemed to understand it, and
I explained that I would need his
signature on it. I put the letter on the
table and went on explaining the way
which Ms. X would be picking up and
bringing his check to him.

Mr. S seemed pleased that the arrangements had been made.

He explained to me that the reason he
receives his mail general delivery was
that one time before his Social Security
check had been taken by a neighbor and
that he didn't get repayment for
several months.

Mr. S related a long fantasy about a two-
way mirror which he thought might have
been put in his apt. by the neighbor.
He said he had lost some money once, and
attributed that to his neighbor also.
He said that he believed that the
neighbor watched him through the
mirror, and when he went out the
neighbor would come into his apt. and
take things. Mr. S said that he saw this
on television, and that that is where
he got the idea. Someone (pt.) in the bed
across the room asked that we keep the
noise down as he was trying to sleep. I
took this opportunity to change the
subject, and reviewed the process by
which his check would be gotten for him.
I then picked up the letter and asked
Mr. S to please sign and showed him where
to sign. He seemed to be having trouble
seeing, and asked if I saw his glasses.
I picked up the glasses and gave them to
him, and he signed and gave me the
letter.

As I read the letter to
Mr. S I questioned
myself as to whether
or not it was relevant
to be reading it to
him. I felt that I
might be overexplain-
ing myself to him. I
think that this might
have been the case,
had Mr. S not been as
alert and interested
as he was. Throughout
the interview Mr. S and
I maintained good eye
contact. I feel that
Mr. S is very inter-
ested in his affairs.

When he began explain-
ing about his apt.
being broken into, I
felt that I had lost
the focus of the inter-
view and was just
letting Mr. S air his
thoughts. I didn't
mind him doing this as
I had no other things
to discuss with him
and didn't mind
listening to him.

I feel that this exper-
ience will teach me the
different situations
where I can let a
client talk, or in
another situation,
switch the focus back
to the subject by
interrupting and
talking about some-
thing else.

When the man asked us
to be quieter, I felt
as though I had
infringed upon his

functioning and limitations.

Let's discuss.

I'm actually surprised he signed the letter— if he were really suspicious of people, he might have hesi- tated. However, if anything goes wrong with the plan for Mrs. X to pick up his check, he will be quick to blame you or her.

Let's discuss.

I explained that I did not work on Friday and that I would try to come by on Monday to see him again.

He thanked me and said that he appreciated my efforts.

I said goodbye and put my chair away and left.

privacy, and that perhaps I was wrong in letting Mr. S talk so long.

Mr. S had some trouble finding the space or identifying where to sign, even though I was pointing out the area for him. I thought for a few moments that he might not be able to sign. His conversa- tion was much more comfortable for him than was signing the letter.

I feel that I need more decisiveness in clos- ing the interviews I've been having.

EXAMPLE 3 Gut-level feelings column used incorrectly for analyzing client's feelings instead of recorder's

The following brief excerpt illustrates the student's use of the third column to give analyses of what's happening in the interview instead of her own gut-level feelings—a sophisticated cop-out to avoid having to face the real purpose of the third column. The recording was done by a graduate student.

SUPERVISORY COMMENTS	INTERVIEW CONTENT	GUT-LEVEL FEELINGS
(What comments would you make if this were your student?)	I said, "Good morning—are you Mrs. J?" She said yes. I said "My name is Sarah Makin. I am a social worker. Do you mind if we have a chat?" She said ok.	Her voice was hardly audible. I wasn't sure whether this was her normal voice or there was some impediment. I took the chair and moved it closer, and client made an effort to sit up, but later returned to her position lying down on the couch. I felt she was trying to communicate and would not react to moving right in.

39

I said, "Your eye sure looks painful."
She said it was and I said "I understand
this happened a couple of days ago. Do
you want to tell me what happened?"

I didn't get any
negative vibrations
and felt the client
could answer any
questions put to her.

EXAMPLE 4 Fourth column added to force recorder to
use "gut-level feelings" column appropriately

Because this student had been using the "gut-level feelings" column inappropriately,
she was asked to include the special fourth column, "analysis" as recommended in
Chapter 5. The following is excerpted from a much longer interview. The material in
the "feelings" column appears exactly as it was recorded by the student.

SUPERVISORY COMMENTS	INTERVIEW CONTENT	GUT-LEVEL FEELINGS	ANALYSIS
	(Client and worker have been discussing a certain plan. It appears to have been worked out and the worker is obviously about to end the interview)	He came up with his own solution. I'm happy now. I hope I can do it. It's already 10:00.	
	He said, "Yes that would be good."		
	I said, "Well, I will check on it and get back to you around noon."		
I'll refrain from comment. You said it—not I!	(I got up and realized as I walked out I had ended abruptly and I went back.)	Fool! You were so excited you forgot your client's needs!	He looked a little disappointed I was leaving—his shoulders drooped.
Good! You redeemed yourself.	I said, "Is there anything else before I go that you wanted to talk about?"		
	He said, "There was something else; I thought of it last night but I can't remember now."	Now I felt bad. Have I let him down by ending so abruptly? Is he doing this on purpose?	
	(I sat down)		
	He said, "I guess it wasn't important."		
	I said, "If you thought about it, then it is something we should talk about."		

	He said, "I can't remember, maybe I'll think of it."	He seems to be telling the truth. This lets my guilt off the hook.	He shook his head.
	(pause...)		
	I said, "Well, if you do, I will be back around noon and we can discuss it then."		
	He said "OK."		He smiled at me and watched me walk away.
Your guilt? His needs? Both?	(I went back several times but he was sleeping. I caught him awake about 4:00. I told him I was making the arrangements and would see him tomorrow.)	I didn't want him to think I had forgotten him.	
	Next Interview Tuesday AM		
I see!	I said, "Good morning Mr. T, did you sleep well?"	If someone said how are you this AM to me for 4 days in a row, I'd probably throw something at them!	

EXAMPLE 5 Same interview process recorded by two people

The following are the first few pages of an interview conducted jointly by two students. They were asked to write separate process recordings without collaborating with each other. The results illustrate the fact that no two people perceive the same interview in the same way. Only the "interview content" and "gut-level feelings" columns are shown. Grammar and spelling are as recorded by the students. Notice that Student A uses the word-for-word style of process recording (and does not use the "gut-level feelings" column), while Student B uses the summary style, in which what was said is paraphrased and summarized rather than quoted verbatim.

STUDENT A		STUDENT B	
INTERVIEW CONTENT	GUT-LEVEL FEELINGS	INTERVIEW CONTENT	GUT-LEVEL FEELINGS
B said, "Mr. A?"		Pat and I went to see Mr. A on 2/9. When we entered the room he was sitting on the edge of his bed.	I was less nervous going to see Mr. A than I was in my first interview. I had no real problem going
He said, "Yes," sitting up, straightening his gown.			

B said, "My name is Bob B and this is Pat A."

There was a pause.

B said "We are from social services." A smile appears on his face. He says, "Oh I'm glad to see you. You see my problem is my check is at the post office and my rent is due. It is my Social Security check. I get it the third of every month, and if my check is not picked up it will go back to Chicago, and it takes 3 or 4 months before you get it. What I want you to do is go to the post office with a card I will give you and pick up my check."

Leaning closer to Bob. "When you pick it up I want you to sign it and cash it to pay my rent."

I asked, "Do you feel you will lose your home if you don't pay the rent?"

He said, "No I live in a housing project for the elderly. They won't through me out" (frowning). Hands moving twisting in his lap. "What I want you to do is cash my check and pay my rent."

I said, "I'm sorry Mr.

I introduced Pat and I as being from social services and gave him our names.

He said "Yes, I was expecting you. My problem is my Social Security check." He described his situation as being that his SS check was at the post office and would be returned to Chicago if it wasn't picked up. Mr. A said, "What I would like you to do is to go to the post office and get my check."

At this point I interrupted Mr. A and told him that it was not our policy to do that sort of service. I asked him if he had any contact w/the social worker at his apt. He said no, that on 1/24 he was hit all of a sudden w/pain while downtown and came straight here via taxi cab.

I told him I didn't mean that day in particular, but anytime previously.

"Oh", he said, "yes I did see her before."

into the room and talking with client.

When Mr. A opened up the conversation I was surprised. I thought it would take more of an explanation.

When Mr. A said this, it reminded me very much of an example which we discussed about things clients would want us to do, but which we do not do.

I felt that by saying this to him I might be turning him off.

I felt he didn't understand my question.

I was glad that he had seen the s/worker so

A, but we can't pay your rent, nor cash your check."

Bob said, "Nor can we pick up your check."

Client frowned, and moved closer to Bob. Bob turned and looked at me. Client also turned away. I said, "I'm sorry Mr. A but we can't pick up your check ourselves. I will speak to my supervisor, and see if we can come up with a solution."

Client nodded, and turned to Bob, leaning close toward him. Bob moved back in his chair.

He said, "The doctors here told me you social workers can do this type of thing." Sitting up in his bed with his head up straight and his hand in his lap.

"You social workers I know do these type of things. This is your job."

Bob said (nervously, hand turning), "We are not supposed to do those kinds of things."

I said, "As I said before we will speak to our supervisor and try to come up with a solu-

I asked Mr. A if he remembered the social worker's name, but he couldn't. Then I explained to him that I wanted to contact that social worker to see if she could pick up his check.

I asked if he was concerned that his rent was behind. He said not really, as he has been living in the apt. where he is now for two and a half years, and the building has been there only 3 years. He said he was not worried that they would put him out, but that his check would be returned to Chicago, and he wouldn't have money to live on when he got out.

I restated that I would try to get in touch with social worker and have her pick up check.

Pat here suggested that one alternative might be to contact the post office and have them hold the check for him until such time as he was able to go himself and get it.

Mr. A said, yes that was a very good idea, and I agreed with him on that.

Mr. A explained to us that he had a personal physician who had

that she might go get his check.

I wondered if there was any possibility of him being evicted anyway.

This struck me as being very real concern.

I thought she made a good point here, one I didn't think of!

tion. Possibly we can contact the post office and inform them that you are in here and see if they can hold your check until you get out. If not maybe someone you know can pick it up."

Client paused for a minute and looked up toward the ceiling.

He said, "No there is no one. You see I am not a friendly person. I see people in my apartment building and speak, that is all. I don't stand in the halls and talk about people's private business."

I asked, "Do you think that's what friends are for or do?"

He said, "I really don't know, I just don't have any friends."

never asked him if he smoked. He also stated that the physician now attending him was upset with the fact that the personal Dr. Mr. A had did not find his physical problem before it became so serious.

I felt resentment towards doctors.

He said that he sometimes has difficulty breathing and told of one time when he was living on "A" st. that the fire dept. brought him to the hospital. He said that he sat in the ER for a while and finally went home.

The length of time he had to wait is ridiculous. The system took advantage of him.

I expressed that I felt that such treatment was unfair.

Mr. A said that for the past two days he had been feeling better, and that he couldn't have anything to eat. The last thing he ate was on Sat. am and that was only a cup of coffee.

Relieved to hear he was doing well.

EXAMPLE 6 Same interview process recorded by four people, with radically different results

The following material was produced by four people participating in a special course for field instructors. Example 1 was acted out and read aloud by two people. The "audience" was instructed to listen carefully but told not to take any notes. They were allowed only ten minutes to record the observed interview from the point of view of the interviewer. This forced them to focus on the highlights only. They had been taught the four-column method of process recording for use with their students and were warned in advance that they would be asked to do a process recording of the acted-out interview. Comparison of the four recordings showed marked differences in the "interview content" column. The other three columns have been omitted in this example.

Go back and read Example 1 before reading the four versions of it that appear below. Notice that three recorders present the client's insistence that he is not a drug user, while the fourth has the client freely admitting to being a drug addict! Notice also that only two out of the four observers mentioned the problematic behavior of the mother towards her son.

Pt. (patient): drinking water. I sat down near pt.

W. (worker): I'm here to see you about getting you to a boarding home.

W.: Are you a drug addict?

Pt.: No, I'm not.

W.: What are you on? (meds?)

Pt.: I took this type of medication.

W.: What is it?

Pt.: I don't know.

W.: Can you remember its name?

Pt.: No, the doctor gave it to me.

W.: Why did he give you that kind of medicine? It is a very dangerous one.

Pt.: I don't know why. All I know is that he gave it to me.

W.: Have you taken this drug before?

Pt.: Yes, but I don't use drugs.

W.: Well, you said you've taken drugs before.

Pt.: Who told you that?

W.: No one. Do you use drugs?

Pt.: No, only what the Dr. gives me.

W.: What was that?

Pt.: I don't know the name of it but I know how it made me feel.

W.: How did it make you feel?

Pt.: Very relaxed all over.

W.: You felt relaxed but don't know the name of the drug. How did you know it was a drug?

Pt.: Because I had it twice before. But I'm not a drug addict and I want to get into a boarding home. I can't go back to my mother's. She'd do things that she would do with a man.

W.: Where have you worked before? How long?

Pt.: As a janitor at _____.

W.: What was your last regular job?

Pt.: I worked for 2 months at a storeroom

I told pt. I'd learned he was an addict and that boarding home would be difficult if he was an addict.

He denied he was an addict and had only gotten drugs on prescription.

I challenged him on his statement and asked on what occasion did he receive the drug.

He gave incident.

Said he couldn't go home because of living situation with mom. No room. His brother said he should stay.

Then asked again if boarding home placement could be done. He was not an addict. Added he knew I didn't believe him.

I said I did.

He said I didn't.

W.: Mr. _____. I am Mrs. _____ I am the social worker. How do you feel today?

Pt.: Well I don't feel well. I don't know where I am going. My body hurts.

W.: You are concerned about your physical health and have to find a place to live. What have the doctors said about these?

Pt.: Well I am ready for discharge but I don't have a place to go; my mother, my sister, etc.

W.: What do you want to do for yourself?

Pt.: I can't do anything. I am a drug addict.

W.: Let us talk about this problem.

Pt.: Yes, but they were drugs the doctor gave me. I'm not a drug addict.

W.: I didn't say you were. But I have to know if you're drug-free in order to get you into a boarding home.

Pt.: Well, I don't use drugs.

W.: Well, let me ask you straight then. Do you use drugs?

Pt.: No, I don't.

W.: Well if that's the truth then I believe it.

Pt.: Well all I know is that I have to go to a boarding home. I can't go home.

W.: Well do you have family?

Pt.: That's what I want to get away from. I was living with my mother and I can't go back there to live.

W.: Why not?

Pt.: Because. It's just the way she is. She talks to you the way a wife talks to a husband.

W.: What does that mean?

Pt.: You know. My sister tried talking me out of going to

(?) but didn't like it but I really need a place to stay in a boarding home. I can't go back home.

W.: O.K.

Pt.: Well, I'm not a drug addict. Can you find me a place? How come you believe others and not me when I tell you I'm not a drug addict?

W.: Let me put it to you this way: Are you a drug addict?

Pt.: No.

W.: If you're telling the truth I believe you.

Pt.: Well, how much longer is this going to last? My lunch is here.

W.: OK, I'll see you later.

live with my mom
but I didn't listen
to her. I was working.

W.: What kind of work
did you do?

He describes. Then
goes on to say he's
hungry and worker
leaves.

EXAMPLE 7 First interview by an undergraduate
student

The following example was produced by a fairly young student in her first field
placement. She had no prior social work experience but had done volunteer work and
had also worked for several years in a medical setting in a position that required
contacts with patients and the public. The interviewer relies heavily on questioning
to get at needed data and also moves rather prematurely toward problem
resolution—two characteristics typical of beginning interviewers. However, she does
keep the interview focused, uses touching effectively, and doesn't come completely
unglued when the student nurse invites herself in to observe the interview. A more
experienced social worker probably would have had the self-confidence to explain
that the interview was a private affair, suggest that perhaps they plan for the nurse to
sit in at a later date, and then see that she left the room. Another alternative would
have been to ask the client whether he wanted this person to be there as an observer.

Note that the supervisor has encouraged the student to use the fourth column to
analyze her interviewing techniques and suggest alternate approaches that might
have been more effective.

SUPERVISORY COMMENTS	INTERVIEW CONTENT	GUT-LEVEL FEELINGS	ANALYSIS
	C (client): (standing up, beginning to walk around bed toward sink)		
	W (worker): Mr. Hartman? (client looks up) I'm Rosetta Myers from social services. I understand you're having some concerns you wish to discuss?		
	C: (speaking tiredly) Yes, yes I do, but I was going to wash my teeth now.		
	W: Oh, OK fine. I'll leave for a few minutes and come back when you are finished. OK?		
	C: Yes, OK. It'll only take me a minute.		

You were prepared!	W: Fine (I leave).	(Great! What a good start—the right place at the wrong time!)	These things happen; anyone would feel more comfortable talking when their mouths were clean.
You handled it real well.	5 minutes later...		
	C: (sitting in chair at foot of bed, facing the bed)		
I like your awareness of sitting—very important.	W: (while taking another chair and placing it in front of him and to his left side about 2 ft. away) Hello again, Mr. Hartman (pulling curtain across slightly). As I said before, I'm Rosetta Myers and I'm with social services.		I was conscious of the way I wanted to sit, so as to be close to him but not uncomfortably so.
	C: (nods affirmatively)		
How did YOU feel about it?	(At that time a student nurse enters the room and states that she will sit in on the conversation because he is her patient) W.: (I nod in agreement) You've got some concerns you wish to discuss?	I wonder what she's going to think about our interview. I wonder what Mr. H. will think about her being there.	I should have asked that she not be present for this first interview, but maybe for the one on Monday. Or I could have possibly asked Mr. H. if it was alright that she be there, though he might have said "I don't care" (whether he cared or not).
Perceptive! What is pt. saying nonverbally? How is he feeling when he says he "feels better"?	C: Yes, yes (eyes cast to the floor, stroking and picking at his moustache with hand). I've been taking my medicine. I feel much better now than I did when I first came in. Doctors think I might have a problem with my gallbladder. They've been taking X-rays. W: I'm glad you're feeling better now (there is a pause). C: It might be different when I have to go home.	He just keeps looking down, maybe he doesn't want her there.	
Good reflective comment!	W: Different? In what way? C: Well... (still looking down at the floor). You know, where I live, it's not too good. The halls are dirty. My room is about half the	Wow—he's really telling me a lot. This is great.	

And you've picked up on it—he's saying he really wants to move.

size of this room here. The lady in charge of the place is nice to me but... (pause). The other day, there's roaches in my room. Not fit to live there... (pause). There's a new skyrise on _____ St., I think. It's better, you know. It's cleaner, the rooms are big.

Was this a question?

Does he need help?

W: Is there someone who could help you out in the place where you're living now, after you leave the hospital?

C: No, no one. They give me a small gas stove to cook with.

Is this difficult? Is he used to having meals cooked for himself?

W: You have to cook your own meals?

C: Yes, usually I do. Ain't no one to help me. There are all men staying there, and they all drink a lot. They don't pay me any respect, don't give me no respect!

Good example of interpretation used here. May consider question or reflection—"respect?"

W: You don't sound too happy to be living where you are now... (pause).

C: No, no, it's no good. Don't tell the lady that I don't like it or she might get mad and throw me out.

Does landlady throw people out often?!

Was it difficult to get this place Why?

W: No, I won't be speaking with the landlady. At least, for the moment, you have a place to go home to. Do you have any friends living with you at the boarding house?

C: Yes, one friend, but all them other guys drink all the time (he looks up at me).

Yes, you changed the subject—do you know why?

W: How much do you pay to live there?

C: I pay $50 month, yes, $50.

W: And you receive $218 a month from Social Security?

C: Yes, that's right. I also get a little check. It's for $8.76 a month from... I'm not sure what agency... just a little old check.

A little humor there about the

Perhaps I should not have changed the subject, but rather ask him his feelings about alcohol abuse by the other men.

W: And after paying your rent and buying food and supplies, do you find you still have enough money?

Enough for what? Suspect he drinks? How much of his check does he want to spend on rent?

C: Oh sure, yes. I hadn't got any problems with the money. There's enough.

Can pt. do some of this?

① Exactly!

W: (taking piece of paper out of his pocket) Let me write down the location that you say this skyrise is and maybe I can check to see if it could be a possible alternative to where you are living now.

little check. Perhaps he's warming up to me.

I wonder what he spends his money on, if what he eats is nutritionally OK?

① Maybe I should have asked more questions as to what he does do with the money left over from the rent and other bills.

C: Well, I think it's on _____ Ave. Yes, it's near the courthouse. It's a big place. They tell me it's real nice inside. Clean and all, you know. (He looks up at me, again.)

Different kind of people there?

I've maintained eye contact as much as possible, but he is still not looking directly at me.

W: You seem to be really concerned about finding a new place to live, so we'll check out this skyrise, and perhaps some other places and then we can decide if you would like to move to a new location. I understand you have a sister, perhaps she could help you in some way?

How much is pt. depending on you?

"We"—you and pt.?

Is there another way to ask this?

C: Yes, I have a sister. I used to live with her, but now I just live at the boarding house (pause).

Boarding—not his choice?

② Let's go over this. Is silence difficult to handle?

② Now what should I say?

③ It never occurred to me to ask why he did not live with his sister. I should have probed further.

W: I see. Do you feel that by moving to a better place, this would help you while you are recuperating from being in the hospital?

③ But you're aware now!

C: Yes, because maybe there would be more help and they could help me get around, people be more friendly.

Is pt. lonely?

W: OK, well, we'll work on that problem of finding a new place for you to live. As far as your hospital stay here is concerned, is there anything you'd like to discuss?

What is he feeling now about his health?

C: (there's a long pause) Well, they're just taking X-rays, check my gallbladder.

I hope he can tell me about any other prob. that may be on his mind.

W: Do you see the doctors often, do they speak with you?

Whoops! I just asked a double question. Too late.

Try to avoid double questions, leading questions.

He changed the subject. Is he worried about his health?

C: Yes, they come in, but they haven't told me about the X-ray I had today yet.

W: Well, perhaps after they have had a chance to read the X-rays, they'll be able to tell you more.

Was he wanting an end to the interview?

C: Yes... so maybe you can check on that skyrise to see if I can stay there? (he looks up at me)

Boy! He really wants to go to that skyrise. I just hope he won't be disappointed.

Good idea of role of social worker.

How will he know the best place?

W: Yes, I can try to get some names of other places also, and then we can check to see which place would be best for you to live in. OK?

C: OK, that'll be good.

Why do you think she left here? Did she ever discuss her reaction to the interview with you?

(At this point the nursing student, who had not said one word the entire interview, got up off the end of the bed and went out the door)

A little rude, if I do say so myself.

W: Anything else you'd like to discuss?

C: No... (pause).

W: Well, if you would like, I will come back on Monday and tell you if I've made any progress in finding some new living arrangement for you.

May be false reassurance.

What's a good time for pt. on Monday?

C: Yes, OK. That'll be OK.

Related to his boarding home?
①
A goal I feel sure you'll accomplish.

W: Then if you think of anything over the weekend that you wish to discuss we can talk about it on Monday, OK?

I'm hoping our relationship progresses further, a trusting relationship.

①
Maybe he will begin to feel more at ease, and will discuss other concerns that he may have.

C: Sure, that'll be OK with me (he nods in agreement, and looks up at me).

W: (I put my hand on his arm and say) OK, then I'll see you on Monday. Let me give you this little card;

Touching is important to me.

Over weekend?	it has my name and the social services office number on it, so if you need to get in touch with us, you'll be able to call (I reach into pocket and give him card).	
	C: OK, fine.	
Felt warmth— sincere comment.	W: (touching his arm again) Well, I'm glad to have met you, Mr. Hartman, and I'll see you on Monday (standing up now, and beginning to move chair back to original location).	Maybe that sounds kind of corny.
	C: (stands up) OK, thanks a lot... let me put this card away, so I don't lose it (as he walks toward bedside stand).	
	W: Bye now, Mr. Hartman (leaving room).	Whew! That wasn't so bad after all!
Generally— appears even with the nurse observer, you established rapport with this pt.—sometimes a difficult task for an experienced interviewer! Your recording was easy to follow— well written. Good insights.

For our discussion in supervisory conference:

1. Focus for next interview with patient.

2. Your role in helping. | C: Bye. | |

EXAMPLE 8 Outstanding interview by an advanced undergraduate student

The same student who wrote Example 7 produced this outstanding interview. Example 7 showed heavy reliance on questioning as the primary interviewing technique. Therefore, the student and her supervisor began to work intensively on other techniques such as clarification, empathy, interpretation, and reflection. They role-played these techniques in supervisory conferences and tried to build on the student's classroom exposure earlier in the school year. One of their educational objectives was that the student be able to label these techniques whenever she used one of them in her process recordings. The student was asked to critique her own interview and state three things she liked about it and three areas she felt could have been improved upon or done differently. A specific plan was then developed for the next interview (see the end of the "supervisory comments" column).

Only five or six weeks elapsed between process recordings 7 and 8. These two examples illustrate the tremendous growth that a conscientious student with some natural abilities and strong, structured guidance from her field instructor can accomplish in a remarkably short period of time. The interview that follows shows effective use of silence, nonverbal communication, reflection, interpretation, and summarization. The level of skill displayed is actually more typical of a graduate student midway through training than of an undergraduate student. This is the student's third or fouth visit with a woman who is hospitalized for a life-threatening illness.

SUPERVISORY COMMENTS	INTERVIEW CONTENT	GUT-LEVEL FEELINGS	ANALYSIS
	W (worker): (knocking on closed door, then walking into room smiling) Hello, Sharon.		
	C (client): (smiling) Hi, You've talked to Bob (patient's husband), didn't you? (begins to laugh)	That must have been on her mind for a while.	
	W: Yes, I have.... Why are you laughing? (smiling, taking chair and placing it near to bed)		That question could have probably been worded a little better, perhaps more of a statement of fact—"This is amusing to you."
	C: Well, I called him up once on Sunday, and then when I called him back later, he sounded different (smiling).		
	W: (puzzled look on face) Different?		I used reflection here.
I wonder what she said to him.	C: The second time I called, he started asking questions like, "Why you think she want to talk to me?" and "What should I say?" (she begins to laugh) Boy, he's gonna give you a hard time.		
Anything else? Did he ask any questions?	W: Well, I explained to him that I would like to meet him, and maybe he would like to discuss any concerns he may have regarding your hospital stay, etc. I explained to him that I would meet and speak with him alone, and then we could set up a time when we could all meet together for a discussion.		I am hoping to clearly state the purpose of my interview with husband.

C: (smiling) Well, I hope you can get him to come in!

W: Your husband explained to me that Tuesday, around 7 pm would be a good time for him to come in, after he gets home from work.

It's like a challenge to her, I suppose.

Do you get the impression she's scaring him off?!

C: If he comes in and talks to you, it'll be something else! You see, the psychologist never talked to him on the phone directly; he used to tell me to talk with my husband, but then my husband won't come. I swear, Bob's so funny. He says, "I'm gonna tell her that you used to drink a lot." But I told him that you already know that, and a lot more. I told him that I tell the doctors and others about my drinking because, now the doctor says that that information was helpful in running tests on me, and stuff like that. I told Bob that I tell the truth about me, all he has to do is tell the truth about himself (pause).

Maybe her husband just needed someone to say they were going to listen to what <u>he</u> had to say.

His problem is that he keeps bringing up old news; he keeps bringing up things that happened a long time ago. Like, one time before we were married, he saw me with a guy, and even now he says things like, "Remember when you was going out with me, and then I saw you going out with someone else?" And we weren't even married yet! And then, the other day he was talking about how my son was caught with two other boys for truancy. Anyway, the other two boys have been in the youth detention facility a lot, and my son don't have no criminal record, so they let him go. But that happened when I first got sick, and the man came to talk to me about it when I was getting ready to take the ambulance to the hospital. So my husband keeps saying that I tried to hide this from him, but I just had other things on my mind, and forgot to tell my husband (now picking and scratching arm, around IV site). The doctors came in this morning.

① YES! Did you think of this at the time?

Was she surprised her husband agreed to come?

What would her husband do? Would he be physically abusive? Interpretation

① She changed the subject. Perhaps she and her son do keep information from her husband. There are two sides to every story!

or questioning needed.

You still pick up nonverbal cues— nice.

Good use of interpretation

W: It seems to me that their visit was upsetting to you... (pause).

(she had been smiling while previously talking, but stopped smiling when last statement was being said).

Attempting to interpret her change in facial expression. The IV seems to be a constant reminder of the reality of being in the hospital.

C: Well.... They discussed the infection I have. One doctor is gonna come back later to talk with me again. They were all talking, and when they finished explaining, I said, "Now tell me in English" (laughter). They talk in all those big terms, and I told them to speak in English (laughter). Then after that, they went outside the door, and I could hear them talking some more. They told me that there is some problem with the blood vessel— ① that the thing is getting bigger and might explode. They kinda hinted on maybe having to do surgery, but I'm not going to go through with that... (pause).

① A lay person's way of describing medical terms never ceases to amaze me.

Do you think she believes this? FEAR.

① Surprised?
② Self-analysis.

W: What you are saying to me then, is that your condition may be getting worse, and that surgery may help, according to the doctors... but that you will not go through with the surgery.

②① Restating and clarifying what she is telling me, so that she may focus more clearly, and to see if I am understanding her correctly.

C: That's right... I gotta leave this world with something left inside of me, after all the surgery I've been through. I'd rather live a few extra days, than to have the surgery and not ever wake up from it.

Interpretation.

W: What I hear you saying is that you do not want to have any more surgery performed because you fear that you may die....

(10 sec. or so pause)

C: (looking down)... Yeah...

Mmnn.... That may have been a bit too strong.

① Could you have shared this?

② Good.

W: You know, it's OK to have those feelings... it's a legitimate fear (pause). Did you feel this way when you had to have surgery before?

① I felt the same way when I needed surgery.

② Trying to assimilate past experiences and feelings with the present.

Does she hear stories about people who get surgery they don't need?

How'd you feel here? Did this take you off guard?

C: (looking at me) Yeah. And with my first surgery in 19__, if I had been a little older and wiser, I wouldn't have needed that surgery. I often wondered if I even needed that surgery. Like this time, all the doctors couldn't decide what I had, in the beginning and then they all agreed. Maybe they can't make up their minds if I need this surgery or not (pause).... Why are we talking about this surgery so much? Did the doctors tell you something that I don't know? (smiling).

Was that the surgery for ____?

Sounds defensive. Maybe she wants you to talk with her doctor? At this point it's fear of unknown.

W: No, I haven't spoken with the doctors, but you have said that there might be a possibility that you will need surgery, and have expressed some fear about it. I'm focusing on this because the possibility of surgery may become a reality in the future, and we will have to deal with that, and your feelings about whether you want to go through with it or not (smiling, but I'm kind of giving the look of "You know what I mean?").

First restating what she has said, but as an answer. Then clarifying reason for discussion of subject, and stating reality of situation.

③ Let's discuss. Why?

Power struggle.

④ YES! Keep this in the back of your mind.

C: Oh (smiling). Well, I was just wondering if maybe they had told you something that they didn't tell me. I don't know. We'll see what the doctor has to say when he comes back in here. Maybe he'll say that I won't need to have any surgery after all... (pause)... the doctors were kinda upset with me this morning because I had left my room last night and I was supposed to be back for my medicine in the IV, but I didn't get back until 11 pm or so, because I went to visit my friend down on one of the other floors. They said that it was important that I take all the medicine because of the infection I got, but I got started talking and

③ It seemed to go right over her head; in one ear and out the other.

④ She is denying the need for surgery, which may become a problem later on.

Does she feel they're punishing her?

pretty soon it was about 11 pm. So I came back, but my IV had infiltrated and they had to start it again over here (pointing to left forearm).

W: How did you feel, to be out of your room and walking around? (smiling).

C: Well, I had done it before, a couple of times, to go see my friend also. But I always got back in time to get the medicine put in the IV.

She didn't answer my question. Maybe if I try another approach....

W: I've noticed that you always keep your door closed. If your friend wasn't here, would you have left your room and walked around?

C: (smiling) No. I'd probably just stay in here. I don't mind being by myself. In fact, people get on my nerves sometime, that's why I keep my door closed. When I first came in here, I used to have the door open. One day this man, another patient, comes in and starts talking and talking, so I told him that I just had taken some medicine to make me sleepy, and I wanted to go to sleep now, so that he would leave. And people walk by and stick their heads in the doorway to see what's going on in the rooms. I know, 'cause I'm guilty of that myself! (laughs)

①
Yes—good control of interview.
②
Good—seeking out more information. Did she answer this question?
③
Did it work?

②
W: You have said that you don't mind being by yourself... is this also true for when you are at home?

C: Well, I do the housework and watch TV. Sometimes I don't even answer the phone all day.

W: Do you have any ideas as to why you feel the need to isolate yourself from others?

C: Well... I would like to get out more. In fact, I used to go play cards at my father's house. But it

I can relate to that.

①
Restatement of what she had said, to show that I'm listening, and to see if she will focus on that statement.
③
I purposely used that word "isolate" to see if she will react to it.

She reacted by putting the blame, of her loneliness

① Right on!

upset Bob, so I don't go anymore. He gets so jealous of me if I go out anywhere. He wants me to be home when he gets home. We used to go to parties and things like that, but the parties get boring after awhile.

or isolation, on her husband. This may be a cop-out, ① and it may take long-term counseling before she can place the blame on herself also.

W: Parties can become boring, and a person can feel alone, even with many people around (pause). Do you feel that your husband has a reason for feeling jealous or upset?

I know the feeling!

Where did she go that upset him?

C: No... (disgusted look). He just don't trust nobody. Not me, not anybody.

How about you?
② Good information for future use.

(There is a knock on the door and a maintenance man comes in asking if the bed has been fixed yet. She tells him yes, that someone has been in already and has fixed it. The man leaves)

I asked this question to see if maybe she could gain some insight as to her behavior and if it may be a ② contributing factor as to why her husband behaves the way he does.

C: They must have called him again by mistake, because there was another guy in here already, unless somehow the bed broke again without me knowing it! (laughs).

W: (nods affirmatively and smiles)

(Then the nurse's aide comes in with the food tray.)

MMnn...the room is beginning to look like Grand Central Station.

C: (to aide) You can just throw those newspapers and things on the floor (pointing to items on bedside stand).

Did you ask him how long he'd be?

(As the aide leaves, one of the residents comes into the room and asks pt. how she is doing. She says "fine." He looks at me, and so I introduce myself. He then starts to lift pts. gown to examine her.)

③ Yes!
④ How did you feel?

④
W: Sharon, I'll leave for a minute while he is examining you. I'll be back.

③ Respecting her need for privacy.

C: (she nods affirmatively and smiles)

(About 3 minutes later)

W: (entering room again, after dr. has left; look of "Well, what happened?" on my face)

① ??

Is this new?

C: He said I would need the IV in for about another week or so. If they stop the medicine now the infection could get much worse, even though I may feel like I'm ready to go home now.

W: Was the possibility of surgery mentioned?

Why didn't she ask?

C: No, he didn't say nothing, and I didn't ask him about it (looking down).

W: To me, it seems as though you may be depressed or worried about all that the doctors have been telling you about your illness... (about a 10 sec. pause).

Was this accurate?

C: (a slight smile, then no smile and eyes looking down) Uh.... Yeah, a little, but I really don't want to talk about that now. Maybe...maybe some other time.

She won't come right out and say it, but the feelings are there.

W: OK, we can talk about that at a later time... (pause). Well, we've discussed your situation with your husband a little more, but we still haven't come to any clear-cut decisions as to your plans for dealing with his behavior. Perhaps, when we've had a chance to all be together, if your husband decides to come in, then maybe the situation will begin to be a bit clearer. This may give him a chance to give his reasons as to why he behaves the way he does, and you may then be thinking of how you want this relationship to improve, or possibly end. We can deal with this as we go on.

Good summary.

Good control of interview. Interpretation, focus, restatement, reflection. Reason for next visit. Questioning—reason for self-insight.

Look at what's new in your interview skills!
1. you focused information.

Perhaps I should have focused on ① her feeling like she's ready to go home, and not bring up the issue of surgery again, but I was curious to see if the doctor had said anything about surgery, what her feelings would have been about what he had said.

Interpreting what I think she is feeling at this point.

Perhaps I was too abrupt in ending that part of the conversation. I should have given more support, then go on to summarizing the interview.

2. used
interpretation
more.
3. restated
information.
4. questioned
with a purpose.
5. reflected.
6. summarized
and now you have
focus for next
visit.

Excellent

Yes!

Is she going
to ask Dr. for
information?

With new talk
about surgery
and fears, is it
realistic? Have
you talked to
Dr.?

3 things student
liked about this
interview:
1. Conscious
awareness of
interviewing
skills to use.
2. Tried to stay
with patient's
feelings more and
less changing the
subject.
3. Stayed with
two goals or plan
for this particular
interview, rather
than getting off
into other areas
and finding it
hard to end the
interview.

C: (smiling) Well, I know something
will happen whether good or bad, if
you can get Bob in here to talk to
you. He may not show up!

W: (smiling) Well, we will have to
deal with that when the time comes,
and you may be right—he might not
show up. You're the person that I'm
mainly concerned with, though...
(smiling) that's why I'm going to
check back with you on Wednesday
to see the doctors give you a report
on your progress and if you would
like to discuss your feelings about
what they may have told you. OK?

C: (smiles, and nods head
affirmatively) All right.

W: And at that time, you may have
been in contact with your husband
again, and we can discuss that. I'd
also be interested to see if you are
up and walking around more, perhaps
even when your friend goes home,
OK?

C: (laughs) OK.

W: (getting up and replacing chair)
I'll see you Wed. morning, then;
Bye!

C: (smiling) OK, bye!

Looking at the
possible reality
of the
situation.

I want her to feel
as though someone
does care about
what she says and
feels and cares
for her well-being,
but at the same
time, I don't want
her to be dependent
on me (trying to
help foster self-
reliance).

Lip service or
will she make an
effort to be out
of bed more?

3 areas student
feels could be
improved or done
differently:
1. Need more depth
in interview.
2. Need more
confrontation.
3. Want it to move
faster toward
goals but seem to
be unable to
accomplish this.

Plan for next
visit:
1. Discussion
of illness
(feelings).
2. Discuss past
health, life
experiences, and
try to have her act
more in touch with
her feelings.
3. See about
talking with
counselor at son's
school (with
permission).

EXAMPLE 9   Directive approach purposely used by a
student in planning for an alcoholic client

The following example was written by an undergraduate student in her second field placement. She had several years of experience as a social worker in an alcoholic program, and was thus familiar with the rather specialized approach that sometimes must be used to help these individuals plan for themselves. Her field instructor also had many years experience working with alcoholics. The approach used is deliberately directive—too much so for other kinds of interview situations. However, this approach is sometimes necessary in working with a manipulative individual who has difficulty in planning for himself. Notice also that the worker does not accept the client's denial of his drinking problem—she knows beyond any doubt that a problem exists (from past records) and moves in at that level, rather than go along with the patient's suggestion that they pretend it doesn't exist. The patient accepts the fact that the worker knows he is continuing to drink, and it is obvious this problem is inseparable from the client's immediate concrete needs. His motivation for rehabilitation is questionable, and it is questionable whether he will follow through with the worker's suggestions and plans. However, the student is experienced enough to recognize that his willingness to see the AA worker may not be genuine.

SUPERVISORY COMMENTS	INTERVIEW CONTENT	GUT-LEVEL FEELINGS
Introduction—your name? Why you're there? etc. The fact you forgot to introduce yourself could indicate anxiety!	W: Good afternoon, Mr. Barlow. I'm from Social Services. How are you feeling today? Pt: One hundred percent better!	I noticed that I felt much more at ease this time than with my other patient.
It's awkward to start asking questions when pt. doesn't know yet who you are or why you're there—it could put some people on the defensive.	W: When did you come to the hospital? Pt: I've been here since Wednesday (the pt. then went into some detail about his medical problem, how he had injured his arm, etc.).	
Nice way of putting it— Lets him know he's in control—you're not making decisions for him.	W: I'm here to discuss with you your plans when you leave the hospital so we can see how my office may be of assistance to you.	
Most doctors don't tell the pt. the reason for the referral to Soc. Serv.—it's good this one did!	Pt: The doctor said you'd be here to talk to me about getting welfare and going to a boarding home. W: Why don't you tell me what you'll be needing when you leave the hospital.	
It would be interesting to learn how the dr. feels about pt's plans for work—if they're realistic or not.	Pt: Well, I need a job. W: What kind of work do you do? Pt: I'm a professional bellhop.	
Good observation and very appropriate feelings. You are not used to this kind of life style, even with your prior experience. Let's hope you never do get used to it and lose your feeling!	W: That kind of work requires long hours of standing and some lifting. Will you be able to do that with your arm problem?	I was afraid of this! How can anybody with a bad arm possibly support himself as a bellhop? I almost cry when I see this kind of situation.
	Pt: Oh yes. W: Have you a place to live?	

How did you react and feel to this rather unusual statement?	Pt: No, I was sleeping in a laundromat before I got to the hospital. W: A laundromat? Pt: Yeah, you know, on one of those tables. That's how I hurt my arm—when I fell off.	
You moved in rather abruptly with this—I would expect him to deny it.	W: Mr. Barlow, have you ever had any alcohol-related problems?	
Then why is he sleeping in laundromats?! Needs exploration.	Pt: Yeah, but I'm in AA now and I haven't had a drink in 6 months. W: Congratulations. It sounds like you're doing OK with that problem.	I wonder about this, but hope it's true.
Don't you believe him? Ha!	Pt: Yeah. I'll _never_ take another drink.	Yeah!!
The medical chart might tell you if he was intoxicated or had been drinking at time of admission.	W: So you weren't drinking at all before you went to the hospital? Pt: Oh no.	
A good plan, but he doesn't agree he needs this because he feels he doesn't drink!	W: Since you're going to need a place to live when you get out of here, I'd like to tell you about the local alcohol program. Pt: I ain't going there! W: Do you know about it? Pt: Yeah. They won't let you work for two weeks and they make you take Antabuse.	I know I'm trying to "sell" this, but it seems like this would be so much better than a welfare boarding home.
"The client" sounds sort of cold and computerized. Reality orientation for patient.	W: Those are not hard and fast rules, Mr. Barlow. In some cases, if the client is well enough to work, they go to work as soon as they want to. The Antabuse is the same way—it depends on the individual. Let me tell you why I suggest the alcohol program. Number one, it's a place to live until you can fully recuperate and are ready to work. And, maybe most important of all, it's a place that will help you stay sober. (The pt. thought about this apparently for a few moments)	

Many alcoholics are easy prey to being mugged on the street. The areas where they live are high risk.

Also, is this his way of manipulating and not going into the alcohol program?

Pt: Is there a chance I could get into one of those places in _____ county? I'll tell you, I don't like it in this county—a guy might get hit on the head here.

I don't know what this means.

W: I don't know about that, but I'll see if I can find out. Are you saying this county is more dangerous?

(Pt. shrugs, gives me a look like "you know")

But he hasn't really agreed to go—are you planning for or with the patient? If you're deliberately using a directive, advice-giving approach (which is appropriate many times with alcoholics), why did you choose to do so?

W: I don't want to give you the impression that it definitely will be possible for you to go into the alcohol program, Mr. Barlow. They may not have any vacancies just now, but I wanted you to have it to consider. If there aren't any vacancies now, the other thing I can suggest to you is a boarding home operated by the county.

What was he living on prior to admission? Was he getting welfare then? If not, why not?

Good response.

Pt: I was told I could get welfare too. How much is that?

W: I don't know exactly the amount of welfare payments or the eligibility requirements, but I can try to get some information for you.

Mr. Barlow, I don't mean to appear to be trying to give you the "hard sell" about the alcohol program, but would you tell me about your association with AA?

Pt: Yeah, I used to go to meetings all the time up on _____ street.

W: Do you have an AA sponsor now?

It's almost impossible for me to understand how someone can survive living as isolated as this.

This apparently is the level he can function with. AA may be less threatening than a structured treatment program.

Pt: No.

W: Do you have any relatives close by?

Pt: No.

W: How about friends?

Sad, sad. The only one.

Pt: My best friend is in (names a far away state). I could pick up that telephone right now and call him.

A good reply.	W: Would you like to talk with someone from AA? I have always been impressed with the fellowship of that organization and how the members help out each other.
A small hope to hang on to!	Pt: Yeah. Have one of them come see me.
Unfortunately, he's very apt not to follow through with your planning. Like many alcoholics, he's kind of going along with you to please you because you are his connection to get welfare and a place to live. It would be helpful to explore his feelings more. However, with alcoholics, sometimes the directive approach that simply assumes you know they are alcoholic and plans from there is most effective.	W: I'll contact someone and see if it can be arranged.

The interview pretty much ended at this point. There was some additional discussion about the fact that jobs are pretty scarce right now and I had a real feeling of futility about anything really useful being done to help this man.

In addition, he is so alone that I think if I were in his circumstances, I'd be hard pressed for a reason to go on, much less remain sober. |
| To deal with any of this, he needs to be in a protected setting so these things can be worked on without his becoming so frightened. | I don't really know what his potential for "rehabilitation" is, but I suspect that it would require vastly more than exists. He needs a decent place to live, good nutrition, medical care, clothes, transportation, money, and extensive vocational training. Plus of course, he needs motivation.

He was very friendly and cheerful when we were talking and didn't communicate any depression at all. |
| Very good recording. I felt I was there too. Your impressions are on the button—a sad and frustrating type of case. | For alcoholics I have worked with in the past, this is fairly typical and represents to me a method of keeping painful reality from getting too close. This is like a shell that would have to be at least partly broken down in order to effect any lasting changes in life style for this client. |

EXAMPLE 10 Reflection and interpretation
techniques used to help client verbalize covert feelings

The following recording was made by a first-year graduate student who was obviously learning techniques of reflection and interpretation. Effective use of these skills helped this otherwise rather nonverbal client clarify thinking and feelings in several areas.

SUPERVISORY COMMENTS	INTERVIEW CONTENT	GUT-LEVEL FEELINGS
	C. My mother's not coming.	Silence.
	Wkr. She won't be here this weekend?	
	C. She called last night and said she wouldn't be able to come, that she couldn't afford it.	Silence.
	Wkr. It costs too much money.	
	C. Yeah, she doesn't have enough money in her check book and the things can't be shut off—electricity has to be paid.	
	Wkr. You feel bad she's not coming?	
	C. Oh, it's OK.	He seemed so sad. The bravado was gone, but he couldn't say he felt bad.
Good.	Wkr. It's alright with you she won't be here?	
	C. I haven't seen her for three weeks and now it will be three weeks more because she'll have to work on the weekends.	
	Wkr. You'd like to have seen her.	
I agree with your comment about not getting into the financial situation at this point.	C. She has to pay the bills. She doesn't have too much in her checking account and I don't have that much in funds so she won't be here.	I know I should clarify his exact financial situation but that didn't seem the most important thing at this moment.
	Wkr. You understand that the money is a problem.	
	C. Yeah.	Silence.
She let you down?	Wkr. Does she usually do this?	I really wanted to say, "You're sad because you need her to be here now," but didn't.
	C. She'd come if she had the money. I'm going to have a big meeting with the lawyers. It's not going to be pleasant. I'm going to say some things that have to be said.	

Wkr. You have some things to straighten out with them.

Who exactly is client talking about here?

C. Yeah. I haven't seen them since I've been here. We've talked over the phone a lot, but this is the first time we'll be meeting here. There's some things to be straightened out. His personality is difficult for some people and that makes it hard for them and they then come back and tell me, and these are people I have to deal with.

They haven't been to see him either!

Wkr. He alienates people who are important to you. How does this happen?

Silence.

C. It happened with my mother. I decided we should have a new refrigerator for the house and she said she wanted the money for it and he said no.

Wkr. That made a problem.

C. She said she wouldn't have anything more to do with him.

Wkr. How does that affect you?

C. She gets angry and won't talk to him.

Wkr. That puts you in the middle. You need him and you need her.

C. I have to work it out. I have to straighten out the finances with him. My bills come to $200 less than is in my checking account.

Wkr. He's in charge of your finances.

C. He signs the checks.

Wkr. Is he a guardian for you?

I believe you're right.

C. I'm not sure exactly how it works. He signs the checks. I can't fire him because he's under contract.

I had a feeling through the whole time of his feelings of helplessness, inability to assert himself and cope with this as he would like to. I think his bravado was gone

Wkr. You feel in a bind?

C. It makes me too sad to talk about it.

Wkr. You're angry with the lawyer?

C. I guess he's OK. He knows his job. He just puts people off.

Wkr. He puts you off?

C. He always returns my calls when he gets the message.

"How does he put you off?"

Wkr. When he gets the message?

C. He's good about that.

Wkr. But there is a problem between him and your mother?

C. So tell me about your day in the wheelchair.

Good! Confrontation!

Wkr. I'll be happy to tell you, but you know, you changed the subject. It was difficult for you.

C. I didn't know I was doing that—I guess I did. I don't feel very talkative.

Wkr. That's OK. You don't have to feel talkative with me. You don't have to be pleasant. This is a hard thing to talk about, isn't it?

You're making a breakthrough.

This was a most unfortunate event.

C. I'd sometimes like to go to sleep and not wake up.

Wkr. We can still talk.

C. Tell me about your day in the wheelchair.

Wkr. Is that what you'd like to talk about?

C. Yeah, what happened?

and he tried to use being mad to escape his feelings.

Silence.

He knows I spent a day in a wheelchair to find out what it is like.

He smiled when I said this. My reason for this was to show that I was aware of his changing the subject and to be in control of the interview.

At this moment some other person came into the room and started talking and called another. My client's roommate and the other guy did a lot of talking, but neither the client nor I said anything. I finally turned my back on them and I said,

EXAMPLE 11 Process-recorded phone conversation
of a crisis intervention nature

This client had been hospitalized in preparation for surgery. At the last minute he left the hospital against medical advice, refusing the surgery. The doctor requested social service help with this problem, as the surgery was really needed. An undergraduate student in her second quarter of field placement had called the patient's home and left a message for him to return her call. He did, and the following interview took place by phone. Notice the effective use of confrontation and interpretation. The approach was definitely unorthodox, but fit well with this particular student's personality, and she was able to carry it off successfully.

SUPERVISORY COMMENTS	INTERVIEW CONTENT	GUT-LEVEL FEELINGS
	Wkr. "Mr. D, what happened?"	
	Pt. "Well, I was going to call you. They came to get me and I decided that I should come home and prepare myself for the operation."	
	Wkr. "Prepare yourself—how?"	
	Pt. "Well, you know, straighten out my affairs and build myself up a little bit."	
Interpretation.	Wkr. "You feel you aren't ready for surgery yet?"	Good, he's undecided—do a good job—maybe he'll come back.
	Pt. "Well, I don't know!"	
	Wkr. "Let's talk about it."	
	Pt. "Well, my doctor told me it was OK to check out for awhile. I have a funeral I wanted to go to and I felt I had to be there. And I need to straighten out my affairs too."	I talked with his doctor and he didn't tell him it was OK. Can I level with him? I'll try it.
	Wkr. "Mr. D, you know the reason I called you is because I care what happens to you?"	
	Pt. "Yes, I know that."	
Strong language!!	Wkr. "Then cut the crap and level with me. I've talked with your doctor and it's hard to believe he would let you go."	
Yes, I'd think there would be a pause!	(pause)	

69

	Pt. "Well, I don't know what they will find."	Good!
It worked! Nice reflection.	Wkr. "You're afraid of what they will find?"	
	Pt. "Yes, I don't know if I'll ever be able to go back to work and I don't want to be a burden on anyone."	
Interpretation.	Wkr. "So you're afraid of something really bad happening?"	(Get back on the track—don't lose that!)
	Pt. "I just wish I knew."	
	Wkr. "What did your doctor say about that?"	
	Pt. "Well he said I should have the surgery."	
	Wkr. "And you don't know what to do?"	
	Pt. "That's right, I have an appointment with the clinic on Friday so I'll be in the clinic."	
	Wkr. "You mentioned you didn't want to be a burden, could you explain that to me?"	Didn't want to lose track of that statement.
	Pt. "You know—a burden on anyone."	
Interpretation.	Wkr. "You mean you don't want to have to depend on anyone?"	
	Pt. "Right."	
Very good.	Wkr. "Have you given any thought to what might happen if you don't have the surgery?"	
	Pt. "Well, not really."	
	Wkr. "Do you think it would be a good idea to look at both sides of the situation?"	
	Pt. "What way?"	
	Wkr. "Well, you're still a young man— if you don't have the surgery what do you think could possibly happen?"	

Pt. "That's true."

Good—you make him say it.

Wkr. "What's true?"

Pt. "It could be worse; but when I left I had felt OK."

Wkr. "How do you feel now?"

Pt. "Still OK."

Wkr. "Well, I hope you continue to feel OK."

Pt. "I'm coming into the clinic on Friday."

He's trying to tell me something—he's reaching out.

Wkr. "What for?"

Pt. "For a checkup."

Wkr. "I'd really like to see you when you come in."

Pt. "OK."

Wkr. "Maybe we could even meet with the doctor and he could explain things in more detail to you."

Pt. "That would be fine."

(pause)

Wkr. "If you need to talk to me before, you can call me here."

Pt. "OK."

(we hung up)

EXAMPLE 12 Effective use of confrontation with client who had been repeatedly rejecting the worker

It was obvious after many contacts with this individual that she had some strong feelings and fears she needed to verbalize. But whenever the student attempted to encourage verbalization, the client rejected her by saying she felt too ill to talk, or otherwise shutting off communication. Until this interview the student had been unable to break through this defense, though student and field instructor agreed this was needed. The BSW student had rather advanced skills, and entered this interview determined to apply some of the techniques she had role-played with her field instructor and used successfully in other situations. The following brief interchange takes place in the middle of the interview and illustrates how the breakthrough was achieved. (In the remaining interview the client revealed long pent-up feelings and was able to cry therapeutically for the first time).

SUPERVISORY COMMENTS	INTERVIEW CONTENT	GUT-LEVEL FEELINGS
	(long pause)	
	I said, "You know Mrs. T., I've been coming in here to see you for some time now and you've been avoiding me and I can understand—I even played along with you but I will only be here a couple of weeks and there's a lot of feelings in you we need to talk about. It's good that you can share your anger with me."	OK—the time has come—don't blow it—confront her.
	She said, "I'm going to miss you; (pause) I have been avoiding you. I'm so afraid."	At the time she paused I thought oh no, I did blow it—but she continued.
	I said, "Afraid?"	
	She said (yelling), "That I'll never get well. I don't want to leave my daughter alone. She has no one but me."	
	I said, "We need to talk about this."	
	She said, "If I die—what will my daughter do without me?"	
Very nice interpretation!	I said, "You're afraid of dying?"	

EXAMPLE 13   Effective use of touching

In this brief segment the recorder uses touching as an effective means of communicating genuine warmth and empathy for her client. Such nonverbal communication should be included in process recordings. Bear in mind that while this particular social worker felt comfortable embracing her client, not everyone would have. Touching can be used effectively only if it comes spontaneously and genuinely. Some people are "touching persons" and others are not. Social workers should not try to be something they are not. Had the worker not felt comfortable with touching her client, she would undoubtedly have found another means of communicating her feelings. (Continued expression of in-depth feelings characterized the rest of this interview.)

SUPERVISORY COMMENTS	INTERVIEW CONTENT	GUT-LEVEL FEELINGS
	Client: "I don't need anyone."	
	Wkr: "You don't need anyone?"	

Client: "No—nobody cares about me anyway; I don't care if he doesn't want to
see me, but I won't talk to anyone."

Wkr: "You feel nobody cares?"

Client: "Even the people that are
supposed to care about me don't."

Wkr: "Let's talk about that."

Client: "Nothing to talk about; they
just don't care. They won't allow me to
cry or yell or anything."

Wkr: "What do you think they feel about
you?"

Client: "They probably are sick of
seeing my face around here—they'll be
glad to get me out of here."

She stopped yelling and started crying.
I put my arm around her.

EXAMPLE 14   Beginning student rejected by client—lack of skills prevent move to a deeper level

This is one of the very first interviews for an undergraduate student with no prior
social work experience. It illustrates how a student can come back from an interview
and state sincerely that "there were no problems" when a more experienced interviewer would probably have elicited more meaningful material, permitting a more
complete assessment of possible problem areas. This example is typical in many ways
of first interviewing attempts.

SUPERVISORY COMMENTS	INTERVIEW CONTENT	GUT-LEVEL FEELINGS
(What comments would you make if this were your student?)	Good afternoon, are you V.M.?	
	Client. Yes, who are you?	
	My name is Albert Smith and I work for social service here. I received your....	Client interrupts me at this point. Anger comes to me because of his interruption.
	C. Oh yeah! Well, I was talking to some others about my financial situation, but young man, I think you won't be able	

to help after I tell you what I have to say.

What may that be, Mr. M.?

C. Well, You see I have always been a self-supporting man, and I have never needed charity or have been on public relief. So to make the long story short, my financial problems as far as food and shelter, they have been accounted for.

At this point he pats on my knee and gives me a wink.

Well, how do you do that, if you do not mind my asking?

C. Simple. I have many friends. Now, the real financial problems I have are my car payments, my rent and my insurance payments. I think you won't be able to help me with that.

It seems like so.

C. Well anyway, thanks for trying but anyway I'm leaving today.

Client shakes my hand as if he was trying to get rid of me as soon and as politely as possible.

OK Mr. M., I hope everything turns out well. Goodbye.

C. Oh, it will, son, goodbye now.

EXAMPLE 15   A struggle with a manipulative client

This interviewer is an individual with several years of experience and some advanced training. The example illustrates how easy it is to lapse into advice giving and false reassurances when the interviewer becomes uncomfortable or fails to concentrate on the use of reflective, interpretive, or other techniques that might have been more effective. The reader can almost feel the tug of war as the client keeps asking for a cigarette and the worker keeps refusing to give her one. Confrontation should probably have been used at some point to draw attention to this behavior and get at the underlying cause—i.e., client appears to be avoiding discussion of certain issues, and asking for the cigarette successfully distracts the worker. Notice that the worker has entered the interview with a prepared approach and goal and has some difficulty deviating from it, even though the situation obviously calls for some alterations in approach.

SUPERVISORY COMMENTS	INTERVIEW CONTENT	GUT-LEVEL FEELINGS
	W: Hello Mrs. Penn, I am Miss Hanks. I understand that your son came to see you this p.m.	At this point I was a little apprehensive and unsure as to what her reaction would be.

C: Yes, that's right.

W: He told me that you had agreed to go back to your son's home—is that correct?

C: Yes, because he told me that there really isn't any place else for me to go.

I was relieved because her reaction was rather calm.

Good. Mild confrontation.

W: How do you feel about this? This a.m. you were pretty firm about not going back there.

Loss of control over life situation. Dr. sounds threatening! I wonder how effectively he handled this. I wonder if she could be saying, "At least he knows I'm not incompetent."

C: Well, what can I do about it? The dr. said if I didn't go, he'd get a court order. At least my son knows me.

I was mentally agreeing with her and feeling somewhat bad about it.

W: Do you understand why the dr. wants you to go to your son's house instead of living with your mother?

Did you let her see that you were feeling bad about her sense of being able to do nothing about the plans being made for her?

C: Yes, because my mother can't take care of me at home.

W: And how do you feel about that?

Good—persisting re: feelings.

C: Sometimes my mother aggravates me.

You might have used reflection here—"She aggravates you....?"

W: Why?

This needs more exploration.

C: She argues with me about little things.

Would it have been better for her to verbalize this rather than your doing it for her?

W: Well, she is kind of old and I guess that might be expected.

C: Well, she's not that much older than me.

You effectively cut off client's expression of feelings! Why? What were you feeling here?

W: She's 25 years older—that's a lot.

You see it as being a lot older because

75

Supervisor comments	Dialogue	Therapist reflections
you're very young—how is the <u>client</u> perceiving it?		
Was there a long silence in here by any chance?	C: Is it? I guess it is. W: And I guess that might be why she said this a.m. that she couldn't take care of you at home.	
Forgive her for what? Does client have feelings of anger toward her mother for a number of things that she needs to verbalize?	C: Yes, I guess so. She's my mother so I have to forgive her (sobbing briefly).	I began to feel that she has accepted reality of situation. My feeling was one of sadness that people should have to end up like this.
Interesting she chose this time to ask for a cig.—perhaps the discussion is getting too heavy for her?	At this point, Mrs. Penn asked for a cigarette. I told her that I'd like to talk a little longer about going to her son's home, so I said, W: You still really haven't said how you feel about going back to your son's home. Are you upset or angry?	I was preparing myself for outburst of crying here. I was surprised at client's complacency.
Helplessness again—does she need to talk more about this feeling?	C: No, what can I do? (I got a cigarette for her) C: You know, they still don't know when I'll go there. The dr. says in a week, but I don't believe him.	
What's she trying to say here?		
Nice platitude, but is this what client <u>really</u> wanted from you?	W: Well, these things take time. C: Yes, I know. W: You will be seeing the dr. at clinic after you leave. C: I will? Oh, good—how do I get a card? W: That's all taken care of—you'll get it when you leave.	
I wonder what this means?	C: OK—you're so nice. I like you so much.	
Did you really mean this or were you	W: Well, thank you—I like you and want to do my best to help you.	I wasn't sure how to respond. Am I

responding automatically to her compliment?

Aha—manipulation?

C: Will you get me another cigarette?

W: Well, I'll be leaving in a few minutes and I'll ask the nurse on my way out.

C: OK.

W: Did your son say he'd be in touch with you again?

Right! But why do you think she keeps asking for a cig. just as you start discussing her going home to her son's house? Confrontation of some sort needed here—let's discuss and role-play.

C: Yes, won't you get me another cig.?

W: Let's talk some more first—so then you'll be going to your son's house as soon as his extra room is ready for you?

By now I was beginning to feel a little manipulated.

C: Yes.

Are you trying to convince yourself she really is agreeable to going—you can't quite believe it?

W: Why don't you think of it as a place to gain your strength and take some time to recover?

I was trying to capitalize on my earlier impression of her facing the reality of the situation.

C: Yes. You know I need the eye drops four times per day, but I can't tell which bottle is which. Will you come see me there—what will I do without you?

What is she really saying? You might have used interpretation— "You're thinking it may be lonely there..." or etc.

W: I'm sure you'll manage fine—think of how nice it'll be to leave the hospital.

Her way of telling me that she really does understand somewhat why she needs to go to her son's home?

Yes!

Are you sure she feels it's "nice" to be able to leave the hospital? Some people would rather stay in the hosp., which has now become a familiar environment.

C: Will you get me another cig.?

W: On my way out, I'll tell the nurse.

C: Tell Mary—she's nice to me.

Re: the above—looks like you were having difficulty relating to her feelings, so

W: You know you said this a.m. that it would be better if everything was over. Why did you feel like that?

I wanted to ask her this, so I just stuck it in here.

convincing myself here?

SUPERVISORY COMMENTS	INTERVIEW CONTENT	GUT-LEVEL FEELINGS
"when you don't know what else to do, give advice (or platitudes)" would apply here!		
	C: Oh, because the student nurses are always going to meetings, they never have time for me, but Sara's nice.	I was surprised at her answer.
What kind of answer did you expect or were looking for?		
I don't think she knows what you are referring to or if she does, is choosing not to respond to it.	W: Do you feel like that often?	
	C: No—won't you please get me a cig.?	
	W: No, but I'll tell nurse. I'll see you probably tomorrow.	I was feeling definitely manipulated and had made up my mind not to give in.
Why not ask her why she keeps doing this?	C: OK.	
	(interview ends)	

EXAMPLE 16   A student is shocked by his client's disclosure

Social workers like to think that nothing can shock them—that they have been exposed to so much of life that nothing surprises them anymore. The following was written by an undergraduate student who had certainly "been around," having seen active duty in service and having a number of other significant life experiences and some social work experience. The client's disclosure was totally unexpected and obviously caught the student off guard, as the client revealed a behavior that many people would condemn or consider controversial. The student had undoubtedly encountered this behavior before. However, the recording shows his struggle to keep his composure, and his obvious concern over how much of his feeling of surprise and shock he should let his client see. The student had been in field placement for several months and had reached the point where he felt quite comfortable in using the "gut-level feelings" column.

The following excerpt starts in the middle of the interview. A number of routine topics have been discussed. The client then started to express her feelings about something, but hesitated to reveal her controversial behavior because she was not certain how the social worker would respond.

SUPERVISORY COMMENTS	INTERVIEW CONTENT	GUT-LEVEL FEELINGS
	W: You never talked about this topic before?	
	C: I have been afraid to.	
	W: Why?	

C: If I tell you, will you promise not to tell anyone?

I don't particularly like your choice of words here—"I can't" would have been better. Do you know why?

W: <u>I don't have</u> to promise that, I can't tell anyone anything about you or our conversation without your permission anyway.

I can't make any promises because I don't know what I will be promising. Besides it will probably be something my supervisor will have to help me on.

Read the material on confidentiality in the Student Room Library for suggestions how to handle this!

C: I know, but promise me anyway.

W: I don't have to promise because I can't tell and besides if you are afraid I might tell then you don't have to tell me.

C: Alright, I'll tell you because I trust you.

W: OK.

Now if she tells me it will be because she wants to.

C: I.... (revealing the controversial behavior in several words).

W: What?

How do you think she felt here?

C: I... (naming the behavior again).

W: What?

How did YOU feel?!

C: I.... (naming the behavior again) Don't you know what that means?

W: Yes.

This is something I never suspected and it shocked the "H" out of me!

C: Does it make any difference to you?

Possibly it does matter—good self-awareness. Let's discuss.

W: No, if that is the way it is with you and you are happy it doesn't bother me.

It really doesn't matter, but why do I feel so uncomfortable—maybe it does matter. This is very shocking, though.

C: The reason I didn't tell you before is because I didn't trust you.

W: I know you didn't.

She might come back later and blame you if

C: I'm sorry, but I do trust you now. If anybody had found out I didn't know how they would react.

This is true because you don't even know

anyone should find out what she revealed.

W: That is understandable.

C: Don't tell anyone OK, and I mean don't tell anyone.

how I'm reacting. I don't know how I'm reacting for that matter.

Why the drastic change in subject? Looks like you wanted out! Understandable under the circumstances— you probably needed to get yourself together before you could proceed!

I empathize with how you must have been feeling.

W: OK. We will have to end this here because I have another appointment.

(following some more brief discussion, the interview ends)

EXAMPLE 17   Strong transference and countertransference cause the student to become the client

The following example illustrates dramatically what can happen when transference and countertransference are not handled effectively. This student knew what was occurring; the "gut-level feelings" column indicates her frustration and anxiety over not being able to control the situation. This particular student normally exhibited very advanced skills, and the interchange in this interview was not typical of her personally or of her usual way of relating to people. The fact that the student reported what happened so honestly shows her desire for help from her field instructor.

SUPERVISORY COMMENTS	INTERVIEW CONTENT	GUT-LEVEL FEELINGS
	S (student). "Do you have anyone to visit you?"	
	C (client). "Yes, I have a lovely daughter, Matilda."	
You're not out of control here—it's OK. Why do you feel loss of control here?	S. "Oh yes, I had heard you had a daughter."	This is where I started losing control.
	C. "Yes, I wish you could meet her, she's a lovely girl."	
Good. Pursue it.	S. "I would like to meet her, maybe I can."	
	C. "I would like for you to."	

S. "Is she married?"

C. "No, divorced."

S. "Oh, and she lives with you?"

C. "Yes, she does. Where do you live?"

S. "I live in _____."

C. "Oh yes, that's a nice area; I live in _____. Do you have family here?"

This is where you started to lose control.

S. "Yes, I have two children and my mother here."

How might you have better answered her question?

C. "You have two children? I don't believe it. You look like such a child yourself."

You fell for it! You must have been feeling anxious and insecure for some reason.
①
Why did you volunteer that you are divorced?

①
S. "Yes, two girls. They are 6 and 7 years old. I'm divorced."

C. "Oh no; I'm so sorry. I know what it's like. My Matilda is divorced too." Do you believe this?

Your need to talk about it yourself instead of exploring client's situation? What is client trying to say?

S. "Don't be sorry; I'm comfortable with it."

C. "I know, but it's hard."

S. "Yeah, sometimes."

She's probably picking up your tone of voice.

C. "You look tired."

S. "I am a little."

What is she saying?

C. "You really don't have to sit here with me. Why don't you go get some rest?" Oh boy!

"Oh boy" is right! What happened??

Do you?

S. "But I enjoy sitting here with you; I am resting."

What does she see the role of the worker as being?

C. "Well, you're lucky you don't have to do hard work in social service."

Comments	Interview	Gut-level feelings
① Good question!	S. "It involves a lot of emotional energy."	① Good grief! What have I said?
Very significant.	C. "Well, you won't have to spend any energy on me. I won't make you listen to me."	
	S. "Well, you talk if you feel like it."	
And she's just found out what your problems are so now she can justify not talking to you.	C. "Nobody wants to hear my problems. They all have problems of their own."	Why didn't I use reflection?
	S. "But it feels good sometimes to talk to someone else."	
What does this mean?? Reflection was needed.	C. "Not really."	
	S. "Well, I'm here if you feel like talking."	
What does she really mean here?	C. "You're lucky your mother lives here."	
Whose needs are you meeting? Yours or the client's?	S. "Yes, I really depend on her a lot. She lives near me—only about 4 miles. I see her a lot."	She's supplying minimal encouragement and I'm talking away!
OK—I accept this explanation—I'd feel uncomfortable with it too after an interview like this.	I can't remember the rest, I was so involved in trying to escape this conversation plus realizing she was getting me to talk. Besides I knew I was going to write this down and wondered how I could avoid it.	This is ridiculous.
I imagine you have some anxiety about how to approach her next time after such a disastrous encounter. Let's discuss.		

EXAMPLE 18   A student experiences difficulty
terminating a relationship

A rather advanced undergraduate student had been following the same client throughout her field placement. It had taken considerable effort (and skill) for the relationship to become established. When it came time for termination, both client and student found it difficult. In the following brief interview the student is introducing the new worker. Such difficulties in terminating are not at all unusual; however, most recorders are not as expressive as this student in the "gut-level feelings" column. It is reproduced here exactly as the student recorded it, preceded by a portion of the next-to-the-last interview.

SUPERVISORY COMMENTS	INTERVIEW CONTENT	GUT-LEVEL FEELINGS
	I said, "How are you feeling today?"	I'm scared to open my mouth—what's the matter with me?
	She said, "Not good; this is awful."	
	I said, "What is?"	
Wait! What is she really saying? Could you have used this as an opening to discuss her fear of death?	She said, "I'll never leave this hospital."	She's in a bad mood—don't push your luck. I won't get anywhere trying to counsel her today. (What I really meant was—I don't want to counsel her today.)
	I said, "Did you see your doctor today?"	
Why did you change the subject?—oh—I see.	She said, "Yes, early this am; he comes in about 6 and wakes me up" (angrily).	
	I said, "Did you discuss these feelings with him?"	
	She nodded yes.	
And she'll miss you too.	She said, "So what are you going to be doing next week when you leave?"	WOW—(my field instructor) was right—she is trying to reject me because I'm leaving.
	I said, "I'll be in school on campus."	
	She didn't answer.	
	I said, "The nurse tells me your son has been sick."	
	She said, "Yes, he has the flu."	
	I said, "You must be worried about him."	
	She said, "Well he's sleeping—I just spoke with him."	
	I said, "How long has he been sick?"	She's not rejecting me today—yet.
	She said, "He went home yesterday from work. I didn't see him."	
	I said, "It's going around."	
	(pause)	I'm really uneasy. Reject me so I can leave.

I said, "Tell me what the machine you're hooked up to does."

She said, "It flushes me out."

I said, "Flushes you out? Are you on foods now?"

Shook her head no.

She said, "No foods—how could I eat? This irrigates me—the impurities in my system."

I said, "I see."

(pause for about one minute)

She said, "Please don't sit there and look at me like that when I don't feel well"—angrily and loud. "It's very annoying."

AHEM! What are you saying with your behavior here?
① Interesting thought on your part.

I said, "I'm not looking at you—I'm reading the notice on the machine."

I'm being defensive— could be guilt because I wanted her to reject ① me (I wonder if I'm having trouble leaving her?).

She said, "Look, please go, I really don't want to talk to anyone right now."

I waited a moment.

I'm not sure what you mean here in your comment.

I said, "I can understand how you feel; suppose I come back when you feel better?"

Sure you will—she'll never feel better as long as I come—it's too useful.

She said, "OK dear."

You were able to escape.

I got up and patted her arm, smiled and gleefully left. Wednesday I'll see her alone—Thursday I will introduce the new worker if possible.

Last Interview

I went in only to introduce the new worker and found Mrs. X sitting up eating her first meal in months. I wasn't looking forward to this, but this situation provided an easy out. The nurse was there also.

Good—I won't have to stay.

I said, "Well, good morning—how
exciting—your first meal."

She said, "It sure is."

I said, "That's good, I'm happy for you."

She glanced at the new worker.

I said, "Well, Mrs. X, I am leaving
today, and I would like for you to meet
Barbara Smith, the social worker who
will be here if you should need her."

(Mrs. X had said to me after I said I was leaving, "I wish you luck" and looked at her tray.)	It's not as bad as I thought it would be.

Barbara—"Mrs. X, if you should need me
for any reason the nurses here know
where to reach me."

Mrs. X—"OK dear, thank you."

I said, "OK, good luck to you and take
care of yourself."

She said, "I will."

I said, "Good bye."

Your feelings are honest ones. It can be very difficult to end a relationship; especially considering how long it took for this one to become established. Many workers probably experience feelings similar to yours.	Barbara and I left. We never sat down (if I had sat down, Barbara would have too).	This showed avoidance on my part. I felt very guilty after I left because I probably could have gotten her to talk. On the other hand, I just wanted out. I'm very disappointed in myself.

EXAMPLE 19   A student is benignly ineffective in his interview

Most beginning students with limited knowledge aren't very effective in their first few interviews. They don't accomplish much, but neither do they harm anyone (Example 20 discusses the differences between a "benignly ineffective" interview and one that actually damages the client in some way). As students gain in experience and knowledge, their interviewing/counseling behavior should begin to move more toward the helping end of the scale.

The following interview took place in a hospital. The nurse on the floor asked a medical social worker to see the patient because "he is worried about a place to live upon discharge and also seems somewhat agitated." The interviewer, a first-year graduate student, had been in field placement only about a month. I have made remarks in the "supervisory comments" column to show possible supervisory reactions to this rather typical beginning interview. The "gut-level feelings" column has been omitted in this example.

SUPERVISORY COMMENTS	INTERVIEW CONTENT
How might you have introduced yourself more effectively? Client is obviously wondering who you are and why you are there.	W.: Hello. (silence) You wanted to see me about a place to live?
	C.: Uh, I'm not sure.
	W.: Well, the nurse gave me this form (shows referral form to client) and asked me to talk with you.
	C.: Oh, you're the social worker I asked to see.
	W.: Oh, yes—I'm sorry, I forgot to introduce myself. I'm Roberta Menig from Medical Social Service.
	C.: OK. Yeah—I do have a problem. You see, my rent was up last week and I haven't paid it and I know I'm gonna have to look for a new place to live when I get out of here. Can you help me find a place?
Are you sure you can find a place for him? Is your role to find a place for him or to help him find it himself? (Beginning interviewers often feel a strong urge to move too quickly toward a solution without adequately exploring the client's situation and needs.)	W.: Yes, I'm sure we can. There are lots of apartments here for rent. I know there are some nice ones not far from here and probably not too expensive.
	C.: Well, I sort of wanted to live in the north section.
	W.: Oh. Well, do you get the daily paper? We can check the classifieds.
	C.: I wonder if they will take me without any deposit. I don't have any money right now.
Fortunately this client is able to express what he wants. What do you think his needs are?	W.: Oh, I see.
	C.: My roommate was working until two weeks ago but he got laid off so now we both have to move. I've got to get a place for both of us.
Now we begin to see what his needs are. Are you hesitant to explore this for fear he might bring up problems you don't know how to deal with?	W.: Do you have any savings?
I wonder what his financial situation has	C.: No. I used them all up.

been? Was he working? How does he usually manage financially?

Did you feel relieved here that you were able to offer something concrete to your client? But is this what he really wants/needs?

Naive assumption there'll be no bureaucratic foul-ups!

Again, false reassurances. You don't know enough about roommate's situation to be able to give this assurance.

(This interview lasted perhaps 10 minutes. The student is probably leaving with a good feeling that she survived this interview and feels she was helpful. How many needs were not examined? Did she deal with what the client really needed? A more skilled interviewer would have elicited information regarding the patient's employment, how long before he can work again, feelings about being broke, determined how supportive (or problematic) the relationship with the roommate is, given more details about the referral, and explored client's feelings about this plan. She might have also given some hints on what to do if client should run into any problems with the referral—i.e., alternate plans or resources available.)

W.: OK. What we can do is refer you to the XYZ Welfare Department. They'll give you temporary assistance till you can get back to work again. You can go there right from here and they'll give you money right away. I'll have the doctor fill out a form for you to take with you.

C.: OK. Can they help my roommate too?

W.: Yes, probably, if he's broke too.

C.: He is.

W.: Well, they can probably help him too then.

C.: OK.

W.: Well, it looks like we're all set.

C.: Yeah. Thanks for stopping by. (He shook my hand and I left.)

EXAMPLE 20   A student harms his client*

This is the nightmare of every social work student: "Will I do something that might harm my client because I don't know what I'm doing?" Most reasonably sensitive, mature, and well-adjusted students do not cause emotional damage to their clients, no matter how naive they might be about human behavior or interviewing/counseling techniques. Clients are quite tough and often well defended against blundering social workers. Most students are benignly harmless in their ignorance—they may fail to pick up on key facts or not know how to deal with certain feelings because they lack the required skills. As a result, they may take three or four contacts to accomplish what an experienced worker could do in one.

What kinds of behavior would actually be harmful to a client? Several factors usually combine to cause this type of outcome. The highly judgmental student with

*This is not an actual interview. However, it illustrates types of harmful behavior that have actually occurred.

87

strong, rigid feelings about various issues or life experience may inflict his views on his client, causing him to build walls to defend against the obtrusive social worker. Guilt feelings may be provoked and reinforced to the point that they interfere with the client's functioning. His negative experience with the harmful interviewer may cause the client to refuse further services and make it difficult for a more skilled practitioner to gain his 'rust and eventually build an effective relationship.

Other students may be personally immature and lack a basic understanding of the meaning of certain kinds of life experiences and how people react to them. A student may have problems of his own that he has not yet worked through that color his interactions with others. He may see his client's needs only through the mirror of his own problems and experiences, and thus be unable to perceive that different people might respond differently to similar life situations. Other students lack a basic sensitivity to people—they regard others' emotions as if they were scientific facts to be elicited, confronted, and dealt with, no matter what the cost to the individual.

Every social worker will encounter interview situations in which he does not respond in the most helpful manner possible because of his own needs at the moment. However, this should occur rarely, and the worker should be so sensitized to such situations that when they do occur, no real damage is done to the relationship or to the consumer's adjustment and coping mechanisms. When interactions with clients prove to be harmful, most supervisors will work closely with the student to examine the cause and to evaluate whether social work is, in fact, the profession best suited to the student's interests and abilities.

The following recording illustrates an interview during which the student has damaged his client. The student is in a unit conducting eligibility studies of people applying for AFDC (Aid to Families with Dependent Children). The applicant is a recently divorced forty-two-year-old woman with seven children. The portion of the interview that follows takes place during a home visit. Notice how the interviewer insists that the client talk about a sensitive area that she obviously doesn't want to discuss. Further on we can see factors in the student's personal life that probably are causing him to press for this information in order to meet some needs of his own.

The interviewer seems virtually insensitive to the applicant's strong verbal and nonverbal communication and plunges ahead in spite of obvious resistance. In the end, the client builds her defenses against the prying worker and becomes so uncomfortable that she withdraws her application, even though she apparently has real financial need and is probably eligible for financial assistance. A supervisor would have no choice but to assign the case to another worker, preferably a highly experienced individual who can communicate a great deal of warmth and acceptance. The supervisor might need to contact the client himself in an attempt to rectify the situation. The most realistic approach might be simply to leave the client alone as she requests, even though this would leave her with many unmet needs. Unfortunately, the actions of the interviewer have been sufficiently damaging that this client is fully justified in feeling that she wants nothing more to do with social workers.

How might the interviewer have handled this differently in order to avoid the unpleasant outcome?

Only the dialogue content is given in this process-recorded interview. The preliminaries of the interview are not included.

W.: How long have you been divorced?
C.: Uh, one year.
W.: Can you tell me what happened?
C.: I'd rather not talk about it.
W.: How come you left him?
C.: Who said I left him?
W.: That's what I read in your case record at the office.

C.: I said I don't wanna talk about it. Do I have to answer any more questions?

W.: Well, I do need to learn about your divorce. It's important we have a complete social history. Did you fight a lot?

C.: Yeah, we fought. Why don't you ask me about finances or something? It's money I need and I don't see what my marriage has to do with that.

W.: I can't give assistance without the complete social history. You must give me more information. Look, if it helps... my parents just got divorced. I know what it's like. My father beat my mother when he got angry and she had to get out of the house for her own protection. Men who do that to their wives ought to be outlawed.

C.: (silence)

W.: So, getting divorced isn't so bad. I mean you probably did the right thing under the circumstances. So, it's OK to tell me about it—I'll understand.

C.: What if the husband leaves you instead?

W.: Well, oh—is that what happened with you?

C.: Yeah. Left me for another woman, the miserable *!#*.

W.: I'm working with another case where that happened. The woman was so upset she had a total breakdown. So, I can understand that that's a pretty rotten thing you've had done to you. How'd it make you feel?

C.: Look, I thought I said I didn't want to discuss this.

W.: Were you having any sexual problems? I mean, a lot of times when there are marital problems, there are sexual problems.

C.: It's none of your business (rising and moving towards the door).

W.: That kind of thing can be hard to talk about. A lot of times sexual problems are really the symptom of other problems that are much more serious.

C.: I've decided I don't want none of your AFDC—I'll beg or steal if I have to. Just get out of my house (showing worker to the door) and don't you come back—you hear?

W.: But I....

C.: Get out of here!

EXAMPLE 21   Process-recorded group session

Tape recording is the preferred method for keeping track of group work activity, since most students will be able to remember only a small portion of the verbal and non-verbal interactions that occur. However, if tape recording is not feasible, process recording can be used as a semidirect method of examining what takes place in group meetings.

In the following example a second-year graduate student is working with a group of mothers of leukemic children. They had been meeting with a different leader for a period of time before she became involved. Notice the improper use of the "gut-level feelings" column. (The recording continues for several pages following the end of this excerpt.)

SUPERVISORY COMMENTS	GROUP PROCESS	GUT-LEVEL FEELINGS
		I arrived early so the room was still dark. I got the lights on and opened the door. As I did this, Mrs. A, Mrs. B, Mrs. C, Mrs. D, and

Mrs. E came in. They prepared their coffee, said hello, and sat down. I sat down at the head of the table.

Good technique to get things started.

I introduced myself. Mrs. A said she had heard I was coming and was glad I could make it. Mrs. B, Mrs. D, Mrs. C, and Mrs. E said the same thing. I then asked Mrs. A what she expected from these meetings and she said she wanted to have someplace to talk about the things that have happened to her and things she is scared of happening and how other people have reacted to what she is going through.

Mrs. D said, "That's so true," and explained that she's been coming here with her child for 3 years—sometimes every day—and other times it'd be 3 or 4 weeks before she had to come back, and she had the feeling she was alone in her misery. "Once in a while another parent would come up and we could talk; you know for a while the only thing they could give our kids was (a specific medication) and no one knew of the side effects."

I asked Mrs. A how long she had been coming here. She said, "Two years. I can also remember that people used to talk about medication and they said there was only one kind and now we have such different medications."

Good. You are relating to her underlying feelings.

I said, "Do all these different medications and procedures worry you?"

Mrs. A said, "Well, yes because the paper always has articles on new discoveries for cures and they all have such different ideas and I am not sure sometimes that we are aware of them and more important, if the doctors are aware of what's new."

I wonder if she's denying reality or if perhaps she doesn't belong in the group or what?

Mrs. C said, "I feel that these meetings are very useful. I come in only once a month, but my child does not have leukemia.

I said I was not sure if all the parents in the group have children with leukemia.

I looked around the group.

They all answered "Yes."

I asked, "What does your child have?"

Mrs. C said, "My girl has XZY disease."

Mrs. A said, "What's that?"

Mrs. C had brought a bag and knitting needles and was comfortably knitting. She stopped for a second and looked to see if others were looking approvingly at her. They seemed to be and I felt they were very interested in what she was saying.

Mrs. C said it is a type of cancer that appears in the "X" part of the body. It is in an unusual place; they tell me and it happens to be behind the eye.

I asked how it has affected her vision and she said that up till now it hasn't.

Silence prevailed for a few minutes here. I felt kind of uncomfortable as I wasn't quite sure what to do with it.

Mrs. A asked where the child was diagnosed and Mrs. C mentioned a facility in another part of the country.

At this point Mr. and Mrs. F walked in very cheerfully and sat down.

This was an abrupt change of subject, cutting Mrs. A off. I wonder if she had more she wanted to say and how she felt about this new person getting the attention.

Mrs. F said, "I have some information on a new form of treatment I want to share with you."
①
I said, "I am sure the group would like to hear it."

Mrs. F was looking at the group.

Ⓘ
Perhaps you shouldn't have answered for the group—maybe they or Mrs. A didn't want to get into this right then. This would have required a more directive role on your part.

You aren't putting many of your feelings on this and the next few pages—did you have any?

Mrs. F then talked about how in another state they use a certain treatment process and give it to children with leukemia.

I asked, "Have you discussed this with Dr. M?"

She said, "I am going to today. I brought in all of this material for that purpose. Isn't this the kind of treatment that John Doe is receiving?

I said I wasn't sure but it seemed like his therapy might be more complicated than what she was describing.

Mrs. F said, "I am not sure how Dr. M will take our reading this material."

Mrs. D said, "Very poorly. He thinks we should do the least possible reading about the subject."

Good—you picked up that they might not agree with it. You might have also asked the group why they thought the dr. didn't want them reading the material. I think you knew the answer yourself and thus didn't ask, but this prevented group discussion.

I said, "What do you think about that?"

Mrs. D said, "Well, in the beginning I agreed with him. I had no idea what terms he was throwing at me, but now I could probably pick up a journal on cancer and read it. It's like a forced education with continued hammering away; unless I was completely dumb, I had to learn what everyone was saying and if a new term comes up I look it up."

Mrs. B said, "I feel the same way. We are living this nightmare and we get pounded at with the same information until you get so that it sounds like you're ordering the prescriptions."

EXAMPLE 22   A process-recorded group meeting is slow in getting started

A group of patients hospitalized with active tuberculosis was meeting for the first time with an undergraduate student. The student had to perform some delicate preparatory work with nursing staff prior to her first meeting with the group. The nurses had wanted to attend the meeting, as they had done with the previous group leader. Unfortunately, their participation had created some difficulties in accomplishing appropriate social work goals, and the student had to find a polite way of making certain the nurses did not attend. This recording illustrates the student's sense of panic when things didn't go exactly as planned.

This recording is also typical in showing how many new groups, or old groups with new leaders, are often slow in getting started. There may be long periods of awkward silence while the leader wonders what to do next to get people talking. Such reactions are common when the group is new or there is a change in membership or leadership. A highly skilled leader might have gotten group interaction going more quickly, but even he would have had to deal with some awkward moments.

Notice the awkward spelling and grammar throughout this recording. Notice also that it doesn't follow the usual way of doing process recordings. This could indicate the degree of mental exhaustion the student was experiencing after the interview, and probably also indicates the struggle she had experienced in trying to get this group going.

SUPERVISORY COMMENTS	GROUP PROCESS	GUT-LEVEL FEELINGS
Good.	I walked in and patients were coming in, as they came in I assured myself of their names and wrote them down so as not to forget.	
Nice way of putting it. However, the second part of your sentence is very confusing!	I introduced myself and said that we were going to make this a time for patients to deal with anything they wanted to let their hair down on and ask for approval.	
	Got zero response.	I said to myself, OH! OH!
	I looked around and said, "We have gotten together here because you all have something in common."	
	(few moments of silence)	
Hooray—a response!	Then Mrs. A said "We all have the same disease."	Thank goodness!
	I said "Yes, you all have active TB."	
	Mrs. A said "Yes, I agree."	
	The other patients nodded.	
Good exploration.	I asked "What does it feel like to have TB?"	
	Mr. A said "I try not to think about it."	
Another response would have been to simply ask "Why?" or use reflection—"try not to think about it?"	I said "Is it more comfortable for you that way?" He said "Yes, I know I have it and they are treating me for it so why think about it?"	

I said "How was it with you?" I directed myself toward Mrs. B. She said "I was shocked but I have to accept." I said "I think I would have that feeling too."

I realized she was dealing on a different level.

What does "going to the TB sanitarium" mean?

Mrs. A said "I was surprised too but once I was told I wasn't going to have to go to the TB sanitarium I was OK."

I turned to Mr. C and asked "How is it for you?"

Resistance?

He said nothing—so I changed the subject.

What am I dealing with?

"One thing we have heard other patients talk about is the feeling of isolation. Has it been this way with you?"

Mrs. D said "Well I am working on a recipe book I have never had time to work on and I watch TV or do some sewing."

I said "It sounds like you have been able to mobilize your energies into fighting that feeling."

Mrs. D said "definitely."

Mrs. A said "I read a lot."

Mr. A said "I can't stand it."

I asked "What do you do?"

I felt good I could zero in on that.

Mr. A said "Well, I get out and walk around."

Mrs. A said "That's for sure he's the only person I always see around."

Ah! Big clue—they don't know each other, but I really cannot introduce them to each other now—I goofed!

You could have still done the introductions by making some kind of comment about "Hey—I just realized not everyone knows everybody—let's pause for introductions."

Mr. E was hiding his head in his hands and squirming in his chair. I sensed a great deal of forlorness. I felt he really shouldn't be here, but I still pressed to see if he would open up.

You were right!

I said "I seem to be hearing from you that you don't know each other." Mrs. D said "I had never seen anyone that's here before today."

Did you go ahead and have introductions here? This gave you a perfect opening.	So I apologized for not introducing them.	
	Then I said "Mr. E I am aware that you are in school. How has that been affected by your being in the hospital?"	
This individual seems quite upset. Will a social worker be seeing him individually?	He answered very quietly, "Someone comes around and I'm trying to keep up."	
	"How does that feel?"	
	(no response)	
	So I backed off and changed the subject.	I haven't touched on anything that's making an impact.
I think you have touched on a couple of important things, but for some reason they are not responding.	"Does it help to have visitors come?"	
	Mrs. F said well, "I have many friends that visit, especially from _____."	
	Mrs. A said "Me too."	
	I then turned to Mr. G, who had not said a word and I wondered why, but he said "I don't understand—I can't speak English."	He has a heavy French accent—oh swell!
	Mr. A said it's OK.	
	"How do your friends feel about your having TB?"	
	Mrs. D said "They are not afraid" and went on about how it is being cured now and no one is afraid any more.	
You might have relayed this observation to him and given him a chance to respond.	Mr. E looked up. I thought he wanted to say something but didn't so I said, "Are the people at the gas station where you work aware you have TB?"	
	He nodded no.	
Gads! No wonder you wanted to exclude the nurses!	Mrs. Williams, who is a nurse, had somehow slipped in and said, "I think Mrs. D because she is older knows how people view TB but I think Mr. E feels guilty for not telling his friends."	Well, I jumped, perhaps more than I should have because I saw the effect of her

In addition to "jumping" I bet you were also angry because of the unhelpful comment she'd just made (?)

Not too bad a way of asking her to leave— you can always get back to her right afterward to explain further.

I said, "Mrs. Williams I am sorry I didn't see you come in, but did you know this group is being held without any nursing staff this time?"

She was embarrassed and walked out saying she was sorry she hadn't been told.

I immediately jumped in and said "Mrs. D how did it feel to have someone say you are old?"

She said, "Well I guess I am. I don't have to hide it." Somehow she was saying this but not really meaning it and then added, "But I have 3 teenage children and I think I know how Mr. H is feeling. They would go up the wall if they had to stay in all the time."

I directed to Mr. H. I said "It seems that some people think they know how you are feeling. Would you like to respond to that?"

Maybe he doesn't feel well physically?

He shrugged, and got his head into his knees for a good while.

Everyone was quiet and it remained like that for a few minutes.

"Are there any unanswered questions about your disease that you would like answered?"

(no answer again)

I said "I am not going to keep you here long but I do want to wrap up what has gone on. I think we have all been aware that people have different ways of expressing their feelings. Mrs. D dealt with it one way; Mr. A another and Mr. E still another. None did it the same way and they are all your own and you have the right to them because they are our own. Do you think that this is so?"

A nice summary that should help set the scene for the next meeting. Your spelling and grammar are rather awkward to say the least!

comments and because she wasn't supposed to be there.

I felt horrible about having to ask her to leave and I did this more out of a feeling that I had to rather than because I was convinced it should be! I also went to her later and apologized for the way I did it.

How dare they!

And I thought maybe silence will work. I fought my interrupting the silence, but I got zero response and came in anyway.

What a cop out for me!

It's time to end. I can feel the resistance and cut through it with a knife.

I felt good about terminating this way.

Good—you may have reached them somehow, though it doesn't show much in their verbal responses.

Mrs. A, Mr. E, Mr. A and Mrs. D all nodded affirmative. Mr. H was out in left field. I thanked them for comming. Mr. D said "When will we meet again?"

I was mentally exhausted!

I said next Monday at 10:00.

Mrs. A said thank you.

EXAMPLE 23 Process-recorded decision-making meeting

The recorder was participating in a meeting of a small group of supervisory-level social workers. One unit is going to be without social work staff for a period of time because of the absence of the supervisor for several months and the concurrent resignation of one of the employees in the same unit. No new workers are to be hired, despite the resignation, and the supervisory group is trying to decide how to provide adequate coverage by shifting staff temporarily from other areas. "A" is the department director and is leading the discussion in this excerpt.

SUPERVISORY COMMENTS	GROUP PROCESS	GUT-LEVEL FEELINGS
(What comments would you make if you were the supervisor of a large-systems student making this recording?)	A. Well we sure have a problem here. I frankly don't know what the solution is. None of them seem ideal by far.	I can feel the discouragement.
	Y. I thought I was going to be acting supervisor of that area and mine too— wasn't that what we had talked about before?	If the problem has already been worked out, why are we having this meeting? I'm confused.
	P. What's this? I missed that. Tell me what was planned.	
But one day you <u>will</u> be in A's position if you pursue large systems!	A. We originally had discussed having Y. take over R.'s unit for the 5 months, but I've been thinking about what that would do to her own unit and I'm not sure that would be realistic. B. would have to increase his caseload to cover for Y. so she could assume the additional supervisory responsibilities and I understand she already has a full caseload and besides, three new patients have been added to the area they're expanding in that unit.	Gads—what a mess. I'm glad I'm not A.
	Y. What could we do then? I agree there would be problems.	

A. Well, it looks like the only solution is for me to directly supervise the people in the unit in the absence of the regular supervisor.

(silence)

I began to get uncomfortable. Maybe this solution wasn't acceptable somehow?

T. That would be an additional burden for you—could you do it?

A. Does anyone have any other ideas?

Please don't look at me!

R. Why not move X. over from T.'s unit and have her supervise the employee. You could then move D. from his area part time to cover X.'s caseload.

T. Wait a minute! That'll leave me with half a caseload uncovered!

A. Do we know if X. would be interested in switching to the other unit?

T. Yes, she knows about the vacancy but has decided to remain where she is.

S. Well, that settles that. Are there any other MSW's we could move from other areas? Or would it be better to move a BA person—in other words, do we want the new person to be the MSW or the BSW worker?

Too bad I don't graduate until next year—I could apply for the vacancy.

A. I don't like having to move people from units that are working well—it keeps things in a constant turmoil and we want to avoid that.

Why don't they move two old-timers from their areas and put the two new people in other units? Oops, now I know.

Y. Why don't we hire two new people— one that would be temporary for 5 months— and the other for the BSW spot. We could make the MSW Acting Supervisor.

EXAMPLE 24 Process-recorded contact with member of another discipline

This undergraduate student is having one of her first professional contacts with a member of another discipline, in this case a nurse in a hospital setting. She was instructed to talk with the nurse prior to her first contact with the patient. She received guidance from her field instructor on appropriate questions to ask, and some role-playing had been done. The column for supervisory comments has been omitted.

INTERVIEW CONTENT	GUT-LEVEL FEELINGS
I said, Hi my name is Ada. I said I was from the social service department and that I was a student.	Felt quite comfortable as though at home.
I said I would like to ask you some questions about Mrs. Marlene Adams.	
The nurse said Okay.	
I said we would like to see the past chart on Mrs. Adams from 1971.	Felt confident about the questions.
She said, someone has sent down for it.	
I said thank you. I said I would like to know how has Mrs. Adams' personality been these last few days.	
She said frowning, she has been not in such a good mood.	Felt confident about the questions.
She said (looking at me), Mrs. Adams has now come to accept that the doctors are going to cut off her leg.	
I said, do you know when her surgery is?	
She said, no I don't know.	
I said do you think I should speak to her?	
She said yes, I think she will talk to you, maybe.	Felt somewhat relieved.
I said, who are the surgeons?	
She said, Roberts, Frankson and another one, I know there is another one (frowning with a puzzled look).	
I said, does she have any visitors?	
She said yes, she has a sister that comes to visit. Her sister came yesterday.	Felt assured that I asked a valid question.
I asked if her husband comes to see her.	
She said, no I have seen a man come to see her but not her husband.	
I said, does she sit up or walk?	

She said she has been going to physical therapy. But she complained about her leg hurting so much. The doctor told her that she would have the operation, so I called down to physical therapy, and cancelled it. We sat her up yesterday and she cried and hollered so much that we had to lay her back down. She did sit up yesterday.

Hoped that she wouldn't ask me to do something so that I would have to go looking for another nurse.

I said, what are the doctors' beeper numbers?

She said Dr. Roberts' number is 184 and Dr. Frankson is 185.

I said, that's all and thank you very much.

Felt more or somewhat relieved.

EXAMPLE 25 Process-recorded conference between student supervisor and his supervisee

Large-systems graduate students sometimes supervise undergraduate students as part of their training. The following brief segment from an actual session illustrates how such a conference might be process recorded. The student supervisor experienced real difficulty writing up this conference and felt unnatural and awkward in the supervisory session, knowing he was going to have to process record it. The experiment requiring process recording was abandoned, and the student subsequently felt much more at ease interacting with his supervisee.

SUPERVISORY COMMENTS	INTERVIEW CONTENT	GUT-LEVEL FEELINGS
	I said, "S., if someone who picked up this record did not know you, what kind of an impression would they get about this worker?" S. said, "One of confusion."	I realized she was trying to be critical of her work.
Good point. You might have also explained how summary recording is different from process recording— i.e., in process recording, she must include her feelings, and now you're telling her not to. That could be confusing.	I said yes, I agreed and "I can appreciate your putting this on paper and risking your feelings to others; however, records may be read by others who may not appreciate what you went through." S. said, "Yes, I see now. I really did show what it was doing to me."	I wanted to be supportive because I feel it important to be able to recognize what you're feeling.

I said, "Many social workers are not able to identify their feelings out loud much less on paper and I think it's really important that you have been able to share those feelings with me and verbalize them without much trouble. However..." and she interrupted, with "I see—they really don't belong here."

Do you think she really understands why?

A nice way of asking her to do it again.

I said that she was right and asked if she thought she might be able to reword this part so that we could see what it was the client was feeling during his crisis. S. said she thought she could. I told her I knew it's hard and it might take some time to get it down pat, but "I think you know what to do now." She said "Yes, I think so." ·

Good supportive approach.

After putting it this way, she might be afraid to reveal it if she really wasn't sure she knew what to do!

I now realized we were approaching a more difficult area.

"So much for feelings," I told her. "Let's go to another area this summary needs." S. said OK. "This is the most difficult. The first time I tried to write a social history it was a total failure and it wasn't until I wrote one a couple (like more than 4 times!) that I got a feel for it."

Good—you helped her see she's not the only one that has to struggle with this.

Her face showed signs of relief.

I well remember! It took some risking on your part to share this. How's it feel to be putting to use your own experiences with a supervisee?

EXAMPLE 26   Detailed supervisory feedback on techniques used in a complicated interview

The following interview was conducted by an undergraduate student only a few weeks away from graduation. The client came complete with a thick case record, full of complicated, problematic, and often very judgmental comments regarding this young woman and her children. The worker's goal was to try to get to know her as a person, rather than simply to zero in on the negativistic areas in an accusatory manner, as had some of her predecessors. Much supervisory discussion and some role playing preceded this first interview with the client. This student had progressed to the point where she was no longer process recording her interviews. However, we both knew this would be a particularly difficult interview to conduct, and thus planned to process record it so that the student could receive detailed supervisory feedback on the actual interview process as well as the overall outcome. This excerpt begins following the preliminary introductory remarks. Notice the unusually detailed supervisory comments and also the student's effective use of the "gut-level feelings" column, which includes not only her own feelings but also some analyses of the client and of the interview. A special summary statement of supervisory comments appears at the end, giving the student guidance on which areas to pursue in the few days prior to the regularly scheduled supervisory conference. The interview takes place during a home visit.

SUPERVISORY COMMENTS	INTERVIEW CONTENT	GUT-LEVEL FEELINGS
	At this time, her little girl came in. She was clean and healthy looking. She picked up a toy, looked me over, then whispered something to her mother and went back outside.	I felt like I failed her inspection.
	W. How are the children doing? Is Maria in Head Start now?	
	C. They are doing OK. Maria is registered and goes back for something on Monday. I guess she'll start then.	
	W. What about Luis?	
"Better" compared to what? What kind of emotional problems? Does it affect him in any way in addition to his speech? Exploration needed. What is the child like at home? How does he respond to her (from her viewpoint), etc.?	C. He is doing better. His teacher said that he is getting along better now. She feels like he has some emotional problems because of his father and this is why he wouldn't talk better. But she says he is beginning to do much better.	She started really talking and I felt very sorry for her.
	W. Does he still get special help with his speech problem?	
	C. Yes, from a teacher at school.	
	W. How often does she help him?	
What exactly does she do to help Luis? For how long? How often? See me re: why this is important.	C. Two or three times a week and I help him with certain words for homework.	I felt like she really wanted to help Luis.
Good. Now you can follow up and talk to his teacher.	W. Where does Luis go to school?	
	C. Down at XYZ School. I wanted to ask if I get a job will it cut my Medicaid	I felt she didn't want

This accident needs exploration. Do you know why this is important? How could you have explored it?

out? I really want to work but I can't pay the doctors if they cut it. I would have a lot of bills especially from Luis because of his harelip and cleft palate. My little girl fell down off the front steps last week and broke her leg.

to jeopordize her financial situation.

How much money would she earn? Doing what? What is she really saying here? Interpretive response desirable. Do you see why?

W. I am not sure if it would cut your Medicaid or not—I don't think so but I'll have to ask someone because I'm pretty new at the department.

Why did you change the subject somewhat here?

W. Does Luis have a lot of medical problems with his mouth?

C. He goes to a doctor for his mouth and ears.

W. Does he have problems with his ears?

What kind of operation? Does his condition affect his hearing?

C. Not much—he has holes in his eardrums but the doctor said they would operate on them when he is older.

W. Can he hear pretty good?

But to what extent is he affected? We need to get this from her and also his teacher, as well as from Luis himself.

C. Yes. He sits up close in school so he doesn't have many problems as far as I know.

I would like to work part time if it won't cut my Medicaid out.

Good! You explore.

W. Do you know where you could get a job?

C. I guess at the ABC grocery. They will need a checkout girl pretty soon.

W. Have you put in an application yet?

She is saying a great deal here re: her needs and anxieties. What feelings are behind her statements?

C. No. I really want to learn a trade because I only went to the 10th grade. What if my husband never comes back? What would I do? He had a girlfriend; I don't know if he married her or not. I don't think so. It wouldn't seem so bad if he would just come and see the

Thank goodness— an answer to an unasked question!

She began crying here.

kids. They need him. People ask me why I want him back after all he's done, but they don't understand. He's their father. He should take care of them even if he doesn't come back. I don't know what to do if he does come back because it will get me in trouble with my welfare worker, won't it? They stopped my checks for several months the last time he came.

I just let her go on talking, partly because I wasn't sure what to say.

I see her point.

A very key statement. I've been around enough to suspect she's putting it this way to really say something else. Can you guess what it is?

A particular interpretive statement desperately needed here! Let's role-play it.

Change of subject—not picking up on underlying feelings expressed above. You shifted from the emotional to the concrete.

W. If he comes back very often and stays they will stop your checks again. That's the reason you get them—because the father is away from the home. You had talked before about getting a divorce. Have you thought about that, in case he doesn't return?

C. Yes.

W. Have you talked to anyone about filing for a divorce?

C. Yes, I've already filed.

Right—it appears she didn't want to talk about the divorce. But there was something else she wanted to talk about. Can you figure out what it was?

W. When does it become final?

C. I don't know.

W. When did you file?

C. It's been awhile.

I don't think she wanted to talk about the divorce.

At this time the door opened and Luis came in. He was just returning from school. He sat down on the sofa and started talking to his mother and looking at me.

She had stopped crying.

Did you introduce yourself to him?

W. How did school go today, Luis?

Luis. OK.

He was very easy to understand (speech).

Luis thinking silently to himself: "Who's

W. What grade are you in?

this stranger asking how I'm doing in school?!"

Luis. I'm in the second.

W. Do you like school?

Good for him! What feeling might have prompted Luis to ask this?

Luis. Yes. Are you a welfare worker?

W. No, I'm from the Make-em-well Agency.

Boy, did that shock me! I didn't know what to say. I was too flustered to make any sense.

How might you have responded differently? I wonder what a "welfare worker" means to him.

Luis. I'm on vacation from school till Monday. Mom, I'm going out.

Luis went outside.

C. He likes to hang around other people.

Good exploration.

W. What do you mean?

But underneath this statement are the same feelings as earlier. What are these feelings?

C. He doesn't know anyone but his father.

Back to the father again—I think she's really confused about him.

A change of subject on your part—I wonder why.

W. Does he not have any friends to play with?

What is she really saying here?

C. Oh yes, he has friends. He just likes to hang around with them and I don't like him to because I don't know if that's normal.

I got the feeling she was afraid he would become homosexual.

Good interpretive statement!

W. Maybe he likes to hang around them and their fathers since his is not here now.

The third opening to discuss the underlying feelings I mentioned earlier.

C. Maybe. It would be better if he could see his father.

W. I think it's pretty normal for boys his age to hang around with others. But it would be good for him to see his father some. How long were you married?

OK. A natural lead into this question.

C. Over 6 years.

A good empathetic statement!

W. That's a pretty long time to live with someone and then have them leave you. Do you have any idea where he is now?

I wanted to find out about the father.

Could you have paused here before asking the question, to let her respond to your empathetic statement?

C. No, he doesn't even tell his people.

W. Do you know his relatives pretty good?

C. Yes, they like me pretty good.

Good.

W. Do some of them live around here?

Does she see them often?

C. Yes, his father's people and some sisters live not far from here.

She told me the town and I never could understand what she said. I was having a hard time understanding her part of the time.

Why were you having a hard time understanding her—did you share this with her?

W. Does your own family live around here?

Aha! The fourth hint at certain underlying feelings.

C. No. I'm kind of by myself—my parents are dead.

W. Did they live around here?

C. No, they lived in another state.

W. Is that where you met your husband?

C. Yes.

The client sat for a couple of minutes without talking. She had stopped crying completely by this time.

A very significant statement!

C. Do you have many people like me?

Very good response! Do you know why?

W. What do you mean?

Yes, reaching for support—and also for something else.

C. That start crying. I don't do it much because of the kids, but sometimes I can't help it.

I felt like she was reaching out for some support.

I think you moved in rather quickly without adequate exploration. It gives the impression here of a little bit of false reassurance—can you see why? Let's discuss and role play.

W. Everyone needs to let it out sometime. You can't keep it bottled up all the time. I realize it's hard to raise several children by yourself and I can see why you need to cry sometimes. We all need someone to talk to sometimes.

OK, she probably was being truthful. But

C. I don't want to give you the wrong idea. I've got friends to talk to and

I felt like she was telling me the truth.

therapeutically, what did she need from you at this point? Please see your fellow student and have her give you the same readings she did on depression (but not the ones on suicide).

A most unfortunate time for this interruption.

Ouch! I'm not sure this was the best timing for you to decide to leave. Were you uncomfortable with her expression of feelings? Can you figure out why your timing was not the best? Look again at her statement, "... and sometimes I cry to them but they don't understand" and your decision to leave, for a hint.

Your confusion is very understandable. You opened up a lot of good areas for further exploration and discussion. In spite of all my comments, you didn't do too badly for your first interview with this complex situation. I think you'll have much to offer her and even if you never had another

sometimes I cry to them but they don't understand—if I catch myself crying I stop because I'm feeling sorry for myself.

At this time Maria came back in and the client stopped talking. When I saw she was finished talking I decided to leave.

W. I will get in contact with the LMN Agency and let you know what you need to do to have them get that special medicine for you (this had been discussed earlier).

C. Dr. Adams said it would cost around $90. I've already got the prescription. When will you let me know?

I feel she is very anxious to get this prescription.

W. I will be out of the office on Thursday and Friday, so I'll come by on Monday or Tuesday. I'll give you my number and you can call me if you need to talk to me before then, OK?

C. OK.

W. Then I'll see you next week. Goodbye.

By the time I left, I was totally confused.

case, you'd learn a
great deal from
working with her.
Please do the
following:

1. Read this through
very carefully. Try
to answer each of my
questions. Use a
different color ink
and write on your
recording if you want.

2. Think. Don't ask
the other students.
Read on the needs of
divorced women and
their children.

3. Go through and
count the number of
times you use direct
question, reflection,
interpretation,
confrontation,
empathy, and other
techniques in your
responses. Write the
totals on the last
page.

4. I'm going to want
you to see this client
twice a week for the
rest of the field
placement.

5. Please plan to
continue process
recording your next
3-4 contacts with this
client.

6. Please work on
everything listed here
and on your recording
and come prepared to go
over it in detail in
supervisory conference
in about two days. You
probably won't have

everything finished by
then (especially the
readings), but that's
OK as long as you're
well under way with it.

CHAPTER 7 SUMMARY RECORDING: GENERAL CONCEPTS

Summary recording is the preferred style for daily social work practice. Regular progress notes, periodic summaries (i.e., intake or transfer reports), and special reports are usually written in summary style, as is the diagnostic summary (see Chapter 10). Many agencies provide outlines that specify the content of formal summaries. Chapter 8 gives suggested outlines to help workers organize and present their material in a logical manner when their agencies provide no guidelines.

Regardless of the purpose for which summary recording is being done or the outline that is being followed, certain basic principles must be considered.

The frequency of recording entries will vary from setting to setting. Agencies may require that entries be made once a week, once a month, or at unspecified intervals. More frequent entries are indicated during periods of intense activity in any given case. Inactive cases that are still open on the books can present a problem if agency procedures do not indicate clearly how often entries must be made. If there are prolonged periods with no activity on a given case, brief notes should be made from time to time. Otherwise another worker or a supervisor may wonder whether the absence of recording means that nothing has been happening or that something has not yet been documented.

A number of settings operate under the auspices of governmental or other regulatory bodies that stipulate the frequency, form, and content of recording entries. Programs granting financial assistance, for example, are required to redetermine eligibility periodically, and the results must be recorded. The Joint Commission on Accreditation (for hospitals), PSRO (professional standards review organizations), third-party payers such as Medicare, and other groups may dictate both the frequency and the content of social work recording. If recording is not done as frequently as required in these settings, the agency may lose money for staffing and program development or reimbursement for services provided. Thus some employers are beginning to specify quality and quantity recording requirements in staff job descriptions; failure to comply with their expectations may be reflected in performance evaluations, and could even result in disciplinary action.

In addition to these situations, most settings require some kind of written report whenever one of the following events occurs:

1. A new case is opened.

2. A case is transferred from one social worker (or student) to another, or from a member of one profession to another professional in an interdisciplinary setting.

3. New information is learned that needs to be entered into the record.

4. Something happens that changes the worker's diagnostic assessment of the situation and/or results in a revised treatment plan.

5. A report is sent to another professional or agency. It is not good practice merely to copy existing record material for transmittal to an outside source. This leads to confidentiality violations and often provides the other party with excess or inappropriate information. A special summary is usually prepared, giving the data requested by the outside setting. You may need to develop your own outline if none is provided for you.

6. Information from the record is released to someone outside the agency.* Some

*See Suanna J. Wilson, *Confidentiality in Social Work: Issues and Principles* (New York: Free Press, 1978), for a detailed discussion of this issue, along with specific guidelines for handling the release of information. It also contains a description of the requirements of the Federal Privacy Act.

settings even require documentation of the fact that a disclosure occurred.* Students and staff in these programs will receive special instructions to insure compliance with federal regulations. In the absence of any federal requirements, the following data should be recorded whenever disclosures are made from case records:

a) Date the disclosure was made.
b) Person/agency receiving the information.
c) Description (or a copy) of the information that was released.
d) Exact purpose of the disclosure (how the receiving agency will use it).
e) Limitations placed upon the receiving agency specifying what they can and cannot do with the material.
f) Copy of a "Permission for Release of Information" form signed by the client should be filed in the record.

7. At the time a case is closed.

COMPARISON OF SUMMARY STYLE AND PROCESS RECORDING

Summary recording is not only much briefer than process recording but differs in the style of writing in the following ways:

1.   It leaves out the "I said," "he said," and does not repeat word for word what the social worker and client said during the interview. Instead, the interview content is summarized.

2.   There is much less reference to what the social worker says and does. The main focus is on the client. The worker includes his observations, feelings, and analytical thoughts under a special heading such as "Diagnostic Summary," "Worker's Impressions," or "Assessment."

3.   Irrelevant details are omitted and even pertinent material is recorded in a much briefer style. Selected parts of the recording may, however, entail considerable detail.

4.   Summary recording describes the outcome but usually not all the steps the worker went through to accomplish the results.

5.   Summary-recorded interviews are not presented in chronological order. Instead, the content of the interview or series of interviews is described under various subject headings. If outlines are not supplied by the agency, the worker organizes his ideas according to subject area and makes up appropriate headings as needed.

Summary recording is the preferred method for ongoing social work practice because it is much briefer than process recording, hence much less time consuming to write and to read. However, summary recording requires more thought and planning on the worker's part because he must decide what to record and what to omit. He must also organize his material in summary format under appropriate headings. Finally, the briefer style means that case records are thinner, less paper is used, and storage problems are reduced.

Look again at process-recording Example 1 in Chapter 6. This same interview done in summary recording style might read as follows:

Second Interview with Mr. A. 3-18-74

Much of today's discussion focused on further exploration of the possibility of his being a drug user. He denied drug abuse and seemed much more concerned with his living arrangements after he leaves the hospital and his conflict over whether he should return to live with his

*Federal agencies under the jurisdiction of the Federal Privacy Act of 1974 must do this. See Public Law 93-579, December 31, 1974 (effective 9-27-75).

mother or not. It was learned that Mr. A. has not worked steadily for almost a year and it appears that he has a rather irregular employment history, which in such a young man might suggest the presence of some type of psychosocial problem. He agreed to follow through with going to a boarding home temporarily after discharge and I will be making specific arrangements for this.*

A few lines of summary recording cover what took several pages to describe using process recording.

CONTENT OF SUMMARY RECORDED ENTRIES

Regardless of the type of interview that has occurred or the specific recording outline being used, certain kinds of information should always be included somewhere in the summary recording:

1. The full name of the client, including any known aliases (false names or nicknames).

2. An identifying number for the client, such as a social security number, patient hospital number, family or financial assistance number.

3. The date of the interview.

4. The date the recording was written.

5. The name of the worker.

6. The purpose of the interview.

7. The content—what occurred during the interview.

8. A description of any problem areas identified by the social worker and/or the client.

9. A description of any services provided by the social worker.

10. The practitioner's professional, analytical assessment of the meaning of what has occurred during the interview, usually under a heading such as "Worker's Impressions" or "Diagnostic Summary." (See Chapter 10 for further guidelines on how to prepare diagnostic statements.)

11. Plans (goals, treatment) for future contacts or follow-up. These are often described under the heading "Service Plan," "Treatment Plan," or "Goals." Subsequent entries then indicate the outcome of these goals and any problems encountered in achieving them.

The content of the recording entry and the style used are generally dictated by the purpose for which the recording is being done and the kind of record it is being placed in. For example, an entry made by a social worker in a hospital medical chart would be quite different from one following an intake interview in a family counseling agency. It is also important to consider who will read the recording and how it will be used in order to determine appropriate style and content. Confidentiality concerns might also enter into this determination.

GENERAL TECHNIQUES OF SUMMARY RECORDING

1. Keep in mind the purpose of all recorded entries. Consider: "Why am I writing this? Who will read it?" Keep entries focused and to the point. Answer the presenting problem or record the key elements of a situation by including significant, relevant information. Exclude inappropriate, irrelevant, or excessive details.

2. Use ink for all recorded entries unless specifically instructed to use pencil. If

---

*Notice there is no mention of the possible disturbed maternal-son relationship. Since the student failed to pick up on this in the process-recorded interview, his summary recording would omit it as the student would not consider it significant enough to report.

entries are being made in records that are frequently copied, use black ink only—other colors do not come through legibly in most duplication processes.

3. Make certain the name of the recorder is legible. If not, the name should be printed beneath the illegible signature.

4. Record exact dates rather than time periods. For example, instead of saying, "Mr. Jones will get his Social Security check in 10 days" (or next week or next month), state that he will receive his check "on November 27, 1979" or "the week of November 27, 1979." Do not say, "Next Monday Mrs. Brown has an appointment with her physician." Instead, record that her appointment is "on October 7." Do not put the reader in the position of having to figure out when you wrote the recording before he can determine the date you are referring to.

5. Be as brief as possible. Recordings do not have to be lengthy to be effective. Even if the material is the best ever done in the history of social work practice, who is going to have time to read it if it is twenty single-spaced typewritten pages? Some recordings that are very long also leave the reader feeling that he still doesn't know much, since such wordy entries often fail to give the essential facts. On the other hand, entries should be as long as necessary to include everything required to achieve the main purpose of the recording. Some outlines are very detailed and will result in comparatively lengthy recording; sometimes the most appropriate entry will be only one or two lines. The recorder should not structure his recording to fit a certain length, but should concentrate instead on achieving quality.

Some settings use forms for social work entries, and these generally provide a limited amount of space. Data that are being computerized or entered onto special three by five cards or face sheets must fit into the space provided. Thus physical restrictions may determine the length of recording in specialized situations.

6. Try not to repeat what has been said previously in recorded entries or on forms. If it is necessary to refer to something said earlier, simply state that "the financial situation as described on page 4 remains essentially unchanged," or something similar.

7. Make subheadings for paragraphs whenever possible to make it easier for the reader to get the information he needs quickly. Avoid long paragraphs that run a full page or more. This is most discouraging to the reader. Make up suitable headings to fit the content. Typical examples might be "Employment Situation," "Contact with School Psychologist," "Conference with Child Welfare," and "Marital History."

8. Avoid uncommon abbreviations, symbols, or social work jargon, especially when making entries in a record that is read by members of other disciplines. (There are exceptions to this, as in medical settings where certain abbreviations are in wide use and officially adopted by the institution, such as c̄ = with; ca = carcinoma, d/c = discontinue or discharge, and so on).

Can you decipher the following entry?

Mr. Jones' S.W. at the DCWD was contacted today. They are concerned that she get her S.S.I. application in right away because she'll need these benefits for NHP or entrance into the HRHC facility. He made a HV yesterday and evaluated her need for FA. He feels she will qualify in view of her HBP, SOB, and COPD. They are also requesting a psych consult to r/o OBS 2° ASHD. He made another HV on 8–11–76 and talked c̄ several members of the HH. The mo. is known to HRS and the DCCAP. The 24 y/o s.i.l. is s̄ funds as is her bro.

Goals:
1. Evaluate for possible OASDI
2. Help her apply for R.R. benefits thru her deceased husband
3. Supportive counseling

4. Get results of means test at JMH C&C office re: eligibility for services there

[illegible scribble], ACSW

CSW*

9. Always give the source of information when recording such material as diagnostic labels applied by members of other disciplines, highly significant social or factual data, and so on. Distinguish among the social worker's impressions, the assessments of other professionals, and information obtained from the client or significant others.

10. Avoid highly subjective words such as "large, overweight man" or "poor housing" when describing persons or situations. In order to understand their meaning, the reader must often have a thorough knowledge of the person who wrote them. For example, a 4'8"-tall social worker who weighs 90 pounds is apt to consider all persons over 150 pounds as "large," whereas a 250-pound 6'4" male worker probably would not describe someone as "large" or overweight unless that person is really huge.

It is acceptable to use general statements, but go on to describe what they mean and why certain adjectives were chosen. Estimate the client's weight; describe how the person got up and paced around the room during the interview, rather than simply stating that the client "appeared nervous." Describe the client's "poor appearance." Excessive detail should be avoided, but enough should be said to present the worker's meaning of the adjectives:

Mr. Jones' appearance was very poor. He was unshaven; tobacco juice was evident on his shirt and his pants were ragged and ill-fitting.

Support any unusual or highly significant observations with some descriptive data. An entry might state that "Mrs. Smith's house was in deplorable sanitary condition." "Deplorable" can mean different things to various workers. Therefore, support such statements with brief details. The following example is taken from an actual recording following a home visit to a recipient of financial assistance:

The floor was covered with dirty clothing and newspapers. During the interview I watched armies of roaches march across the dining room table where the family had just eaten. There was a strong odor of urine present and the infant child was crawling on the floor through the debris. Dirty dishes and clothing were piled all over.

11. Be very careful in the use of diagnostic labels. Terms such as "alcoholic" and "mentally retarded" should not be put into writing unless the diagnosis has been clearly and professionally established. It is better to state "patient appears to drink heavily, consuming 8–10 cans of beer nightly" than to say "patient is an alcoholic." Such labels are often misinterpreted and tend to follow a client for years once entered into a formal case record. On the other hand, professionally trained social workers are qualified to make some direct diagnostic assessments of their own. These often consist of analyses of behavior patterns and underlying as well as overt emotions and needs, e.g., "Client appears to be quite dependent and...." This is quite different from saying "client is schizophrenic" or "Mr. Jones is a homosexual." Students and practitioners who are uncertain how to express diagnostic assessments in writing should seek supervisory guidance.

*All these abbreviations stand for something real:

S.W.: social worker
DCWD: Dade County Welfare Department
S.S.I.: Supplemental Security Income
NHP: nursing home placement
HRHC: Human Resources Health Center
HV: home visit
FA: financial assistance
HBP: high blood pressure
SOB: shortness of breath
COPD: Cardio-pulmonary disease
psych: psychiatric
r/o: rule out
OBS: organic brain syndrome
2°: secondary to
ASHD: Arteriosclerotic heart disease
c̄: with
HH: household

mo.: mother
HRS: Health and Rehabilitative Services
DCCAP: Dade County Comprehensive Alcohol Program
y/o: year old
s.i.l.: sister in law
s̄: without
bro.: brother
OASDI: Old Age and Survivors Disability Insurance (Social Security)
R.R.: Railroad Retirement
JMH: Jackson Memorial Hospital
C&C: Credit and Classification
ACSW: Academy of Certified Social Workers
CSW: Clinical Social Worker (or Certified Social Worker)

12. Do not be afraid to say "I don't know" in writing. Many social workers tend to avoid mention of an area in their recording when they feel uncertain as to the meaning of what was said or observed. The worker must be certain before he uses diagnostic labels and statements, but total failure to mention something means that the reader will be unaware that it ever happened. When uncertain, the worker should note the information with the comment that the meaning is unclear. For example, "Mrs. Smith's extreme anger was unexpected and it is unknown exactly what precipitated it." Such unknowns often lead to a treatment plan recommendation that the area be explored further.

13. Make certain that subsequent entries explain the outcome of all recorded plans or goals. Avoid leaving the reader hanging with incomplete recording. For example, the frustrated reader may mumble to himself, "Six weeks ago the worker talked about helping the mother deal with feelings of rejection toward her daughter. It's never mentioned again in the recording—I wonder what's happening with this?" Similarly, if a plan is changed in midstream, recording should reflect what happened and why and describe the new or alternate plan. For example, the worker might be striving toward nursing-home placement for a client. Suddenly the entries talk about the person returning to his own home instead. What happened to the nursing-home plan and why was it changed? Try to give the reader some sense of continuity and follow-through with social work planning and goals.

14. Use summary recording to describe more than one contact with a client. It is not always necessary to do a separate recording for each contact; instead, make an entry in the margin or a subheading that states the time period covered. For example, "11/17/77 to 1/10/78." The first sentence of the recording might then read something like this: "During this time I had numerous contacts with Mrs. Smith and also with Gloria's teacher at the XYZ School." Then the recorder can go on to summarize the results of these contacts without having to describe separately what took place in each.

There are a few exceptions to this guideline, primarily in protective services settings where it can be extremely important to document the exact date that an event happened or an attempt was made to contact a client. The pattern formed by these entries over a period of time will stand out more significantly than it would if the information had been summarized rather than listed in separate entries. This form of documentation can also be essential when attempting to secure a court order for someone's protection. Social work staff and students working in these settings usually receive specialized instructions on the required recording format.

15. Avoid recording too much "process." The outcome or the results of social work activity are usually more important than the detailed steps the practitioner went through to accomplish something. When a worker becomes totally absorbed in resolving a problem, it is tempting to record the success story in detail. Consider the following typical example of this kind of recording:

Mr. Blackstone called me this afternoon to tell me he didn't get his S.S.I. check—or rather, it was $14.38 less than it should have been he thinks. I called the S.S.I. office and was told I had to speak to Miss Williams. Her secretary said she wasn't in the office then but would be back at 11:30. When I called about 11:45, she had gone to lunch. She called me about 2pm in response to my message. She didn't know what had happened to Mr. Blackstone's check, but promised she'd look into it and call me back. When I didn't hear from her in 2—3 days, I called again and she told me the computer had made an error and they would issue a supplementary check which Mr. Blackstone would receive in about 2 weeks. I thanked her for the information. Mr. Blackstone called me the next day and I gave him the information.

This is more process than summary recording and boring to the unfortunate person who must read it. Of what significance will all this detail be six months or three years from now? The fact that a contact occurred with the S.S.I. office in Mr. Blackstone's behalf is important and should be recorded. However, it should be presented in brief, summary style:

Mr. Blackstone called me on 8–14–76 advising that his S.S.I. check was $14.38 short. I spoke with Miss Williams at the S.S.I. office who discovered a computer error. She promised that a supplementary check will be issued for Mr. Blackstone—he should receive it by 8–31–76. He was advised of this plan.

It is important to record the name of the person contacted—if Mr. Blackstone fails to get his supplementary check as promised, someone will need to follow up on it. Notice that exact dates, rather than days of the week or time periods, are recorded. It is also important to note that the plans were conveyed to the client.

16.   Recording must be kept current and complete enough for the worker's supervisor or another staff member to pick up where the recorder left off, should he be absent unexpectedly from the job. It's easy to think, "Oh, I don't have to worry about that—it'll never happen to me," but an unexpected crisis is always a possibility. Many practitioners would require a solid week just to get their recording up to date so they could leave for a planned vacation!

THE EFFECT OF GRAMMAR AND SPELLING ON SOCIAL WORK RECORDING

> *It don't matter weather I can writ good or not—the main thing is that I be able to help my clients—they is really in need of my serfices.*
> Undergraduate social work student

This section should not even be here. Persons who train BSWs and MSWs as students and hire them as social workers should be able to assume that such individuals can read and write. Unfortunately, many students are moved through junior and senior high school with poor training in basic English. These individuals are often bright and, because they possess basic skills in relating to people, make it through college with very little improvement in their communication skills. In graduate schools of social work, some students are rewarded with A's because "the idea was good" or because "a lot of work obviously went into that paper," in spite of awkward grammar, spelling errors, poor sentence structure, and other abuses of the English language. Unfortunately, these students often graduate believing that their skills are adequate or even exceptional, when in fact there are serious deficits that will cause problems for them as social work employees. Deficiencies often show up most dramatically in the area of social work recording.

The question is often heard: "Do I have to be a good writer to do good social work recording?" Some people obviously have more facility for expression than others. However, excessive symbolism, poetic phrasing, and picturesque descriptions can actually detract from, rather than add to, the clarity and purpose of social work recording. On the other hand, poor spelling and sloppy organization of thoughts can negate what the social worker is trying to say. Obvious misspellings, incorrect tenses, and other writing errors typical of the uneducated will cause the reader to question not just the writer's knowledge of English but the content of the recorded entry. This can be a real problem in interdisciplinary settings where social workers, physicians, psychiatrists, and others are making entries in a common case record. There is little tolerance for the inability to communicate clearly, using good English (though there is a surprising tolerance for illegibility).

There are several levels of communication. Some people can communicate effectively orally but not in writing. However, if a worker consistently produces poorly organized, vague, and unclear recordings, the supervisor will wonder how he can communicate clearly with his clients during interviews.

Problems with reading comprehension often go hand in hand with difficulty in expressing oneself in writing. Inadequate writing skills may affect the ability to document or describe social work activity and can cause the worker to spend so much time on recording activities that he is unable to see the required number of clients and carry a full workload. Failure to read at a normal rate with an appropriate degree of comprehension can also severely handicap the worker's services to his client. Reading in connection with social work practice may consume a disproportionate amount of time. Partial comprehension may lead to poor diagnostic assessments and treatment planning. Summaries written for other professionals may be incomplete or inaccurate. The meaning of words and phrases may be altered by misspellings and grammatical errors, causing others who take action on the written report to think or act inappropriately. Thus reading and writing skills are virtually inseparable.

There are students and social work practitioners who do not have a college education. If there is a genuine differentiation of roles and tasks, these individuals are often involved in more concrete services, requiring minimal reading and use of basic and highly structured recording styles. If these individuals do record, they must be able to get their information across clearly; however, the expectations would not be as great as for those with more formal education.

If deficits in writing ability make it impossible for the worker or student to communicate the fact that he is doing effective social work, situations will arise in which it really won't matter whether his skills are any good or not. How others perceive a person is reality for them—not what the person thinks he is. Thus if a worker's supervisor, professional colleagues, quality control reviewers, and others see only poor, unclear written communication as a reflection of his skills, it will be difficult to convince them that the individual is actually a highly skilled professional.

CHAPTER 8

SUMMARY RECORDING OUTLINES

These outlines provide a structured format for organizing information when specialized summaries are required. Many agencies provide their own outlines; in their absence, the outlines in this chapter may be used. They will not meet the need of every type of social work setting, but are presented in a manner that should make them easily adaptable to most settings.

INTAKE SUMMARIES

The intake summary is usually prepared following an agency's first contact with a client or person seeking services in a client's behalf. The purposes of the intake interview are to permit the voluntary client to express his needs as he sees them and to state what he would like from the agency and/or worker. It also enables the worker to explain the services the agency has to offer and to discuss the reason for contact with a consumer who did not seek the agency's services but was referred by someone else. Basic identifying data and social history information, especially as it pertains to the presenting problem, are gathered. The worker and client attempt to determine if the agency can meet the client's needs. A decision is made as to whether there is a need for further contacts and by whom. Roles are defined. This could include discussing fees, scheduling appointments, and other basic items. The intake worker may pass the case on to a social worker (or member of another discipline) who will provide ongoing services.

Following the intake interview, the worker does a diagnostic assessment of what was learned and observed and makes recommendations for further treatment and/or services. His report may follow an outline provided by the agency or it may use a special form. The following data are usually included in an intake recording:

1. The worker's name, the date of the initial contact, and/or the date that the intake summary was prepared.

2. The client's name, address, phone number, and identifying number.

3. Other persons the worker may have talked with as part of the intake process, and their names and relationships to the client (e.g., family members may have participated in the interview or the contact may have been initiated by a phone call from a referring agency).

4. The reason for the contact with the client. This might also be called the "presenting problem."

5. A summarized description of pertinent background and social history information related to the primary problem area(s).

6. The nature and/or pattern of previous contacts with the agency, if any.

7. A diagnostic summary statement.

8. A treatment plan describing short- and long-range professional treatment goals.

9. Some agencies include a final heading of "disposition" to indicate the specific outcome; i.e., "Case is being transferred to Sara Jones for continuing casework services," or "case is closed because . . . ," or "Mrs. Jones will be seen by the clinic psychiatrist for evaluation of possible suicidal tendency; the social worker will interview family for pertinent social history and Tony will undergo psychological testing with Mr. Smith."

TRANSFER SUMMARIES

When a case must be transferred from one worker to another, it is important that the new counselor get a complete picture of the client's situation, problems, and strengths, plans made, progress toward achieving goals, and unfinished matters. The new worker must be able to move in quickly and establish rapport with the client. The transferring worker should always explain to the consumer that a change in workers will be occurring and prepare him for this process. If time and circumstances permit, the old worker should introduce the new person to the client; a joint interview might be one way of making the transition. During such a conference, the departing worker or student could review what he and his client have been working on in their relationship and involve the new worker in setting goals for continued services.

The following information is usually included in a transfer summary:

1. The worker's name and the date the transfer summary is being written.

2. The client's name and identifying number.

3. The reason for and the date of the initial involvement with the client by the worker and/or the agency. If it is a case that has been opened and closed several times, a brief summary of the dates and reasons for the openings and closings should be given.

4. The presenting problems at the time the case became active.

5. A heading of "case activity" or "services provided" to describe what has been happening with the case since it became active.

6. A description of the client's present situation.

7. A diagnostic summary.

8. A discussion of any pending treatment plans.

9. The reason for the case transfer, to whom it is being transferred, and the effective date of the transfer (if different from the date the transfer summary is written). A statement can be included to indicate whether the client is aware of the transfer.

Occasionally a worker who is transferring a case is aware of some highly confidential information about the client that he does not wish to put into writing. He may therefore choose to tell the new worker the information orally rather than put it into the transfer summary. He should also indicate whether or not the client is aware that certain information is being passed on to the new worker.

CLOSING SUMMARIES

Whenever an active case is being closed it is important to have something in the file that documents why the agency got involved with the client, what was done, what the final outcome was, what problems could or could not be solved, and why the case was closed. This often proves invaluable when the client contacts the agency at a later date and the case is reopened. Often the worker who writes the closing summary is no longer with the agency or has himself forgotten the details of the case. Thus the new worker must rely entirely on the closing summary for a comprehensive picture of the previous case activity. The new worker may have time only to glance through the closing summary while the client is waiting to see him. Therefore, it must be clearly and concisely written, with headings used wherever possible to make it easy for the new worker to locate the information he needs.

If there is a chance that the individual will become known to the agency again in the future, this is often indicated, along with any pertinent recommendations. The official closing summary often forms the basis for summaries to other agencies (with the client's permission, of course) and a starting point for intake workers in the same agency who may have contact with the individual at a later date. Thus the closing summary often becomes the single most important document in a case record once it has been closed.

A suggested outline for a closing summary, which could be adapted to fit individual agencies, would include:

1. The worker's name and the date the closing summary is being written.

2. The client's name and identifying number.

3. The reason for and the date of the initial involvement with the client by the worker and/or the agency. If it is a case that has been opened and closed several times, a brief summary of the dates and reasons for these openings and closings should be given.

4. The presenting problem(s) at the time the case became active.

5. A heading such as "case activity" or "services provided" to describe what happened on the case while it was active.

6. A description of the client's situation at the time of the case closing.

7. A diagnostic summary statement. It is important to mention any unresolved problems remaining at the time of the case closing and give an indication of why they persist.

8. The reason for and the date of the case closing (if different from the date the summary was written).

9. Some agencies request that the worker include a statement indicating the probability of the case becoming active again in the foreseeable future.

GENERAL SOCIAL-HISTORY SUMMARIES

It is difficult to provide a general social-history outline that would be applicable to all or even most social work settings. Most ask their staff and students to pull together a complete social history at some point in their relationship with the client. Certain subjects are invariably included, such as family relationships and financial situation. However, some areas will be emphasized while others may be entirely absent, depending on the focus of the agency and the nature of the presenting problem. For example, if a young couple comes for marital counseling, there will generally be considerable emphasis on family relationships, psychosexual development, and related areas. If the presenting problem is financial need, economic factors will be thoroughly explored, along with employment background and potential. If a young child is a behavior problem at home and is undergoing neurological testing for possible brain damage, the social worker will obtain an in-depth developmental history dating back to the mother's pregnancy. Family relationships would also be explored. If the patient is a middle-aged man facing radical surgery, there is heavy emphasis on medical-surgical aspects and how the patient views what is happening to him, as well as how the experience will affect various areas of his life.

The following outline is in use in a medical social work setting and is therefore slanted toward this speciality. However, it should give some idea of what a complete social history might include. Students and beginning practitioners are urged *not to copy this outline blindly*—it would not be appropriate for settings that do not provide medical social work services and would need modification.

Social History Outline (for an Inpatient, Medical Social Work Setting)*

Date and Reason for Referral	Self-explanatory. Include also the source of the referral.

---

*Taken from Jackson Memorial Hospital, Medical Social Services Procedure Manual, Miami, Florida, 1975. Headings in parenthesis are alternate ones that are often used.

Medical Situation	State patient's age. Briefly describe how patient came to be injured or admitted to the hospital and if admission is due to trauma or an unplanned occurrence. Give the date of admission, patient's primary diagnosis, and any other significant medical problems. Describe how patient's medical problems are affecting his ability to function mentally and physically (i.e., sleeps most of the time, is ambulatory, incontinent, confused, unsteady on his feet, bedridden, etc.). Indicate the prognosis for recovery (if known) and anything known about what the patient's level of functioning is expected to be at the time of discharge. If known, include a statement indicating how much the patient and/or significant family members have been told about the patient's diagnosis and prognosis. If this is not known, state this.
Family Situation	State whether the patient has any family or close friends. Names, addresses, phone numbers, relationship to patient, and the degree of closeness between patient and these persons should be indicated.
Living Arrangements	Describe the patient's living situation. This is usually obtained from the patient and family. What type of facility does patient live in—an apartment, rooming house, alcoholic halfway house, private home, outdoors under the expressways, etc. Perhaps he has no permanent residence and lives in abandoned cars. Try to paint a picture of his life style. Depending on his mental and physical condition, factors such as whether he lives alone, upstairs or downstairs, and closeness to the hospital could or could not be important.
Economic Situation	List the amount and source of patient's income and give some indication of his monthly expenses and any unmet needs. If patient appears eligible for or has already applied for financial assistance, this should be described.
Background Information	Place of birth, ethnic or cultural factors, education, and early history—anything that appears significant in view of patient's current situation and social service planning. Include a brief description of past or present employment (often the pattern of employment is more important than the actual dates and places of employment), marriages, children, etc.
Worker's Impressions (Diagnostic Summary)	If not already covered in a previous item, include here your analyses of what you believe to be the primary feelings and needs of the patient and/or his family. Include any diagnostic impressions that may not be readily apparent to the casual observer.
	Mentally review all that is known about the patient and his situation from the items above. What feelings would a person in this situation be apt to have? What feelings might his family have? What feelings has the patient expressed about his illness, his situation, his

future, etc.? Does he have any feelings that perhaps have not been verbalized? Indicate attitudes of family members or significant others in the patient's life toward the patient, and the medical or social service treatment plan.

Casework Goals (Treatment Plan)   Based on the previous two headings, describe specifically what social service activity is recommended to meet the needs the worker and/or the patient and others have identified. Mention short- and long-term goals, any community resources that might be utilized, and obstacles that might delay or prevent the carrying out of the plan.

GENERAL INTERIM SUMMARIES

A social history, often including detailed background information, is usually prepared when a comprehensive picture of a client's situation is required. Once this has been accomplished, there is usually no need to repeat information that is not subject to change. Interim summaries are usually done on active cases where it is necessary to pull together day-to-day social work activities into a summarized format. They are often used to update information and treatment activities following the original intake and/or social history report.

The following outline for an interim summary spells out when the summary is required and provides some guidance on how to do the summary along with the actual outline. This particular outline was prepared for use by medical social workers in a hospital* and is included in the department's procedure manual. However, it could be readily adapted to other kinds of social work settings:

introduction

Interim summaries are to be done as required by the social service department, by Medicare, or by other third-party payers, or whenever the individual social worker or supervisor determines that a great deal of information about a patient is rapidly changing and needs to be pulled together in a comprehensive manner to facilitate interdisciplinary communication and social work planning.

If the headings in the following outline are used, criteria for recording for the social service department, Medicare peer review, and audit can all be met.

In addition to the specific data called for in the outline, the following guidelines should be observed:

1. Review existing social work entries and summaries to avoid unnecessary repetition and to determine:

   a) what needs to be said that has not been said;
   b) what information has changed;
   c) whether progress/problems and outcomes have been recorded for all previously stated social work goals and plans.

   Information on all three areas will need to be included in the interim summary.

2. The summary should clearly indicate the sources of your information (i.e., doctor, family, patient). It should also make obvious to the reader whether your main contacts have been with patient and/or family.

3. If any specific data called for in the outline are unknown, say so, adding whatever brief explanation might be needed. The reader should not be left wondering if family know the prognosis, or if the sister is not mentioned because there has been no further contact, and so on.

*Jackson Memorial Hospital, Miami, Florida.

Interim Summary Outline

Date and Reason for Referral	State date case originally opened to social service, and reason for initial referral or case opening. If case has been opened and closed several times, briefly describe dates and reasons. Comment on any obvious patterns (e.g., "Case has been closed twice when patient left the hospital and refused further services").
Medical Situation	Briefly describe patient's initial presenting problem and any changes since the case was opened. Describe the individual's current level of physical functioning and any significant limitations, and anticipated treatments, procedures, or complications that could be of significance physically or emotionally.
Patient/Family Response to Illness	Review any previous summaries or social work entries and update this information. How much has patient/family been told regarding diagnosis and prognosis? What kind of understanding do they have of treatment procedures and medical or surgical planning? Has patient and/or family been taught self-care procedures in preparation for discharge? Describe patient's and/or family's emotional and attitudinal response to patient's illness or hospitalization. Has this created any problems in providing medical or social work services? If patient's or family's attitude or emotional response is unknown, this should be so stated.
Family Situation	If previous recording does not do so, list pertinent family members, including a description of their involvement with, and relationship to, the patient.
Living Arrangements and Economic Situation	This data probably appears in previous entries. If not, update and include it here. Be certain to note any changes, or possible changes, in living arrangements or finances that might affect social service or discharge planning. If earlier recording mentions a referral to SSI (Supplemental Security Income), foodstamps, or other community resource, comment on the status of the application—was it approved, rejected, or still pending? If rejected, why was this action taken, and will it have any significant repercussions for the patient?
Background Information	Add any pertinent information that has not been previously recorded.
Social Work Activity Thus Far	Describe the type of social work activity up to the time of the interim summary. Include a brief summary of: 1. Frequency of contacts and with whom (e.g., "We have seen patient once weekly until two months ago when he became comatose. Contacts with patient's sister were infrequent until September 1975; since then they have occurred several times weekly. I have had no contact with patient's brother.") 2. Nature and purpose of contacts: what approach

was used to achieve the purpose of the contacts (e.g., casework, group work, supportive counseling, many brief "how are you today" contacts with a few in-depth sessions; reality-oriented treatment; application of principles of behavior modification)? What approaches have been tried but were unsuccessful?

3. Briefly describe goals that have been accomplished as well as unsuccessful planning efforts. Mention primary problems encountered in achieving past goals.

Diagnostic Assessment

Review all that is known about the patient and his situation. What do the recorded facts and behaviors *mean*? What coping mechanisms are being used, and how effectively? What feelings do the patient and family have? How are they dealing with or expressing these feelings? Can you comment on how the feelings and behaviors could affect medical or social work planning? Avoid repeating facts—include as much in-depth diagnostic assessment and analysis as is possible and appropriate. Comment also on the patient/family's attitude and response to social work involvement. The worker's impression of the appropriateness or inappropriateness of behavior on the part of the patient/family/significant others should also be included.

Current Treatment Plan

Whenever a factual summary and diagnostic assessment of known facts about a patient's situation are prepared, the treatment plan must also be revised. Include:

1. A statement of each social work goal. Be as specific as possible. Avoid vague terms such as "supportive contacts," which have little meaning to interdisciplinary team members.
2. The desired outcome of each goal.
3. Any existing or anticipated problems or positives that could affect the accomplishment of the goal(s).
4. Clearly indicate whether the planning has been discussed with patient and/or family. Comment on their response to it and their willingness and ability to follow through.
5. If any short- or long-term goals have changed from what was recorded previously, indicate the reason for the change.

SPECIALIZED INTERIM SUMMARIES

Occasionally there is a need for a specialized recording outline that sets up specific guidelines governing the purpose and content of the material to be written. As agencies implement peer review, many are setting up recording criteria for staff and reviewers to ensure that agency records comply with established standards. Reviewers may use a form or a checklist of items that must be covered in the social worker's recording. This list is sometimes referred to as a "protocol."*

An example of such a protocol and the accompanying guidelines for recording

*The idea is adapted from an article by Kris Ferguson et al., "Initiation of a Quality Assurance Program for Social Work Practice in a Teaching Hospital," *Social Work in Health Care* 2nd. 2 (Winter 1976–77): 205–17.

appear below.* The setting is a medical social work department in a large hospital that contains many specialized areas, including units for burn patients, cancer patients, intensive care, pediatric and renal dialysis, transplant patients, and the rehabilitation center. The social workers assigned to each unit specialize in servicing that particular kind of patient. All are MSW's. The department felt that the recording expectations for the areas listed above should be different from other areas of the hospital. Accordingly, staff members worked together to develop the ideas for the "Protocol for Adult Specialty Units" that follows. The protocol lists items that must be addressed in the worker's recording. When records are pulled for review, social work entries must show that these various areas were explored, evaluated, and dealt with in some manner. Thus it is a protocol for social work practice as well as for recording.

Following the protocol are "Guidelines for Social Service Recording in the Rehabilitation Center."† They state the purpose of social work recording in that particular area and set up definite quality and frequency of recording expectations that can be measured easily in peer review and audit activities as well as when assessing individual worker performance. Notice that the guidelines refer to the department's procedure manual and other recording outlines that must be followed.

Protocol for Adult Specialty Units

I   *CRITERIA FOR REFERRAL TO SOCIAL SERVICE.* All patients are automatically seen by the social worker.

II   *PROTOCOL*

A. *Assessment*

1. Description of patient's physical situation; length of time patient has had the illness/condition; general condition; presence of other illnesses; prognosis.
2. Patient's general attitude toward and adjustment to his illness. This would include description of feelings/behaviors such as denial, acceptance, depression, anger, etc.
3. Patient's living arrangements prior to admission.
4. Patient's family composition; their response to patient's illness and/or hospitalization; their health and any other factors that might affect patient's recovery or care post-discharge (such as employment of family members that would cause patient to be home alone after discharge, etc.).
5. Patient's employment background and potential for future employment; patient's motivation to return to work or enter a rehabilitation program; patient's and family's financial situation.
6. Patient's and family's usual response to loss, role changes, pain, stress, and other crisis situations.
7. Anticipated discharge date and confirmation that patient and/or family as well as medical staff are aware of discharge date and plans.

B. *Goal Setting*

1. List of problems/needs as seen by patient, family, medical staff, the social worker, and significant others.
2. Goals established with patient, family, relevant staff, and significant others along with indication that these individuals are aware of these goals and that they have been communicated to medical staff as well.

C. *Implementation of Plan*

1. Indication that referrals are being, or have been, made to appropriate community resources and that patient is aware of this planning.
2. Description of discharge objectives (if pertinent) and indication that all persons involved with this planning are aware of the goals and their role

*Taken from material developed by staff of the Medical Social Service Department, Jackson Memorial Hospital, Miami, Florida.
†The rehabilitation center houses primarily long-term patients with spinal-cord injuries (paraplegics and quadriplegics), strokes, and amputations. The average length of stay is over three months, and social workers follow many of these multiproblematic patients and their families very intensively.

in facilitating the plan (e.g., completion of appropriate papers by the physician, etc.).

3. Reinforcement of medical information and need for particular treatment or follow-up after discharge. Indication that patient/family are aware of these plans and what is required. Referrals to medical personnel for instruction when needed. Indication that tangible arrangements for transportation, follow-up appointments, and other essentials have been made.

D. *Recording*

1. Consult reply (if applicable) in chart; make progress note entries at least once per month. Sign and date all notes and show worker's title.
2. Special summaries and reports completed as specified in the recording guidelines for the particular unit and/or in the department procedure manual.
3. The recording should reflect/describe the assessment, planning or treatment involved in working with the other items described in this protocol.

III *UNEXPECTED COMPLICATIONS*

A. Patient discharged prior to being seen by social worker.

B. Patient/family refuse services.

C. Patient leaves against medical advice.

D. Abrupt changes in family composition or other support systems.

E. Patient's death.

F. Unavailability of community resources, which delays or hinders discharge planning.

G. Medical changes in patient's condition that alter or delay social service plan.

H. Psychiatric problems that complicate or alter the course of social service planning.

I. Family difficult to contact, not living in the area, or otherwise difficult to involve in planning.

IV *CRITERIA FOR TERMINATION OF SOCIAL SERVICE INVOLVEMENT.* Termination will occur when:

1. Goals have been reached.
2. It appears that goals cannot be achieved.
3. Patient leaves against medical advice *and* cannot be located and/or absolutely refuses services *and* there are no significant others whose needs would require social service involvement.
4. Death of the patient does not necessarily result in termination, as social service may continue to be involved with family or significant others. Death results in termination only when the primary involvement has been with the patient and there are no goals or needs involving other persons that would require social work involvement.

Guidelines for Social Service Recording in the Rehabilitation Center

I *Purpose.* The functions of social service recording in a long-term area such as the Rehab Center include the following:

A. To share with interdisciplinary staff pertinent psychosocial background information regarding the patient and his family.

B. To share with interdisciplinary staff the patient's/family's emotional response to injury/illness/loss, their adjustment to the Rehab Center itself, and their plans for the patient after discharge.

C. To share with interdisciplinary staff the contract goals established between patient/family and the social worker along with the specific treatment plan and an anticipated time frame for its implementation.

126

D. To share and document obstacles encountered in achieving these goals as well as to record successful outcomes.

E. To help interdisciplinary staff understand the role of the social worker in a Rehab Center.

F. To facilitate supervisory guidance related to casework/groupwork skills, case management, and discharge planning.

II *Protocol.* The social worker will use the Medical Social Service Department's "Protocol for Adult Specialty Units" in formulating the content of his recording.

III *Implementation*

A. Within one week of patient's admission or transfer to the Rehab Center, the social worker will do an initial assessment using the "Social Service Report Form" (C-465).* This should include a brief description of the patient, his medical status, and initial reaction to the Center, along with presenting problems as identified by the patient, his family, hospital staff, and/or the social worker. Recording should reflect specific short- and long-range treatment and service goals. If the patient is to be considered "inactive" because no appropriate goals can be established at the time of this evaluation, the worker will indicate this in his recording and indicate when periodic reassessments will be done.

B. At the end of the patient's first month in the Rehab Center, a detailed social history will be done and placed in the medical chart. The "Social History Outline" provided in the Procedure Manual† will be used for this purpose.

C. At least once a month, the social worker will record in the progress-notes section of the medical chart. All significant occurrences should be documented. These entries should describe progress (or lack of) in goal achievement and modification of existing goals as well as the establishment of new goals. The patient's/family's current emotional status and its effect on progress in achieving Rehab Center goals should be included. Refer to the Procedure Manual for additional guidance on how to write appropriate progress-note entries.

D. An interim summary is required at least once every three months. Use the "Interim Summary Outline" for preparing this report.

E. A closing summary is prepared when the patient is discharged from the Rehab Center. The "Closing Summary" outline provided in the Procedure Manual is followed. If there is a plan to continue working with the patient after discharge (as an outpatient), the Closing Summary is still required; however, it should stress the reasons for continued social work involvement and describe treatment goals.

F. If a former Rehab Center patient is being followed as an outpatient, recording will be done according to the Procedure Manual guidelines for outpatient specialty units.

OUTLINE FOR RECORDING GROUP SESSIONS

Staff and students who use group work as a treatment method often must develop their own method of recording. It is usually impractical to make entries in the individual records of every participant in a group each time the group meets. Thus it makes more sense to maintain a special record or folder, labeled with the name of the group, in which various kinds of entries pertaining to group activity can be recorded.

---

*This is a mostly blank sheet of paper prepunched for filing in a medical chart. It has a line down the left-hand side and across the top to form margins. The name of the form and its identifying number are printed on the bottom.

†This refers to the procedure manual in use in the social work department that developed these "Guidelines for Social Service Recording in the Rehabilitation Center."

To illustrate this type of outline, let's suppose that a worker is assigned to a special service unit that works with AFDC (Aid to Families with Dependent Children) mothers. The worker is meeting weekly with a group of these women to discuss common problems and needs. A recording outline might appear as follows:

AFDC Mother's Group—Recording Requirements

I A separate record will be set up and labeled with the title of the group ("AFDC Mothers Group").

II A face sheet will be filed in this record, indicating the following information about the group:

    A. *Purpose.* Why was the group formed? What goals are the worker and/or the clients hoping to achieve?

    B. *Membership.* How were members selected? What criteria were required, if any? Were any types of individuals specifically excluded from membership?

    C. *Initial Membership.* List the individuals who are members of the group as of the first meeting.

    D. *Place, Frequency, and Times of Meetings.*

    E. *Beginning and Ending Dates.* When will the first meeting be held? Is the group time-limited? At what point will it terminate? What must be accomplished before the group disbands?

    F. *Group Leader's Approach.* Briefly describe the primary techniques you plan to use to accomplish the goals outlined for the group. Include any outside resource persons or materials that will be used.

    G. *Anticipated Complications.* Are there any complications that could hinder the achievement of goals or result in premature termination (e.g., you may know in advance that you will be out of town for three weeks and may be concerned about the effect a substitute person will have on the group)?

III A separate piece of paper will be used to record the highlights of each group session. Information should include:

    A. The date of the meeting.

    B. The number of the meeting (e.g., the third meeting of this group thus far).

    C. The names of those present and absent.

    D. A brief description of the interaction of individuals in the group. Significant comments, feelings expressed, or possible areas for further discussion and exploration should be noted. Only the highlights should be recorded.

    E. A brief summary and analytical statement about the overall group interaction.

    F. The plan or agenda for the next meeting.

IV Once monthly the worker will make a brief entry in each group member's individual AFDC case record, noting the fact that the individual is participating in the group sessions and including any pertinent data or observations that his/her caseworker needs to be aware of. Treatment goals (through the group process) should also be included.

V Whenever an individual terminates membership in the group, an entry will be made in the appropriate AFDC case record. It should describe briefly the nature of the group and the individual's participation. Problems in achieving goals should be described, along with the goals accomplished. The reason for termination should be included, along with any pertinent recommendations for the individual caseworker's consideration.

VI At the time the entire group terminates, a summary will be done. One copy will be placed in the group folder and one copy will go in the AFDC case record of each individual who was a group member at the time of termination. The summary should include:

A. Points A, B, D, and E from the face sheet.

B. A brief summary of the main topics discussed in the group sessions.

C. A brief description of significant goals accomplished or problems encountered that interfered with treatment goals.

D. The reason for the group's termination.

E. All of the above items would be the same for each individual group member. A final paragraph can be added to describe briefly the individual's participation in the group. The copy that is filed in the individual AFDC record should contain only information on that particular person—no data on other group members should be included.

VII The special group folder will be filed in a storage area designated for inactive group records.

SUMMARIES FOR OTHER AGENCIES

When a worker receives a request from another agency for information about his client, it is often submitted in writing. The client's permission to release the data must be obtained first, of course. Usually the agency requesting the information will specify what it wants. If not, it is important to ask. The other agency should be sent only the information it needs—no more and no less. Some workers take the easy route and simply duplicate everything in their record or send a copy of their latest special-purpose summary. This is poor social work practice. First, it gives the agency more information than it really needs. Second, it violates the privacy of the client; release of information, with or without his permission, should be kept to a minimum, and blanket copying of preexisting materials goes against this principle. In most instances a special summary must be prepared specifically for the agency to which the information is being released.

It is impossible to provide an all-purpose summary format for these reports. The worker must determine what information the agency is seeking and try to get the agency to provide an outline or at least some guidance or help in preparing the summary. No information should be sent unless this can be obtained. Requests for "everything you have on Mrs. Jones" should not be granted. Instead, explore why they want the information and determine which data are relevant for their needs. It is highly recommended that summaries be stamped "confidential" so that the receiving agency will refrain from passing the information on to a third party without the client's permission.

LETTER WRITING

There is no set outline to follow for writing letters. However, a few basic guidelines can be helpful.

Letters can form an important part of the case record. Usually they are to or from the client, various community resources, and other interested persons. Letters written by workers tend to be brief and either give out information, request information, or confirm appointment dates or other data. Regardless of why a letter must be written, several basic principles should be kept in mind:

1. Letters to community agencies should always be typed. With very few exceptions, correspondence with consumers should also be typed.

2. Do not send postcards if they contain any information that could embarrass the receiver should someone else read it. If the postcard indicates that a client is known to your agency, an embarrassing violation of confidentiality could occur.

For this reason, many agencies use return addresses that do not mention the name of the setting.

3. Even in the regular letter sealed in an envelope, avoid putting into writing highly personal or confidential things that the client might not want another member of his/her family to read.

4. Employ language that the client will understand. Many workers tend to use lengthy words buried in long sentences that are virtually unintelligible to the client with little formal education. On the other hand, it could be insulting to use oversimplified language when corresponding with a verbal, well-educated person.

5. Use your appropriate title. Students will need to check with their field instructor to determine how they are to identify themselves in written correspondence and recorded entries, as opposed to oral exchanges.

6. Most consumers should be addressed as "Mr.," "Miss," or "Mrs." "Ms." is often used if the marital status of a women addressee is unknown or unclear. Only children and clients with whom the worker has an unusually close relationship are addressed by their first name.

7. Always make a copy for the case record.

SPECIALIZED RECORDING STYLES

Most social work settings have their own specific recording requirements. These vary depending on the nature of the clients served, accountability and funding-source mandates, internal peer review and research activity, record-keeping practices, kind and amount of clerical support, disciplines and training of staff, consumer accessibility to the records, and so on. However, a few settings, particularly the medical setting and Title XX social service programs,* have developed recording styles that have received nationwide publicity and been implemented in hundreds of settings, either voluntarily or under professional or legal mandates. Most students and practitioners will encounter one or more of the three most common types of specialized recording, and thus a brief overview of them is presented here.

COMPUTERIZED RECORDING

Many large, sophisticated social service systems use data bank systems of some type. These can range from a simple mag card typewriter through a comprehensive word-processing center to a complex set of computer hardware. An agency may maintain data only for itself—no other organization has routine access to its computerized information. However, the trend today is for groups or networks of agencies to cooperate and compile their data into a combined, and often massive, computerized data bank system. Thus all Title XX programs in a given state may routinely send certain types of information to a statewise computer terminal. All branches of the NYS Department of Mental Hygiene may be required to feed certain client data into a statewide data bank system.† The Multi-State Information System (MIS) is another example of such a system; it compiles mental health information from numerous states. Many social service agencies have no computer system of their own, but send data to state-maintained registries—births, deaths, child abuse, tumor diagnoses, and other data may be submitted from a wide variety of service delivery systems.

Computerized record keeping has two primary purposes: it can *replace* the traditional social work case record and become *the* method for maintaining records on individual clients; or it can *supplement* the traditional individual social work record and amass statistical data for use in research, accountability, budgeting, and other administrative purposes. The second function is by far the most common in social work practice today. A brief description of this approach will be provided, followed by a more detailed description of a specific system developed for use by hospital social workers.

The simplest data bank system consists of the agency secretary, who receives information submitted to her by social work staff and then manually compiles it into a form useful to administration. She may be aided by a mag card typewriter. Many agencies employ a similar type of statistical record-keeping system. The next most advanced system would use word-processing equipment. These systems maintain the data in a familiar format, merely storing the information conveniently. The typist or terminal operator feeds the data into the machine, records it the way it should

---

*The "services" part of state and federal financial assistance programs. Some clients receive services only, without direct financial assistance.

†In fact, a recent lawsuit involved several professionals and a social worker in New York who challenged the state Department of Mental Hygiene, maintaining that its computerized data system did not provide adequate safeguards to protect the confidentiality of patient names and identifying data that employees were required to submit to the system. Unfortunately, the court ruled that because the plaintiffs had no evidence that damaging confidentiality violations had actually occurred (they were primarily concerned with the possibility of this happening), there was no violation of patient privacy rights, and employees were required to continue submitting the data. *Volkman* v. *Miller,* 383 NYS2d 95 (Supreme Court, May 13, 1976), p. 95.

appear, then sends it to "storage" on special cards, disks, or tapes. Massive volumes of data can be recorded in an amazingly small amount for space. For example, some word-processing equipment can store several hundred pages of typed data on a disk smaller than this sheet of paper, and only a few times thicker. Data retrieval is simple, and the equipment can be keyed to flash data on a screen or print it out in a variety of formats.

These systems do not drastically alter the method of recording used by the social worker. He can write or dictate his social service notes as usual, but instead of typing them into a case record, the transcriber might enter them directly into the data system. Such systems can also maintain lists of caseloads by worker, client names and addresses, referrals, and other statistical and identifying data. Thus, staff often complete special cards to provide the desired identifying data. Instead of maintaining these in a manual master card file (i.e., in a filing cabinet or file box), the data are entered into the word-processing system, where they can be updated daily and retrieved to the viewing screen or printed out on a moment's notice. Many such machines can also be instructed to search for a particular client's name or other information while the operator works on something else. All this is done from common styles of recording—hardly any special computer language is needed. If the social worker fills out a data card with a client's name, address, and presenting problem, this is what gets fed into the system, though some settings use a simple coding system whereby types of presenting problems, for example, are assigned a number, and only the number is entered into the system.

The more sophisticated computerized system often necessitates special reporting forms and styles. Some become so cumbersome that the worker may feel that he is spending as much time coding his services for the computer as he spent actually providing the service. These systems are designed to accept a special mark entered between two boxes, or a number placed on a computerized punch card or form to report the social worker's activity. The worker's actual recording is never entered verbatim into the equipment. Thus, if the agency is compiling data on the nature of services provided to clients, the recorder must consult special sheets that describe all possible services that could be provided, determine which one fits most closely the service he actually provided, look up the code for that service, and enter the code onto the special data-reporting card or sheet. If a regular social service record is also being maintained, there will be some duplication of effort, as one set of forms must be completed for the computer operator and normal recording done for the regular record.

For example, a worker in a mental health setting that employs a computerized recording system may be supplied with a six-page list of common psychiatric diagnoses, with a brief paragraph defining and describing each one. In order to report his patient's diagnosis to the computer, he would review the list and select the appropriate item. However, the worker may have fifteen other lists to consult as well, in order to code factors such as type of treatment provided, frequency of contacts, time spent per contact, the nature of each contact and with whom, family members, treatment goals, problems or barriers in achieving the goals, final outcomes, etc.

The System for Hospital Social Work Departments

The American Hospital Association (AHA) and the Society for Hospital Social Work Directors recently published a document that sets forth guidelines and forms for uniform reporting of medical social work activity.* Directors of hospital social work departments across the country have long felt a need to compare statistics among departments. Unfortunately, each department had a different method of defining and recording case activity, making meaningful comparisons virtually impossible. A committee was established to develop something everyone could use, and all members of the society had opportunity to contribute ideas. The reporting system is set up

---

*American Hospital Association, *A Reporting System for Hospital Social Work,* 1978. Copies can be obtained from the AHA, 840 N. Lake Shore Drive, Chicago, Illinois 60611. The reporting system is undergoing some revisions.

so that the results can be tabulated manually or entered into a computerized system. It employs a coding system and would be used in addition to regular records and documentation of social work case activity. Thus this system was developed primarily for administrative purposes, rather than as a means of recording daily social work activity in formal case records. The introduction to the reporting system states that the primary purposes of the system are:

- To determine the need for and contributions of social work services

- To study the kinds of patient services that are needed

- To assess staffing needs of the social work department

- To document the activities and accomplishments of the social work department

- To provide a measure of accountability to the hospital administration, the clients, the social work profession, third-party payers, and the government

- To aid in budgeting and cost accounting

- To serve as an administrative tool*

The system uses five basic documents:

1. A code sheet This lists and codes many different types of identifying data and social work activity. Items under the following headings have been coded: patient status, patient location, source of referral, interventive method(s), problem(s) identified source(s) of payment, service(s) completed, department activity, service-related activity, teaching activity, community activity, research activity, intraorganizational activity, and courtesy.† For example, under "source(s) of referral" the following items appear:

Item	Code
Physician	1-3-1
Nurse	1-3-2
Family member	1-3-3
Friend	1-3-4
Administration	1-3-5
Self	1-3-6
Social work rounds	1-3-7
Automatic social services	1-3-8
Health and welfare agency	1-3-9
Team	1-3-10
Early case finding	1-3-11
Other hospital staff	1-3-12
Other _____	1-3-13‡
Describe	

2. Opening sheet This is very similar to a traditional face sheet. It asks the worker to write in the patient's name, address, age, marital status, and other basic identifying information, including a listing of family members. The second part of the sheet lists various sources of referral, problems identified, and sources of payment by name and code number and asks the worker to put a checkmark by all applicable items.

3. Transfer and closing sheet This is similar in format to the opening sheet and asks the recorder to list traditional identifying data and to check some coded items to indicate the nature of social work activity, problems identified, status of the problem, and payment sources.

*Ibid, p. 1.
†Ibid., pp. 4–8.
‡Ibid., p. 4.

DAILY WORK SHEET

PATIENT'S NAME (Last, First)	DIRECT SERVICES				SUPPORTIVE SERVICES							
	Patient Status Code	Patient Location Code	Interventive Method(s) Code(s)	Number of 15-Minute Time Intervals	Department Activity Code	Service-Related Activity Code(s)	Teaching Activity Code(s)	Community Activity Code(s)	Research Activity Code(s)	Intra-organizational Activity Code(s)	Courtesy Code(s)	Number of 15-Minute Time Intervals
Smither, Mary	1-1-1-1	1-2-3	1-4-1	2		2-2-6 2-2-7						
					2-1-1							
Total												

Social Worker _____ Date _____

Reprinted, with permission, from A Reporting System for Hospital Social Work, published by the American Hospital Association, copyright 1978, p. 18.

4. Daily work sheet This form goes hand-in-hand with the code sheet. The worker completes the work sheet on a daily basis, recording various types of activity for each patient seen. Most of the headings listed on the code sheet also appear on the daily sheet, and the worker is asked to fill in the proper code number to correspond with his activity on each patient. It also incorporates a time element (coded), requiring staff to indicate how much time they spend in certain activities. This sheet is shown in the accompanying figure.

5. Monthly tally sheet This special form summarizes all the identifying and service activity data reported on the worker's daily sheets for an entire month. All the monthly tally sheets for individual workers can then be added together to arrive at a monthly total for the entire department. When this stage has been reached, it is possible to say, "This is what this social work department did this month." This data can be kept for a period of several years, enabling an individual department to compare its activities from year to year and to look for significant trends. It can identify peak and slack months of the year and compare, for example, July to July of each year with December to December to see if different patterns are evident at different times of the year on a recurring basis. A department could take its annual budget (overhead, salaries, and so on), divide it by the number of workers or the number of time units of activity reported, and arrive at a cost per unit of activity figure. Raw data numbers can be converted to percentages, and one department can compare itself with others across the country to determine, for example, if it is usual or atypical for its workers to spend an average of 60 percent of their time in direct services to clients, as opposed to paperwork, meetings, and indirect service activity.

Such a uniform reporting system has many obvious advantages from an administrative, funding, accountability, and research perspective. Unfortunately, in reality, the average grass-roots social worker often has difficulty identifying with these broad perspectives. He is concerned with meeting the daily needs of his clients, feels overworked, and often has little time, interest, or energy to look beyond his immediate caseload. He may view complex or alien-appearing reporting systems as added burdens that detract from time he could spend with his clients, rather than identifying with the larger process and advantages of such a system.

Thus departments that implement such systems must involve nonsupervisory personnel in developing the system whenever possible, and help staff understand the broader purposes of this additional demand on their time in order to elicit their full cooperation. Many highly sophisticated and well-meaning reporting systems have been sabotoged by bitter, frustrated, uninformed workers (and students) who see them as "more paperwork and a waste of time." Departmental and national totals will be meaningless and large-scale policy planning inappropriate and futile if line staff resort to making up numbers to fill in the blanks, guessing at monthly totals at the end of each month instead of keeping accurate daily total sheets, and so on. Yet staff often hurt themselves by such activity. Failure to report every client contact could cause the department administrator to feel the worker *should* be able to carry eighty-five cases. If he knew how many contacts the worker was actually having, he might be able to assess more realistically the caseload the individual is capable of carrying and servicing with quality.

Hospital-based social work departments often compete with other departments for a limited amount of funds for the annual budget. Accurate, properly maintained statistics can go a long way in helping the social work director demonstrate and verify the department's need for more staff, or assist him in establishing that the presence of social work staff in the hospital saves the facility funds by bringing about more rapid discharge of patients, and so on.

Unfortunately, with computerized statistical data systems there is often a very fine line separating the comprehensive, highly sophisticated, and ideal instrument that will produce meaningless results due to worker resistance, from a simpler, more modest system that will, in the long run, produce reasonably accurate and meaningful data because of full cooperation on the part of those staff who must live with it on a daily basis.

GOAL-ORIENTED RECORDING (GOSS)

The goal-oriented approach to social services and social work recording was embraced with much enthusiasm by state services programs for recipients of financial assistance in the early and mid 1970s, when separation of services and financial eligibility took place. The federal government, through the Social Security Administration, took over the financial assistance programs for aged, blind, and disabled adults. This is referred to as the Supplemental Security Income (SSI) Program. However, states retained responsibility for all other social work services to these individuals, including child welfare and AFDC programs. Thus there was much interest in exactly what services workers would be providing and in developing some kind of uniformity in social work recording. The Department of Health, Education, and Welfare wanted to develop a nationwide system for reporting social service activity by the various states. Thus Goal-Oriented Social Services (GOSS) was set up to accomplish *both* purposes of computerized recording: maintenance of the direct client record and statistical reporting. It did not succeed in all respects, and specific procedures of the reporting process were soon abandoned or altered.

However, the basic approach and concept remains in effect. Some of the basic concepts of GOSS draw upon other approaches to social work practice and recording and can be seen in recording practices used by agencies and individual staff who may or may not be consciously aware of their use of the goal-oriented approach. This approach also has an impact on interaction with the client. In order to record what it asks for, a worker must use a "contracting" approach to service delivery—an approach that has become quite popular and proved highly effective in many treatment situations. The alert reader will also note some strong similarities between GOSS and problem-oriented recording.

Under GOSS, basic social history and background information is gathered and recorded. However, there is considerable emphasis on including the client in the assessment process, and in setting goals and developing specific plans for reaching the identified goals. In some instances a formal verbal or even written contract is developed between worker and client, outlining the presenting problem and plans for dealing with it.

States provide their service workers with standardized lists of broad goals. Services to all clients must fit under one of these goals. The worker then identifies and records barriers that would block or hinder achievement of the goal; these may be obtained from a coded list. A service plan is then formulated that states specifically what worker and client plan to do to work toward accomplishing the goal. An itemized list of services is provided and workers are asked to select one or more that come closest to describing how they plan to accomplish each stated goal. Staff are asked to indicate a time frame giving the length of time it will take to complete each goal. Finally, periodic reassessments examine progress in achieving goals and determine outcomes. Recording of social service activity, using the GOSS outline, takes place in the usual manner in the individual case record. The standardized and coded lists of broad goals, barriers, and specific service activities are used by the worker to complete computerized data forms.

The GOSS approach leads to uniformity in recording and statistical reporting practices among social workers, and forces staff to include the client as an active participant in the planning phases of service provision. It also asks workers to include assessments analyzing the meaning of data they have gathered. This is a new and anxiety-producing role for many state social service employes who have limited professional training in human behavior and hold degrees in English, education, philosophy, history, and similar disciplines, yet are employed as social workers. The use of standardized goals and service activities also forces staff to make the client's situation fit the recording criteria, rather than the reverse. This can be an awkward, frustrating process for a conscientious social worker attempting to service his client properly and yet continue to meet agency recording and reporting requirements and be fully honest in reporting what he does. In a system already overwhelmed with bureaucratic paperwork and high levels of worker resistance to additional such responsibilities, GOSS has met with considerable resistance and a significant amount of manipulation on the part of individual workers in their computerized reporting of case activity. However, the basic concepts are valid and can lead not only to effective recording, but also to more effective services provision when GOSS is viewed as a tool to assist the worker in helping his client in addition to providing an outline for organizing and presenting the information he gathers.

PROBLEM-ORIENTED RECORDING (POR, POMR, SOAP)

Problem-oriented recording is a specialized approach that was developed for use in interdisciplinary medical settings. Several different names and abbreviations have been used to refer to the same basic approach to recording—POMR (Problem-Oriented Medical Record) and the more common SOAP (Subjective Data, Objective Data, Assessment, Plan). In simple language, this system requires the recorder to identify problem areas, assess them, and then state what he plans to do about each problem. This particular approach is useful in interdisciplinary settings because many different disciplines may be working on the same problem. For example, a female patient may be hospitalized following a heart attack. She may have various medical problems. If obesity were one of her medical problems, it would be stated as such. A physician might work on the problem by prescribing a low-calorie diet and some medication. The dietitian might attack the problem by counseling the patient on proper nutrition, meal-planning, and calorie-counting techniques. The social worker might assess emotional factors related to the obesity and provide counseling to increase the patient's self-image and encourage development of defense mechanisms other than eating during times of stress, loneliness, or depression. Finally, a chaplain might remind the patient that her body is "a temple for the dwelling of the Holy Spirit" and thus encourage her not to abuse her body, since it belongs to God. All four disciplines are working on the same problem, each going about it in an entirely different manner, yet all must work together as a team. In addition, the social worker may identify problems that only he will work on, and the same could hold true for other members of the interdisciplinary team.

Some disciplines have developed a uniform list of standardized problems. A specific disease (e.g., tuberculosis) may be known to produce or be accompanied by specific problems or complications. A physician might review this list to select the problems that pertain to his particular patient. The standard protocols for identifying and treating TB may also indicate a time frame, i.e., TB patients with certain problems should require no more than ____ days of hospitalization. If more inpatient treatment is required, the recorder must document the problem areas that would justify the extended care. Social workers in medical settings often do this when arranging discharge planning. As a member of the medical team, they must document any factors that might prolong the patient's stay. Third-party payers, peer reviewers, PSRO, and others concerned with quality control, cost accounting, and similar matters then review the recording and concur with or challenge the staff member's treatment activities and goals. A social worker's failure to document justifiable reasons for delays in arranging a nursing home placement could, for example, result in Medicare's ceasing to pay the hospital for an eligible patient's care.

The social work profession has not developed a standardized master list that says, "When a client has this ____ problem, no more than ____ referrals to outside agencies and ____ days of casework services should be needed. The following problems may complicate the client's situation: _____." Thus individual social work departments and staff usually develop their own criteria as to what areas must be evaluated and serviced when clients have certain types of diagnoses, or presenting problems. These may form the basis for protocols that state the kinds of psychosocial information that should be gathered, the nature of services to be provided, and what must be included in the record.* These protocols often provide a guide for both practice and recording and may be used by peer reviewers and others as they read records to determine how effectively the department is meeting its established standards.

The ideal use of POR is for all disciplines to record on the same form in the same interdisciplinary record. Indeed, most medical social work departments have now done away with the separate social service record and record only on the primary medical chart. This trend began in the late 1960s and early 1970s and initially caused much anxiety, as social work staff felt helpless and impotent without their professional security blanket—their private case record. However, staff soon discovered that time spent on paperwork was cut virtually in half as the need for duplicate recordings was eliminated and clerical filing and typing tasks were cut drastically. One of the primary purposes of recording in interdisciplinary settings is for documentation, but it is also intended to provide a means of exchanging information. If one discipline is hoarding its own records, located far away from where the patient is being treated, this purpose is negated. When all disciplines record in one central record, everyone can see at a glance what each team member is doing with all identified problem areas.

Under the SOAP approach, some problem areas are identified in the initial contact with the patient. Additional problem areas may surface in subsequent contacts and be

---

*See Chapter 8, under "Specialized Interim Summaries," for an example of a protocol for practice and recording.

recorded in daily, weekly, or regular progress note entries. Once a problem has been identified and assessed and a treatment plan outlined, subsequent record entries must refer back to that problem area and comment on progress in achieving the plans outlined in earlier entries. Transfer or closing summaries would list each problem area individually and summarize the nature of the problem, assess it, and comment on progress, hindrances, and results in achieving the treatment plan that was developed. Let's examine the SOAP approach in more detail and provide some examples of how it might be used.

Somewhere in the worker's recording (following an outline provided by the social work department) he will be asked to make a heading of "Problems" and, for each problem identified, list the four elements of SOAP recording. This could come at the end of an initial social history or interim summary or could recur throughout ongoing progress notes.

S = subjective data   The worker would write "S" and then describe the subjective data. Subjective data refers to the client's statement of the problem as he or she sees it. The viewpoints of significant others may also be included. Consider: what are the client's thoughts and feelings about his situation and problems?

O = objective data   This section asks the worker to record factual data and observations. The client's behavior and/or personal appearance are described, but *not* analyzed or assessed. For example, "The patient paced back and forth across the room as I interviewed him," or "Mrs. Jones cried as she told me about her husband's drinking problem." If the client has undergone official testing for medical or psychiatric diagnoses, the results of these evaluations can be included as factual information. Details concerning the client's living arrangements, financial situation, and so on, can also be included if they are relevant to the particular problem area being discussed.

A = assessment   This is where the worker *analyzes* the meaning of the factual observations he has recorded and the client's perceptions of the problem that he has written down. Do the client's and worker's perceptions of the problem agree? If the objective material stated that "The client cried as she talked about her husband's drinking problem," what does the worker think this *means*? What does this observed behavior tell the worker about the client? See the section on the Analytical Thinking Model (Chapter 10) for additional ideas on how to arrive at analytical assessments.

P = plan   Based on the gathering of facts, awareness of the client's feelings, and assessment of what all this means, the worker states what he or she plans to do to work on the problem that has been identified (this is very similar to what is commonly referred to as a "service plan" or "treatment plan" in many recording outlines).

Let's return to the situation of the woman who has just been hospitalized with a heart attack and see how POR might look in her interdisciplinary medical chart.

Medical social workers often get referrals on patients from medical staff who see the patient and identify possible problems that social service needs to evaluate. Most hospitals use special "Consult Referral" forms whenever a member of one discipline wants to refer his patient to a specialist or member of another discipline. The form usually gives basic identifying data, the patient's primary diagnosis, and the reason for the referral. The social worker then writes directly on the form, giving his response to the reason for the referral, based on preliminary contact with the client or significant others. He often includes additional pertinent psychosocial information on the form. This is filed in the medical chart, and officially opens the case. The medical chart also contains "progress note" sheets—blank sheets of ruled paper on which all members of the treatment team record daily notes regarding their diagnostic and treatment activities. In most progressive hospitals, social workers write directly on the progress note sheets, alongside physicians, psychiatrists, and others.* An early entry will usually identify one or more problem areas and might appear as follows:

*A few settings relegate social work entries to a separate section of the record, or even forbid social workers to make entries in the interdisciplinary chart. Facilities reviewed by the Joint Commission on Accreditation of

5-15-79 social service note

Talked with Mrs. Smith and her husband today. Social service has identified the following problem areas:
1. obesity
2. inadequate income
3. depression
4. social isolation

The entry would then go on to give the SOAP elements for each problem area. In some settings the physician initiates the problem list for each patient. He may give four or five medical problems he intends to work on. Several of these may be things that also necessitate social work activity. If the physician names five problems, the social worker may, in his entry, add inadequate income, depression, and social isolation as numbers six, seven, and eight on the master list of problems. Thus, whenever any member of the treatment team has something to say about any of these problem areas, he merely refers to it by number in his recording. A subsequent social service entry concerning one of these problem areas might look like this:

5-21-79 problem #3—obesity

S—Mrs. Smith states she was normal in weight until four years ago when her daughter died of leukemia. She has attempted many diets without success and says she feels useless, rejected by her husband, and ugly now that she is 125 pounds overweight. She wants to be thin, but doesn't know if she can do it or not.

O—Mrs. Smith is a short woman who appears much heavier than she actually is because of her small bone structure. Most of her weight is around her abdomen, giving her a rather unusual appearance. She talked freely about her weight problem, but cried when expressing her feelings of hopelessness about being able to control it.

A—Mrs. Smith appears quite depressed. Her feelings that her husband is rejecting her because of her obesity appear realistic—the couple has ceased sexual relations and Mr. S. appears frightened and at the same time, judgmental toward his wife for her obesity. It does not appear that they have openly discussed their fears and feelings with one another, however. Mrs. Smith's daughter was her only child and she seems to have some awareness of eating as her defense mechanism for dealing with her loss and subsequent depression. She appears to have many unresolved feelings about herself and her marriage.

P—1. Referral to the dietitian for dietary counseling.
2. Supportive counseling with Mrs. S. individually to encourage ventilation of feelings and development of alternative methods for coping with her feelings.
3. Joint counseling with Mrs. and Mr. Smith to improve marital communication.
4. Referral to an organized diet group post discharge, but only when Mrs. S. expresses willingness to participate.
5. Staff need to be very supportive and nonjudgmental in relating to Mrs. Smith and in reacting to her obesity. She needs, of course, medical facts concerning the impact of her weight on her health, but strong criticism and exhortations to lose weight will lead to increased feelings of inadequacy and greater dependency on food to make her feel better.

Jane Brown, BSW
Social Worker

Hospitals are in violation of mandated policies if social workers cannot record in the medical chart: "Adequate records relating to social services rendered must be included *in the patient's medical record*" (emphasis added) (*JCAH Accreditation Manual for Hospitals,* 1970, Standard III). The "Standards for Hospital Social Work Departments" adopted by the Society for Hospital Social Work Directors of the American Hospital Association in 1976 state that "Progress notes and other social work entries in the patient's medical record should be such as to permit regular communication with physicians and other personnel involved in the patient's care. Notes should be clear and concise and should indicate the worker's social appraisal, observations, proposed corrective measures, actions taken, and results.

"Entries by social work personnel in medical charts can include information relating to nature of the social problem and situation, relevant historical information regarding the patient and family, plans for social work services, outcome of planning, referral to other resources, final summary of problems and services."

The worker will make periodic entries to report on progress and new developments in the case and will comment on each problem area individually whenever appropriate in subsequent entries. In follow-up to the obesity problem, such an entry might appear as follows:

6-2-79 problem #3—obesity

O—Mrs. Smith is beginning to take more interest in her personal appearance. Her hair was fixed attractively this morning and I saw her with makeup on for the first time.

A—Patient is responding favorably with increased self-concept and feelings of hope as result of 12-pound weight loss from her diet. Her husband has openly expressed his feelings about her obesity for the first time and appeared unaware of how deeply troubled his wife has been over his reactions to her weight.

P—1. Continued joint counseling with Mrs. and Mr. Smith.
2. Dietitian to talk with Mr. and Mrs. Smith jointly re: dietary techniques so he can be involved in the process and be a source of support for Mrs. Smith.
3. Visit from Weightwatchers representative will occur prior to discharge as Mrs. Smith has accepted this referral and initiated contact with them.

Jane Brown, BSW
Social Worker

Notice that the "S" part of the recording is missing—the worker obviously had nothing to say under this heading, and so it was not used. Notice also the use of incomplete sentences. This is typical of entries in interdisciplinary charts. A great number of abbreviations and symbols are also used, but have been excluded from these examples to avoid confusing the reader.

The SOAP approach to POR has been implemented in many inpatient hospital facilities. Most commonly, medical staff have adopted the approach, but social service staff and other disciplines have not followed suit. Some facilities have adopted, then abandoned the approach. The Veterans Administration developed an excellent document for implementing the POMR system in its social work departments throughout the United States, and then abandoned it at the last moment due to ambivalent feelings on the part of key personnel regarding the new approach.* In reality, many social work settings are already using a problem-oriented approach to recording, though they may not be referring to it as such or attempting consciously to teach it. There are some definite benefits to this style of recording. It facilitates interdisciplinary communication and forces the social worker to organize his thinking and to provide written follow-up for all treatment plans developed, so that the reader knows exactly what happened with each plan. It can bring about a uniformity of recording that facilitates internal and external quality review processes. However, POR emphasizes problems rather than strengths and positives. The process of having to list the four SOAP components for each problem area can become quite cumbersome in multiproblem situations. Thus the POR approach has not yet found wide acceptance among social workers, especially outside of the medical setting, and will need to undergo further study and adaptation before it is adopted as a significant and common form of social work recording.†

*Documenting Quality Social Service Utilizing the P.O.M.R. System (Washington, D.C.: Veterans Administration, Social Work Service, June 1976); 48-page Xerox copy obtained through Eleanor Kyle, Chief of Social Work Service.
†Several articles have appeared in the social work literature reflecting efforts to examine and adjust the POR approach to social work practice. See "Selected Readings" at the end of the book.

CHAPTER 10

THE DIAGNOSTIC SUMMARY AND TREATMENT PLAN

Most recording of interactions with clients consists of facts, observations, and other information that could have been picked up by a tape recorder and a camera. What the tape or video recorder cannot do, however, is react to, analyze, diagnose, and assess what has been observed. This is what the diagnostic summary is all about. All professionally trained persons engaged in a helping capacity with clients should learn to put into writing their professional opinions about and analyses of the facts and information gathered. What the helping person thinks about a client and his situation determines what treatment plans are made. Much of this thinking process should take place during the interaction with the client so that the counselor can adjust his approach and techniques according to his ongoing diagnostic assessments. In the quiet of his own office, the practitioner may want to apply the "Analytical Thinking Model" (shown later in this chapter) or a similar method of analyzing the case dynamics in preparation for writing the formal diagnostic summary and treatment plan.

Writing a diagnostic summary statement forces the worker or student to organize his thinking and give some in-depth thought to a case situation. Thus, diagnostic summaries should be written not just to satisfy recording requirements but also as a tool to help the worker develop appropriate treatment planning and provide better services.

The diagnostic summary provides an opportunity for the worker to set down his professional impressions, reactions, and concerns about his client. Put into writing, these ideas can be helpful to other staff who work with that individual at a later date as well as to the person making the entry. There are also times when it may be therapeutic to share diagnostic assessments with the consumer. A diagnostic summary enables a supervisor to learn quickly about the needs of the clients his staff are serving. Casework treatment plans that are formulated without the worker's having gone through the diagnostic thinking process are often inappropriate, superficial, unrealistic, and/or do not meet the client's needs. The worker must learn how to think diagnostically before he can provide meaningful helping or therapeutic services.

Diagnostic summaries are often included when information is being shared with another agency. However, these should not necessarily analyze and comment on *every* aspect of the case situation. They usually focus on the problem area(s) of concern to the agency or individual the information is being released to.

It is not necessary to write a diagnostic summary or treatment plan whenever the worker makes a recorded entry. On the other hand, there are times when it is essential that this be included, such as when a case is opened, reopened, transferred, or closed (see the special summary outlines for these and other types of case activity in Chapter 8). Diagnostic summaries are also needed when a significant change occurs in the client's situation and/or the worker's or client's perceptions of needs and problems.

There are times when diagnostic summaries should be *omitted* from the written record:

1. If information is being released to a setting that does not need in-depth diagnostic material to provide a given service (e.g., referral to a nursing home) and/or does not employ staff trained to interpret diagnostic statements, such material should not be transmitted.

2. If it is known or suspected that a given case situation is of legal interest and stands a greater than average risk of being subpoenaed by the courts, highly sensitive diagnostic material should be withheld unless the worker feels it would be essential to his own defense (if he is the defendant) or for serving the client's best interests.

3. If the client has access to the record and his viewing certain diagnostic material would have a negative effect, such material might not be recorded.

WHAT THE DIAGNOSTIC SUMMARY SHOULD INCLUDE

A diagnostic summary is an *analysis* of what the worker knows about the client and his situation. This means that the practitioner must spend time thinking about his client before he starts writing or dictating. Let's say that it will take thirty minutes to prepare an in-depth diagnostic summary of a fairly complex case. Perhaps fifteen or twenty minutes should be used to review mentally all that is known about the case—questioning what, why, what if, suppose, I wonder what that really means— and *then* the remaining ten minutes spent writing down on paper what has been thought out. If this advance thinking is not performed, the worker's diagnostic summary will be superficial and meaningless.

A good diagnostic summary analyzes why things are the way they are and focuses on feelings and attitudes of the client, significant others in his life, and the views of the worker regarding the case situation. Such a summary will usually include the following material:

1. *The problems and needs as seen by the client.* What does the client think are his main needs and problems? When the worker does not agree with the consumer's stated needs, he often omits the material. No matter how unrealistic or incomplete they may sound to the worker, the needs as seen by the client must be recorded. If the individual states that he has no needs or problem areas, this should be recorded.

2. *The problems and needs as seen by the worker.* What do *you* as the treatment person think the client's problems and needs are? This will not always be the same as what the consumer says they are. Point out any differences between your feelings and those of the client and indicate what you feel are his real needs. This is where the worker's understanding of the psychodynamics of human behavior is crucial to achieving depth in analysis of meanings hidden behind the client's statements and nonverbal actions.

3. *The client's feelings about his situation.* What adjectives would you use to describe how the client is responding to his needs and his situation, and why do you use these particular adjectives? Is he depressed, apathetic, unmotivated, ambivalent, worried, highly anxious, accepting, striving, confused? Does he say one thing ("My hernia doesn't really bother me") but you think he really feels differently ("I think he is really afraid of surgery and doesn't want to admit that his hernia bothers him")? If so, say so and why.

If for some reason you do not know or are unable to determine your client's feelings and attitudes about his situation, state this. It is perfectly acceptable for the social worker to say "I don't know" as part of a diagnostic summary. The fact that we cannot pinpoint what is happening is often as important to record as would be a specific explanation or analysis of a situation.

4. *The appropriateness of the client's feelings and behaviors.* Are they appropriate or inappropriate in view of the crisis or situation the client is facing? Are the feelings exaggerated or unexpectedly absent? For example, it would be normal and appropriate for a man to cry when he is grieving over the loss of his wife. On the other hand, it would usually be abnormal for a young adult who has just learned he is dying of a terminal illness to smile constantly and philosophize on how "we all have to go some time" without expressing some feelings of anger, denial, or depression.

5. *Efforts the client has made to solve his problem.* Has he done anything to try to resolve the problems or needs he has presented to you? What do you think about these efforts—are they realistic or unrealistic? Have they been effective? What else might he do to solve or alleviate his problem?

Practitioners and students often use outlines that force them to say *something* under a "diagnostic summary" heading. No one likes to admit he doesn't know how to do something. Thus, rather than leave this item blank, the anxious practitioner will often include material that does not belong under "diagnostic summary" or "treatment plan" headings.

The diagnostic summary is *not* a statement of facts, even though they may not be recorded elsewhere. The "diagnostic summary" heading is reserved for analytical statements, not a description of facts.

The diagnostic summary is *not* a repetition of information about the client or his situation that has already been stated under other headings in the recording. It is *not* a catchall place to write things the worker forgot to include in the earlier part of his recording. If necessary, provide a special "Miscellaneous" heading at the end of the recording and describe whatever factual information was omitted. Do not clutter up the diagnostic summary with this material.

THE TREATMENT PLAN

After going through the thinking process required to prepare the diagnostic summary, the worker is ready to develop a treatment plan to deal with the needs and problems identified by him and his client. In some settings this part of the diagnostic summary is labeled "goals" or "objectives."

1. *Describe the ideal manner of meeting each of the needs described in the diagnostic summary.* It does no good to develop a treatment plan that is impossible to accomplish because of limitations on the part of the client, the community resources, the treatment person, or other essential participants. The worker must train himself to think consciously of the differences between the ideal treatment plan and the one that can probably be accomplished. Too many records describe beautiful treatment plans that are virtually meaningless because no discussion is included of any reality factors that may or may not make the plan workable. On the other hand, some workers consider even thinking about the idealistic plan a waste of time. Either extreme has its drawbacks. Often a review of the idealistic plan will force the worker to come up with new ideas and resources that he would not otherwise have discovered. If we do not keep in mind the ideal approaches, we will not have a standard or a goal to strive for in our professional practice, and the quality of services provided will suffer.

2. *Describe specifically what you, as a treatment person, plan to do to help the client meet the needs and problems you and he have identified under the diagnostic summary.* This is where the worker indicates the realistic plan for meeting the identified needs. If a need exists that nothing can be done about, or which the worker decides deliberately not to tackle, this should be stated in writing.

For example, an idealistic goal might be to "arrange for Mr. and Mrs. Hansen and their seven children to get into public housing in order to relieve the crowded housing conditions in their two-bedroom apartment." In reality, however, there may be a three-year waiting list to get into public housing and other, more realistic goals may have to be substituted. There may even need to be recognition of the fact that the housing situation is one problem that cannot be solved.

3. *Briefly describe the client's willingness and ability to carry out the treatment plans described in 2 above.*

4. *Describe any progress (or the lack of it) since the last treatment plan was written.* Have there been changes in the client's needs and situation? Has the worker's or the client's perceptions of these needs changed? Have new problems arisen?

5. *Conclude with a statement of what is going to happen to the case (if anything) as a result of the analysis of the current problems and needs and the proposed treatment plan.* Will the case be transferred to another unit or a different worker? Is a special contact planned? Is the case being closed?

THE ANALYTICAL THINKING MODEL

A professional helping person must learn how to think analytically before effective diagnostic statements can be produced. Analytical thinking refers to the ability to take a situation apart so that its dynamics can be studied meaningfully and the appropriate "solution" selected. Achieving this ability does not mean that the practitioner will also be able to diagnose. Even after the worker has learned to analyze a situation, he may not be able to select the appropriate diagnostic label to apply to what he is recording or observing. His ability to do this will depend upon his knowledge of the dynamics of human behavior. However, the analytical thinking process will lay the groundwork for application of this knowledge.

The following method is suggested for analyzing case situations. The professional or student should put himself through this process in preparation for writing the diagnostic summary and treatment plan that will be placed in the formal case record. As the worker goes through the process, his "answers" should be put in writing on a worksheet and then summarized to make up the formal diagnostic summary and treatment plan. This process could easily take several hours, obviously impractical for daily social work practice. The goal is that the worker learn the thinking process and eventually be able to do it automatically, in his head, as he works with clients and prepares written diagnostic statements. Once learned, the Analytical Thinking Model (ATM) approach should take no more time than that currently being used to arrive at diagnostic assessment and service plans.

1. *Review mentally everything that is known about the case* up to the point that you are preparing to do a diagnostic summary.

2. *List, in outline form, ten to fifteen key facts known about the case.* Do not give impressions or analyses. Try to select only the major facts that are known about the client and/or his situation. This requires sorting out what is relevant from what is not. If some significant information about the case is unknown, this could be a key fact that should be listed.

3. Review the list of facts you have written down. *THINK: What feelings might the client be experiencing, knowing what I know about him?* Focus on the client *only*— do not describe feelings of family members or others, though the client's attitudes toward these people might be included here. List individually each feeling you think the client might have, and *for each feeling:*

(a) *State who or what the feeling might be directed at.* This will not be appropriate for all feelings (such as guilt or depression), but would apply to feelings such as anger, resentment, and love.

(b) *State why you think he might have the feeling.*

(c) *State how the feeling might be manifested behaviorally.* In other words, how might the client express his feeling? What kinds of behavior or actions would tell you that the feeling is present? It might be helpful to review mentally the common ways that most people might deal with, express, or not express, the feeling, and then consider how your particular client might express the feeling.

You will get your ideas about the kinds of feelings your client may be experiencing and the ways in which he might express them from several sources:

(a) Your own personal life experience. A review of how you have handled certain feelings may help you identify feelings and potential behaviors on the part of your client.

(b) Your professional work experience. This has put you in touch with many people, experiencing and expressing many diverse feelings. If you have several months' experience, you are probably able to identify patterns that tend to produce certain kinds of feelings or cause people to express them in certain ways.

(c) Your knowledge of the client's specific situation. This could include what others have told you about him, past case records, statements he has made, or nonverbal communication you have observed.

(d) Your knowledge of human behavior in general. Classes taken, preparation for a professional degree, attendance at workshops or training sessions given by an agency, and readings could inform you how most people in the client's situation would probably feel or behave. Bear in mind that you are thinking theoretically at this point. You are not wholly certain your client has the feelings you have identified, but are simply listing all possible feelings he *might* have. As you get to know him better, some of your ideas will either be substantiated or eliminated.

It is important in this step to list *all* possible feelings you think your client might have. This means you may need to read some literature about the environmental, physiological, emotional, or cultural factors that are known to be affecting your client in order to determine what kinds of feelings and reactions a person in your client's situation might be expected to have.

4. *Consider who are the "significant others" in the client's life.* Select one or two persons with whom he relates most closely and go through step 3 with them. In view of the key facts known about the client and his situation, the possible feelings he might be experiencing as a result, and the associated behaviors, what are the major feelings that these significant others might be having? Look at and describe the actual or possible interactional patterns between the client and these other persons. Bear in mind that the professional helping person can also be a significant other with feelings.

5. *Develop a treatment plan.*

(a) *List all possible case outcomes or treatment goals, regardless of whether they appear realistic or unrealistic.* (For example, "get Mr. S. to go to a nursing home"; "remove six-year-old Sarah from the home"; "help Mrs. J. prepare for her death due to her illness." These should be broad, basic objectives or outcomes. Do not list subgoals or steps for achieving the outcomes listed.

(b) *Label each plan or outcome suggested in (a) as either realistic or unrealistic.* Also determine which outcomes or goals are unrealistic to plan for consciously, but may happen anyway due to circumstances beyond the client's or the worker's control. For example, Mrs. S. has been an alcoholic for fifty years and is now seventy. It is not realistic to expect her to stop drinking at this point. But, as her health deteriorates, she may be forced into an inpatient medical facility where she is unable to obtain alcohol, thus bringing about an involuntary withdrawal from alcohol.

(c) *For each realistic goal: (1) state the goal; (2) break it down into subgoals that must be achieved before the overall goal can be accomplished; and (3) state exactly what specific treatment techniques will be used to accomplish the goal or subgoals.* For example, a realistic goal might be for Mrs. C. to gain better control over her children and use more effective parenting techniques. However, a subgoal might be to help her alleviate her depression and feel better about herself as a step toward helping her relate more effectively to her children. If a treatment technique such as "empathy" is listed, state exactly *how* you would communicate empathy to this particular client in this particular situation. What would you say or do? Or, exactly how would you get your client to "ventilate unexpressed feelings of anger" if you have put that down as one of your goals or treatment plan objectives?

(d) *Rank the treatment goals in order of priority.* Which ones will you work on first? Watch for some goals that, if accomplished, would automatically bring about accomplishment or progress toward achieving other goals.

(e) *For each treatment goal, give an estimate of the length of time you feel it will take to accomplish the goal.*

6. *Finally, write a diagnostic statement that summarizes your main thoughts in steps 2 through 4. Also make a heading of "treatment plan" and summarize what you came up with in step 5.* Only the written material you produce in this final step should be placed in the official case record. The worksheets from steps 1 through 5 should not become part of the permanent case file. They should be kept in a secure location in a separate folder until no longer needed by the worker, at which time they should be destroyed.

Application of the Analytical Thinking Model to a Supervisory-Administrative (Large-Systems) Problem

Supervisory and administrative staff in the helping professions are often faced with difficult decisions. Human elements can make such decisions most difficult for the individual who is especially attuned to human needs and is professionally trained to "be a helping person." When such decisions are rendered, the employee, the supervisor himself, upper-level administrators, consumers, and others may be affected. What is needed is an objective, *structured* method of attacking the problem.

Analytical thinking refers to the ability to take a problem situation apart so that its dynamics can be studied objectively and meaningfully and the appropriate "solution" selected. Until the analytical thinking method is learned, the supervisor-administrator should write each step out on paper. This forces thinking to be definite, organized, and to the point. The basic steps are as follows:

1. *Review mentally everything that is known about the situation or problem.*

2. *List ten to fifteen key facts known about the situation or problem.* Use outline form. Do not give impressions or analyses. Sort out the relevant from the irrelevant factors in the situation.

3. *What feelings might the key person in the situation be experiencing? List each feeling individually, and for each one:*

(a) *State who or what the feeling might be directed at.* If you have listed "anger" as a feeling that your supervisee might have, state who or what he might be angry at, and so on.

(b) *State why you think the feeling might be present.*

(c) *State how the feeling might be manifested behaviorally.* How might the supervisee express his feelings? What kinds of behaviors or actions would tell you that the feeling is present? What are some of the ways that supervisees deal with and express feelings of anger, for example, toward a supervisor?

4. *What feelings might the person who will have to make the decision or take the necessary action have in this situation?* (In a supervisory problem this would be the supervisor; in an administrative situation it could be the administrator or perhaps the department or agency collectively.)

5. *What feelings might significant others be experiencing in this situation?* Select *only* significant others whose feelings are *relevant* to the problem at hand. A number of significant persons may have feelings (e.g., the family of the employee in a supervisory problem), but these feelings might not necessarily affect the handling of the problem. Consider: *should* family feelings about a supervisee's dismissal determine what action the supervisor should take? Typical significant others whose feelings might be relevant could include co-workers, the administration, clients, other agencies, the community, the taxpayers (in a government agency), or funding and accrediting bodies.

6. *List all possible solutions or actions that might be taken to resolve the problem.* List all possible alternatives, even those that may seem undesirable or impossible. Do not permit the reality constraints of the system to limit your creative thinking in this step.

7. *For each possible action listed in step 6, list all possible repercussions, both positive and negative, that might occur if the action were to be taken.* Be sure to consider the reactions of persons identified in steps 3, 4, and 5 as you work on this step. At the completion of this step, label each possible action as realistic or unrealistic, desirable or undesirable.

8. *Select the option, solution, or possible action that comes closest to resolving the problem and has the fewest potentially negative factors that would make it impossible or undesirable to accomplish or implement.*

Teaching the Analytical Thinking Model in a Group Situation

This section is included for those staff development or classroom instructors who may want to teach the Analytical Thinking Model to learners through group analysis of a case situation. The group goes through the Analytical Thinking Model step by step to arrive at the assessment and treatment plan. The most important concept to teach is the Analytical Thinking Model itself. It is easy for learners to get so involved with the case situation that they lose sight of the thinking process that they are learning. The instructor must keep the discussion focused on the thinking process rather than try to achieve a complete understanding of the case example.

The following steps should be followed in giving this instruction. Those preceded by an asterisk are optional, depending on time. The exercise, minus the starred items, will take three to four hours of a single day, in addition to any time allowed for breaks. If the items with asterisk are included, time must naturally be added for each.

1. Explain to the group that they will be learning a structured, step-by-step method for taking a case apart analytically and developing a diagnostic assessment and treatment plan. Comment that this technique is lacking in social work practice and, as a result, many social workers cannot perform meaningful diagnostic thinking and treatment planning.

2. Explain that time will probably not permit going through each of the steps of the Analytical Thinking Model. However, enough will be done so that participants can become familiar with the thinking process and apply it to other cases they are working with.

3. Explain that this thinking model is not necessarily the sole approach to diagnostic thinking. It is only one approach that a number of people have found helpful.

4. Explain that the Analytical Thinking Model exercise that they will be doing can easily take two to four hours. Therefore, it is not a practical method for working with every case in a caseload. However, once the thinking process has been mastered and two or three cases have been put through the model in its entirety, the process will become more or less automatic and much less time consuming.

5. Distribute the case example to be studied. Allow sufficient time for everyone to read it. This should take no more than five minutes, since the case example is usually a one- or two-page summary.*

*6. (Optional) Have group members write a diagnostic summary and treatment plan based on the case summary they have just read. Ask them to be very specific in

*See Chapter 14 for case examples that can be used in this exercise. Trainers might also want to make up examples of their own.

their treatment plan as to what techniques they will use and what goals they hope to accomplish. Fifteen to thirty minutes will need to be allowed for this exercise. Ask people to put their names on their products, and collect them. Explain that they will be returned later in the training.

7.   Distribute the Analytical Thinking Model outline. Allow as much time as necessary for everyone to read through it quickly.

*(Optional)   While the group is reading the Analytical Thinking Model handout, look through the initial diagnostic summary efforts that were collected earlier. Take a quick survey of the treatment plans given. Write down the primary goals suggested by the members of the audience. For example, one goal might be to "get him to go to a nursing home" or "get him to accept surgery." Each time a different major goal is suggested write it down on a large piece of paper, and then note how many people suggest that as a goal. The results will usually show conflicting goals. Some people will state "get Mr. A to go to a nursing home" while others will say "Mr. A should not be pushed to go to a nursing home." The contradictions will be quite interesting.

   *(Optional)   When the group has finished reading the Analytical Thinking Model handout, share with them the results of your brief survey. Do not comment on the quality of the product offered by the group, but simply list how many people suggested the various goals. Make a comment such as "Isn't it interesting that there are so many different ideas as to what should be done with this client?" The group will usually respond with equal interest. (Your goal as instructor is to point out how professionals possess various degrees of skill and view a client's situation in various ways. You realize that after they have gone through the analytical thinking training and produce a second diagnostic summary at its conclusion, there will be much greater consistency in their goals and plans for the client. However, you do not share this knowledge with the group until the very end.)

8.   Have someone from the group read step 1 from the outline ("Review everything that is known about the case"). Explain that this has been accomplished by their reading the summary that was distributed.

9.   Have someone read step 2 ("List key facts known about the case"). Ask people to take a minute to review the case summary and think about the *key* facts that should be listed. Solicit ideas from the group and write them on the blackboard. Have someone take notes of what is being written so that it can be erased and referred to later if necessary. Guide the discussion so that group members do not just list everything they can think of about the case—force them to be selective and list key facts only. If you know of several important facts that the group has failed to include, give them hints and use other techniques to encourage them to supply the missing items. If they cannot, list them yourself. There should be a total of about ten to fifteen items when this exercise is completed. Move quickly so that it takes no more than five or ten minutes.

10.   Have someone read step 3 from the outline. ("Feelings the client might be experiencing based on what is known about him"). Explain that knowledge of these feelings can come from several sources: e.g., knowledge of the client specifically and knowledge of the general psychodynamics of human behavior, normal and abnormal psychology, and coping and defense mechanisms. Explain that the more knowledge and training one has in these areas, the greater the depth that is possible in this step of the Analytical Thinking Model.

   Comment also that much of this will be hypothetical—we are trying to list every possible feeling that the client might have. We will not know until we get to know him better whether he actually has these feelings. They will be confirmed or discounted as we work further with him. However, it is important to have these thoughts in mind so that we can be alert to possible feelings as we work with the individual.

Ask the group to list all the various feelings they think this client might have, using only one or two words for each. This will take only a minute or so. Most groups will list such feelings as anger, fear, anxiety, and depression. Write them on the blackboard. When five or six feelings have been listed, including the major ones that you have in mind, stop the discussion. Explain that there will be time to go into depth in only two or three of these feeling areas. You make the decision as to which areas will be discussed. The first feeling to be discussed should be one that is manifested behaviorally in rather obvious ways. Anger and denial are good ones to start with. Try also to start with feelings that will build on one another to result in yet another feeling being suggested. For example, when anger and guilt are discussed in depth, the group may be able to recognize that the client could also be experiencing some depression. Then take depression and work through it. This helps the group see how feelings can build on one another, enabling them to come up with additional feelings. This portion of the discussion will probably take half an hour to forty-five minutes. Use a directive approach and do not allow the group to get sidetracked or so wound up in the case that they forget the thinking process they are learning.

When one feeling has been completely worked through on the blackboard, go back and ask the group to think about how the feeling might be manifested behaviorally. "How would we know that this individual has this feeling—what in his behavior or actions will tell us that this feeling is present?" Proceed to list these ideas on the board. Time will probably permit going through only one or two of the feelings that have been worked through.

11. Ask the group to read the next step in the process (feelings of significant others). Explain that time will not permit going through this step in detail but that the thinking process is very similar to what has just been done regarding the client's feelings. Ask the group simply to list who the significant others are in the individual's life, and write these on the blackboard. If there is strong interest in pursuing one of these key figures, this can be done if time permits. Some groups will choose to explore the feelings of the professional helping person as a significant other. If the group suggests this, it should be pursued if time permits.

12. As this discussion is taking place, be alert for ideas that directly suggest a treatment plan, and comment on this. This is important to help the group see the connection between their analyses and the treatment plan they will subsequently be developing. Trainees need to see that these two processes are not isolated from one another but are actually interwoven.

*(Optional Break) A natural time for a break is just prior to discussion of the treatment plan. If the training must be broken up into two sessions on separate days, this is the place to do it. The instructor should have the notes from steps 9–11 typed up so they can be distributed at the second session, since the learners will need this material to refer to as they develop the treatment plan.

13. Explain that the group will now develop a treatment plan. Ask the members to review the notes that have been developed in the previous discussion. Explain that one of the most difficult things about a treatment plan is determining the main objective. Ask the group to list all of the idealistic goals (e.g., get the man to stop drinking, get him to accept nursing home placement, get him to enter a vocational rehabilitation program, help the couple reunite). What do we really want to accomplish as professional helping people in working with this individual? List the idealistic suggestions on the blackboard. Keep them brief and use phrases only. Comment on why they are idealistic and that the client's motivation, the feelings that have already been identified by the group, and other external factors will determine whether the client is able to follow through, or whether the goal is even desirable or workable.

Engage the group in a discussion to select two or three realistic goals. Explain that it is important to think consciously of idealistic versus realistic goals so that we do not automatically select goals that turn out to be unworkable. List each realistic goal suggested by the group.

14. Take each realistic goal separately. Write the first goal on the blackboard. Comment that a goal is admirable, but we need to talk about how we are going to accomplish it. Force the group to be very specific during this part of the exercise. Do not allow them to get away with textbook generalities that cover up lack of knowledge of specific social work treatment skills. For example, if the group suggests that one goal is to "help client ventilate his feelings," ask how we will accomplish that miracle. Someone may suggest "by being empathetic." Write that down and explain that empathy is kind of a subgoal. How does one go about communicating empathy to a client? Elicit specific ideas such as "sitting close to the client" or "making comments such as 'I can see why you're angry.'" Use outline form to list these things on the blackboard. Go through as many of the realistic goals suggested by the group as time permits.

15. Summarize for the group the experience they have been through during the past two to three hours. Comment on how they have moved from a complex presenting situation where there were multiple problems and confusion about which to approach first, to developing a rather specific assessment and treatment plan. Review again how important is one's knowledge of the psychodynamics of human behavior in social work assessment and treatment. Comment again on the fact that, while learning the process, learners should write out the exercise on long yellow sheets of paper, and that it may take several hours. Explain again that this is not realistic in day-to-day social work practice but that, once the thinking process has been mastered, it will take no more time than whatever nonstructured process they are using now, which probably results in less effective assessment and treatment planning. If the group argues, "We don't have time for this," the response is simple: "If we don't have time to relate to our clientele in this way, then what are we here for?"

*16. (Optional) If time and group interest permit, ask group members once again to write a diagnostic summary and treatment plan now that they have gone through the Analytical Thinking Model. Ask them to write the diagnostic summary in summary style as it might appear in a case record. Explain that they are to take into consideration the ideas that have arisen from today's discussion. Do not make any reference to their first effort at the beginning of the exercise (if this was done). Allow at least forty-five minutes for completion of this portion of the exercise.

*17. (Optional) When everyone has finished writing his diagnostic summary and treatment plan, return the original efforts from the beginning of the training session. Ask them to compare the two. There should be considerable verbal and nonverbal feedback from the group indicating their recognition and awareness of the improvement they have achieved. Comment on how the treatment plans and goals that the group identified in the beginning are quite different from the ideas developed by the group following the analytical thinking process (many diagnostic summary efforts at the beginning of the training come up with unrealistic goals, as opposed to more realistic goals presented at the conclusion of the training). If time permits, read a few of the final products to the group.

*18. (Optional) Offer to give individual feedback on the second diagnostic summary effort. Collect both the first and second diagnostic summary efforts of those who are interested in your critiques. Be honest in your comments, pointing out factual statements as opposed to analytical remarks, unrealistic goals and planning, as well as giving specific positive feedback regarding something that is appropriate, very analytical, or well expressed. If you should wish to retain some of the examples for use in training, secure permission from the author.

19. Distribute copies of a bibliography of pertinent readings on diagnostic-analytical thinking. Devise the bibliography yourself, making certain that the readings included are readily available in your agency or local library. The group should be ready to receive this and eager to pursue additional research now that they realize the importance of increased knowledge of human behavior in achieving proper assessment and treatment planning. Comment that the bibliography is only a sampling of the kinds of material that are available.

EXAMPLES OF CASES THAT HAVE BEEN WORKED THROUGH THE SMALL-SYSTEMS ANALYTICAL THINKING MODEL

1. The "James Peters" Case

A group of about twenty MSW's and graduate and undergraduate students applied the Analytical Thinking Model during two three-hour group discussion sessions and came up with the worksheet thinking that follows. Notice how their approach clearly specifies why the feelings of the client and significant others might exist. This group selected the social worker as a significant other and examined his possible feelings. A few explanatory comments on the part of the discussion leader have been included.

Following is the case summary that the group read before starting the Analytical Thinking Model itself.

background

Mr. Peters is a fifty-two-year-old white male alcoholic who has been living "in the streets" for at least ten years. It is known that at one time he was married, had an intact family, and worked at a fairly skilled job. He does not have a lot of formal education, but it is obvious upon talking with him that he is an intelligent man. It appears he has had a problem with alcohol for at least twenty years, has been in and out of various treatment programs, and has received just about every kind of alcoholic counseling and treatment the community has to offer. About five years ago he simply refused to participate in any more of it, preferring instead to live in the streets.

In 1-77, Mr. Peters came to the emergency room of a hospital, complaining of pain in the mouth and jaw area. Medical workup upon admission revealed cancer of the jaw. Some surgery was performed, including removal of most of his tongue. Due to Mr. Peter's life style, the physicians recommended nursing-home placement. Instead, Mr. Peters left against medical advice (AMA), with his feeding tube still in place.

Within a few days the hospital began getting complaints from the community regarding a "poor, sick man lying in the streets who just looks terrible, but I can't get him to go to the doctor." He was observed pouring alcohol down his feeding tube. Mr. Peters persistently resisted efforts to get him back into the hospital; when police would pick him up and bring him to the emergency room, he would simply walk out before he was ever seen. One day a call came from a nun in a Catholic school regarding "a sick, drunk man lying in the street in front of our school, vomiting." Again, efforts to hospitalize him failed.

After about six months, Mr. Peters came on his own to the emergency room, complaining of intense pain and increasing weight loss. He agreed to be admitted so that his symptoms could be alleviated. Examination revealed metastatic cancer with radical neck dissection recommended. Mr. Peters strongly refused and left AMA once again. A review of the medical chart revealed a prognosis of six months or less life expectancy, with or without the recommended surgery. It is not known whether Mr. Peters was informed of this.

the counselor's role

What can be done in this situation? What are Mr. Peters's needs? What counseling approach should be used? What should be the goal of the counselor's involvement?

key facts

1. Mr. Peters is fifty-two years of age.

2. He is homeless and lives in the streets.

3. He used to have a family.

4. He has a diagnosis of being an alcoholic for twenty years.

5. He has a past history of unsuccessful treatment for his alcoholic problem.

6. His medical diagnosis is metastatic cancer* with six months or less life expectancy.

7. He recently had his jaw and part of his tongue removed surgically because of the cancer.

8. Since the surgery on his jaw, he has repeatedly refused medical treatment, including additional surgery.

9. It is unknown if Mr. Peters knows his prognosis.

10. He repeatedly leaves the hospital against medical advice.

11. He has refused nursing-home placement several times.

12. There have been repeated complaints from the community regarding the patient when they observe him sick and in the streets.

13. He recently came to the emergency room on his own, complaining of pain that resulted in readmission to the hospital.

14. We know that he is intelligent from the way he expresses himself.

feelings that Mr. Peters might be experiencing based on the key facts known

The group listed the following feelings and then chose four to work on in more detail: anger, fear, isolation, guilt, denial, powerlessness, anxiety, inadequacy. For every feeling identified, they listed what (or whom) the feeling was directed toward, and why he might be experiencing that feeling.

feelings of anger

TOWARD	WHY
1. The world.	1. It has done him injustice.
	2. He may have unresolved anger from childhood.
	3. People force him to do things he doesn't want to do.
	4. None of the treatment programs has worked for him.
	5. The world consists of healthy people and he is not healthy.
2. Doctors.	1. They are not curing him.
	2. They make him feel impotent— they took out his tongue.
	3. They have the power to make him do things against his will (medical surgery, etc.).
3. His family. Himself.	1. He contributed to his own situation by not following medical advice.
	2. (What others could be added here?)
4. Whatever supreme being he believes in.	1. Why me?
	2. Projection of anger onto the supreme being.
	3. Why hasn't the supreme being cured me if he is powerful?

*The cancer has spread and can no longer be treated effectively. Mr. Peters will eventually die.

(If it is not socially acceptable to be angry with one's god or supreme being and Mr. Peters had these feelings, it could result in guilt feelings.)

5. The social worker.	**1.** He may view the social worker as another person who makes him do what he doesn't want to do.
	2. The social worker is healthy and he is not.
	3. He may have had negative experiences in the past with social workers.
	4. Certain feelings related to sexual identification may be aroused depending on the sex of the social worker.

feelings of guilt

Why

1. He is angry at himself for various reasons.

2. If he is angry at God, this could result in guilt feelings.

3. He was once productive and now is not and is dependent.

4. He is engaging in self-destructive behavior (leaving against medical advice, refusing surgery, etc.).

5. He is not meeting society's expectations—maintaining a family, working, etc.

6. He may have a continued sense of failure—he has not experienced success in various treatment programs and has not cooperated and could therefore feel responsible and guilty.

feelings of isolation

Why

1. There appear to be no significant others in patient's life except fellow drunks on the street. It is actually unknown whether there are family or relatives.

2. He has had disfiguring surgery that could cause others to avoid him.

3. He has loss of tongue resulting in speech difficulty that would increase difficulty in communicating with others.

4. His physical living arrangement indicates and contributes to isolation.

feelings of fear

WHAT HE IS AFRAID OF	WHY
1. Death	**1.** This is shown by the fact that he seems to be trying to wash everything away with excessive drinking —a way of avoiding.
2. Life	**2.** Nothing has worked in the past and therefore nothing will work now—a sense of hopelessness for the future and his future life.
	3. There are indications that he wants to die:

(a) He has refused treatment in the past for his drinking problem.

(b) He has refused surgery, has left the hospital against medical advice, has refused nursing-home placement—all things that might contribute to physical recovery.

(c) There appears to be a great deal of denial concerning his condition and prognosis.

feelings of depression

Why

1. We know that he might be angry at himself. Psychodynamics of human behavior tell us that anger turned toward oneself or internalized can result in depression. If this is severe enough, the patient may become suicidal.

2. Drinking may give him a temporary sense of power and self-esteem that he uses to counteract or combat his real underlying feeling of depression. Therefore, his drinking constitutes a form of escape from his sad feelings.

3. Many things tell us that he is or has withdrawn from many aspects of life, and we know that depressed individuals do this.

4. Mr. Peters has suffered considerable loss and we know that loss leads to situational or chronic depression. He has lost family, self-esteem, home, job, his physical health, etc.

(Notice that the group did not deal with how these feelings might be manifested behaviorly—what behaviors on Mr. Peters's part might tell us that he has these feelings?)

feelings that significant others in Mr. Peter's life might be experiencing

The group identified four types of possible significant others: his drinking buddies, the doctors, his family (if they exist), and the social worker. The group chose to deal with the feelings of the social worker in this situation and how these feelings might affect the worker's behavior as he interacts with his client.

FEELINGS OF THE SOCIAL WORKER

1. Hopelessness and helplessness.

2. Frustration over inability to help or cure.

3. Anger:

   (a) At the patient.
   (b) At himself for not being able to be effective as a social worker.
   (c) At the doctors whom this worker may feel need to tell patient medical aspects and prognosis. There may also be anger because doctors are recommending mutilative surgery (radical neck dissection).
   (d) At the system because it has not been successful in curing

BEHAVIOR

1. The worker might respond to his own feelings of helplessness and hopelessness by avoiding the patient, becoming very structured, or using advice giving in order to impose control, or he might experience a reaction formation and advise the patient to go to a nursing home.

2. The worker may express his feelings nonverbally—frown, body language, intellectualization, not listening.

3. The worker may project his anger onto someone else; or use displacement—do something to another person when he really is not the

the client of his alcoholism or his physical illness.

4. Guilt because social workers are supposed to make people well. Also, we can observe that Mr. Peters may have some suicidal tendencies and behaviors—what is the responsibility of the social work profession to intervene and prevent this? How far do we go in allowing patient to exercise his right of self-determination?

5. Sadness.

(Notice that all the above feelings are negatives. The group was asked to come up with some positives.)

6. Empathy

7. Concern or caring.

8. The challenge of distinguishing between unrealistic and realistic goals.

9. Awareness of one's own feelings.

one who deserves to be the object of anger.

treatment plan

The first step was to list all *idealistic goals:*

1. Nursing-home placement.

2. Get patient off alcohol.

3. Reunite patient with family.

4. A peaceful death (help patient prepare for this emotionally).

5. Secure his cooperation with all medical treatment.

These are goals that society and/or helping persons might view as totally desirable. However, reality factors outlined in the previous sections would indicate that most of these goals are simply not going to be accomplished with this particular individual.

realistic social work goals

1. Help patient accept and express his feelings and/or life decisions.

2. Help patient see alternatives regarding surgery and living arrangements. Alternatives might be nursing home, boarding home, continuing to live in the street, rent a hotel room, enter an alcohol treatment program. Make certain patient is aware of the various alternatives and making intelligent, informed decisions as to what he wants to do.

3. The social worker may have to accept the fact that this patient does have self-destructive feelings and behavior and that we might not be able and perhaps should not try to alter this against the patient's will.

It was decided in this case that we would have to allow this intelligent, competent individual to exercise his right of self-determination and control over his own life even though we recognize that he is choosing, in his own way, to hasten his death.

The next step is to examine each of these goals and look at how we might go about achieving them.

155

goal one: help patient accept feelings or decision about his life

1. Allow patient to ventilate feelings:

   (a) Through nonverbal behavior. Nodding of the head, allowing him to cry if necessary, etc.

   (b) Verbalize feelings for the patient—"I'm sure you have been feeling pretty angry"; "You must be feeling pretty bad that you left the hospital and people make you feel guilty about it."

   (c) Questioning to elicit feelings and information.

   (d) By being a role model. If patient sees social worker expressing his feelings, he may feel more comfortable talking about his own feelings.

   (e) By listening.

   (f) By getting some history that will probably elicit feelings in connection with the facts that are brought out.

2. Show empathy. Empathy could be communicated by listening, nonverbal behavior such as sitting close, nodding of the head, maintaining direct eye contact, and giving feedback about what is being heard.

3. Engage in frank discussion regarding death and life as it pertains to patient's behavior and plans.

4. Engage in frank discussion with patient regarding repurcussions of his various actions.

   The group had time to examine only the first treatment goal in depth.

2. Mr. and Mrs. Raymond

In the following case situation, an individual worker has completed all the steps in the Analytical Thinking Model.

key facts known about Mr. and Mrs. Raymond

1. Mr. Raymond is sixty-six; his wife is believed to be in her early forties.

2. Mr. Raymond has been hospitalized for cancer of the prostate which has spread to the penis. As a result, the penis was surgically removed.

3. Mr. and Mrs. Raymond moved here from some distance about two years ago.

4. They have no family members living in the local area.

5. They are financially independent and able to pay for all medical care required.

6. Physician recommends that patient be discharged home as he can be managed there medically. However, Mr. Raymond wants to remain in the hospital.

7. Mrs. Raymond is at the patient's bedside from 10 A.M. until 8 P.M. daily.

8. Mrs. Raymond comes to the social worker frequently with small, seemingly unimportant requests.

9. Mrs. Raymond has expressed revulsion at the thought of having to provide any kind of nursing care to her husband and has refused to help with his care while hospitalized.

10. Mrs. Raymond has been told everything regarding the patient's diagnosis, prognosis, and medical treatment (he has a five-year life expectancy).

11. It is unknown what the patient has been told regarding his diagnosis, prognosis, and medical treatment.

12. This couple has been married for twenty-five years and has a daughter living in another state.

13. Prior to patient's hospitalization, Mrs. Raymond never had to do anything on her own—her husband ran the household and took care of everything (according to her statement).

14. Mr. Raymond refuses to talk to the social worker (or anyone else). He either pretends to be asleep or turns his head and body toward the wall whenever the social worker enters the room.

feelings that Mr. Raymond might be experiencing

(The patient has refused to speak to the social worker. This behavior, along with our knowledge of his physical situation, suggests some rather strong feelings that he could very well be experiencing. Go on to the next step, which examines Mrs. Raymond's feelings, and then go back and see if you can identify feelings for Mr. Raymond.)

feelings that Mrs. Raymond might be experiencing

1. *Fear.*

   (a) Fear that she will lose her dependency role.

   (b) Fear that she won't be able to take care of her husband after he's discharged from the hospital.

   (c) Fear of loneliness and isolation either from husband's incapacity or his eventual death.

   (d) His illness may be causing her to experience fears regarding her own death.

   (e) Fear that she somehow caused his illness and the resulting sexual problem. Perhaps a feeling that it's because there's something basically wrong with her.

   (f) Fear that she will have no purpose in life after Mr. Raymond has died.

   (g) Fear of rejection by her husband because he'll see her as being inadequate to meet his physical and emotional needs (a role she has not been expected to play previously).

   (h) Fear she'll find she has no identity of her own after he's gone.

   (i) Fear of being alone with her husband at home and having something happen to him (i.e., death).

   (j) Fear of the unknown because of the alteration in him physically, which will affect their sexual relationship.

2. *A feeling that she is being, or will be, rejected by her husband.*

   (a) He won't talk to anyone.

   (b) He is making it very clear that he doesn't want to go home.

   (c) Mrs. Raymond knows and admits that she cannot get herself to look at her husband's physical wounds or to take care of him. She may anticipate that he is rejecting her because of this (her own guilt).

   (d) The patient's feelings of sexual inadequacy may cause him to reject his wife before she has a chance to reject him. Thus she may experience real feelings of rejection because this is actually occurring.

   (e) Mrs. Raymond doesn't want to be burdened with the physical care of her husband when he's discharged home. Thus, to prove to his wife that he loves her, one would expect that the patient will try hard to recover and to cooperate with medical care so as not to leave Mrs. Raymond with more responsibility than she can handle. However, he is not doing this—he is uncooperative with medical care and is not making sufficient effort to do things for himself. Mrs. Raymond may view this as his way of rejecting her.

3. *Mrs. Raymond may be experiencing feelings of rejection toward her husband.*

   (a) The patient's physical condition and appearance are repulsive to Mrs. Raymond.

   (b) His illness has inconvenienced her tremendously.

   (c) His illness is forcing Mrs. Raymond to give up her dependency role and to realize, for perhaps the first time in her life, that she has never developed a meaningful life, skills, or abilities of her own.

   (d) Mr. Raymond has failed to equip his wife for the role of widowhood.

   (e) He's no longer whole sexually.

   (f) She may not need her husband financially.

   (g) A certain amount of feelings of rejection toward Mr. Raymond would be considered normal in this situation and would be expected.

   (h) By rejecting her husband, Mrs. Raymond postpones responsibility— reinforces her denial and postpones the time when she must confront and deal with anxiety-provoking issues caused by his illness.

   (i) She is very angry at him (for all the reasons listed above; anger leads to rejection as a defense mechanism in some people).

   Mrs. Raymond will probably *not* openly or directly verbalize any feelings of rejection or anger toward her husband because:

   1. It is not considered socially acceptable to reject one's husband, especially when he is sick.
   2. She probably doesn't know how to verbalize these feelings.
   3. These feelings may be subconscious—Mrs. Raymond may not be aware that she has them.
   4. Perhaps Mrs. Raymond's daughter would reject her if she were to verbalize feelings of rejection toward the sick father.
   5. Mrs. Raymond is not the kind of person who communicates directly and openly regarding *any* emotion.

4. *Feelings of guilt.*

   (a) We know that when people experience feelings that are considered socially unacceptable, e.g., anger and rejection toward one's sick husband, this creates feelings of guilt.

   (b) Now *Mr.* Raymond is the one who is dependent and needs Mrs. Raymond and she knows she should meet his needs. At the same time she fears she cannot and perhaps doesn't want to, which would make her feel guilty.

   (c) Part of Mrs. Raymond may wish that he would go ahead and die and get it over with and relieve her of all this misery. Some of these feelings would be considered normal under the circumstances. As this is a socially unacceptable feeling, guilt will result.

   (d) When a person with a lifelong dependency pattern is forced abruptly out of this role, it is very traumatic. Feelings of anger, regression, and guilt would be considered typical and to be expected.

5. *Feelings of depression.*

   (a) We know that many people react to losses with depression. Mrs. Raymond has experienced a number of losses, including:

   (1) loss of dependency role.
   (2) loss of her husband's physical well-being.
   (3) loss of normal sexual relationship.
   (4) loss of self-esteem and/or status (her husband is no longer someone to be proud of).

(b) We know that when people have feelings of anger that they are unable to express openly, they often turn this anger against themselves. When this occurs, depression results.

(c) Feelings of isolation can lead to depression. Mrs. Raymond is isolated emotionally and physically from her husband; she is isolated geographically from her family, who might offer her needed support.

(d) Some feelings of depression in this kind of situation would be considered normal. We are unable to evaluate at this point whether or not Mrs. Raymond's depression is within normal limits or is excessive for the situation she is facing.

Note: The reaction of the patient and Mrs. Raymond to the patient's physical loss of sexual functioning is totally unknown. It is unknown how they functioned together maritally and sexually prior to the illness. It is unknown how he feels regarding this loss to his masculine self-image or how he feels his wife might be responding to this.

comments regarding the diagnostic thinking process thus far

Notice that the first feelings listed are the more obvious ones that we would expect Mrs. Raymond to be experiencing. After two or three feelings have been explored, it is possible to start building on them to establish how a person with these feelings might be feeling or reacting. For example, we were able to determine that feelings of guilt and depression might exist because of some of the other feelings that she might have.

There has not been a detailed breakdown of the effects that the loss of the penis might have on the patient and his wife because too little is known at this point about the nature of their marital-sexual relationship. Any diagnostic thinking along this line would be highly theoretical. It is hoped that the worker is thinking in general about the effects that the loss of a penis could have on a man and his wife and is planning to explore this area further. It would be very important to determine how Mr. and Mrs. Raymond were relating sexually prior to this surgery. If they have not had sexual relations for some time *and* neither has been upset by this—it has been by choice—there may actually be a sense of relief in both partners that now neither can be expected to perform sexually.

Notice that some of the reasons given for the feelings Mrs. Raymond might be experiencing are based on general knowledge about human behavior, while other reasons given are based on specific knowledge about Mrs. Raymond and her husband. The social worker with limited understanding of the dynamics of dependency would not be able to produce an in-depth diagnostic summary analysis of this case until he had done some reading on the subject of dependency. Also, an understanding of what is happening to Mr. Raymond medically is crucial to the diagnostic understanding of the case dynamics.

This particular case example does not go into an analysis of the significant others in the patient's life in the usual sense. The wife is the significant other and the analysis has focused first on her instead of on the patient, which is the reverse of the way it would normally be done. As the worker establishes communication with Mr. Raymond, it is hoped that another diagnostic exercise can be done to look at his feelings.

how Mrs. Raymond might be showing her feelings behaviorally

1. She is spending many hours at the patient's bedside. We know that someone rejecting a loved one may appear unusually devoted as a means of covering up and denying these feelings to himself and others.

2. Her constant "simple" requests of the social worker indicate a bid for attention and direction. This behavior may also indicate her inability to express her underlying feelings directly.

3. She may become increasingly anxious as specific plans are made for the patient's discharge home and may actually oppose this plan because of her own fears or her inability (or unwillingness) to care for her husband at home.

4. If she becomes too emotionally overwhelmed by her feelings, she may suddenly stop visiting her husband in the hospital (avoidance).

5. She may leave her husband (separation or divorce). She may seek another marital/sexual partner to fulfill her needs.

6. She may apply pressure on her daughter (unrealistically) to meet some of her dependency needs now that her husband can no longer do so.

treatment approaches

1. *To deal with Mrs. Raymond's feelings of fear:* Encourage Mrs. Raymond to verbalize some of her unexpressed feelings of anger, anxiety, guilt:

   (a) Let Mrs. Raymond talk. Do not give advice or false reassurances.

   (b) Use empathy. This is communicated by:
       (1) Nonverbal means—nodding of the head, moving close to Mrs. Raymond, maintaining direct eye contact, etc.
       (2) Say, "I can understand how you must feel," etc.

   (c) Do some interpretation: "That must make you very angry . . ." or "It must be difficult to see your husband this way. . . ."

   (d) Give approval and withhold any judgment regarding what she has to say. Let her cry if she needs to.

   (e) Make her feel comfortable by offering privacy for the interview and by being informal and relaxed yourself.

   (f) Be available when she needs to talk, keeping in mind that her contacts with the worker regarding "silly little things" could be guided into the in-depth discussion that she needs and is actually seeking.

   (g) Gather past history regarding Mrs. Raymond, Mr. Raymond, and their life together. As she relates these facts, there will be opportunities for her to open up and share feeling content as well.

2. *To deal with Mrs. Raymond's feelings of being rejected by her husband:*

   (a) The same techniques listed above for helping her verbalize her feelings would be applied here as well.

   (b) Gather some information on past history to increase understanding of how this couple has functioned together prior to the husband's illness and to get some insight into Mrs. Raymond's adjustment and functioning as an individual.

   (c) At some long-range point, you will need to facilitate communication between Mr. and Mrs. Raymond regarding these feelings of possible rejection. On the other hand, you may determine that their communication pattern has been dysfunctional for some time, perhaps rendering this goal unrealistic.

3. *To deal with Mrs. Raymond's feelings of rejection and anger toward her husband:*

   (a) The technique of generalization will be used to help Mrs. Raymond feel free to verbalize these feelings that are considered "socially unacceptable." This can be done by making comments such as, "Many wives are quite dependent on their husband and have quite an adjustment when something happens suddenly to the husband," or "Family members often find it hard to visit their loved ones and see them sick . . . ," etc.

   (b) Use the same techniques described in (1) above.

4. *To deal with Mrs. Raymond's feelings of guilt and depression:*

(a) As the worker concentrates on the first three feeling areas identified, these will begin to take care of themselves. Increased verbalization of socially unacceptable and troubling thoughts and feelings will help to alleviate some of Mrs. Raymond's anxiety and guilt feelings and at least bring them out into the open, where the worker and Mrs. Raymond can deal with them directly. It would be premature to attempt to move in on the underlying feelings of guilt and depression first without attacking the other, less complex, feeling areas first.

(b) Likewise, as the above four areas are dealt with, the depression, if it exists, will come out and the worker will be able to work with it at that time. It will also be possible then to determine if it is within the normal ranges for a person facing the life crisis that Mrs. Raymond is grappling with.

comments regarding the treatment steps discussed thus far

Notice that these also build on one another. It is important when writing this part of the exercise to decide which feeling area must be dealt with first. Study all the feelings listed to determine if some will resolve themselves or will come out in the open once some of the others are worked with. That is the case in this example. Some of these latter feeling areas are very long-range and won't be dealt with until some time later in the treatment process. It would be pointless to go into lengthy abstract thinking regarding how the worker might handle them. When this later stage in the casework treatment process is reached, the diagnostic summary thinking exercise should be repeated, with emphasis on these long-range areas.

Now the worker must state priorities and attempt to indicate how much time will be required to accomplish the treatment plans.

treatment approaches, continued

1. Mrs. Raymond's feelings of fear will be dealt with first. These are most immediate and pressing to her and least difficult for her to verbalize. Getting her to verbalize these feelings should occur in one or two interviews. This should establish a pattern that will enable her to continue verbalizing these fears as they arise in the future.

2. The feelings of being rejected by her husband would be dealt with next. Some of these may surface while working on the first area. This should occur within the first few interviews; setting up any joint marital counseling sessions with the husband may not be possible while he is still hospitalized and therefore may not happen at all unless a community resource can pick up on this after discharge. The other desirable alternative is to prepare Mrs. Raymond for more effective communication patterns with her husband so that she can do much of this on her own at home. This may not be possible, however, if there is a long-standing pattern of dysfunctional marital communication.

3. The feelings of rejection and/or anger toward her husband would be dealt with next. This is saved until later to enable the worker and Mrs. Raymond to develop rapport before moving into this area, which will be more difficult for Mrs. Raymond to talk about and may be partly subconscious. It is doubtful that worker will be able to work through all these feelings while patient is still hospitalized.

4. The feelings of guilt and depression will be treated last. However, some of the guilt can be dealt with at the time of discussion regarding feelings of anger and rejection toward Mr. Raymond. As she releases some of her guilt and anxiety in the other feeling areas, depression may lessen. A longer-term relationship would be necessary to deal with any severe underlying depression, and the worker will not be able to achieve this. If depression is identified as being present to an abnormal degree, referral to a community resource for follow-up on this area would be indicated.

Following is the regular diagnostic summary that would go into the social service case record. It is based on the analytical thoughts developed in the preceding steps.

Mrs. Raymond is currently facing many anxieties due to her husband's rather sudden illness, which is forcing her out of the dependency role which she has filled for many years in their marital relationship. Thus far she has been unable to verbalize her anxieties directly and instead has come repeatedly to the worker with seemingly insignificant questions that in reality represent her bid for structure, attention, and an opportunity to ventilate. She appears never to have developed an identity of her own as a person, and the loss of her dependency role is very threatening to her. She also faces some practical problems regarding financial management and making arrangements for her husband's physical care after discharge. Her feelings toward doing so are ambivalent at best, as she undoubtedly has feelings of anger and rejection toward her husband because of her feelings of inadequacy and anxiety.

It is unknown what effect the loss of the penis will have on their marital relationship, and this needs further exploration. Mr. Raymond's refusal to talk with people is probably an indication of his overwhelming sense of loss, which appears to have produced a situational depressive reaction evidenced by his withdrawal.

treatment plan

Mrs. Raymond is most actively, though indirectly, reaching out for help at this time, and thus our initial focus will be with her. It is hoped that in the next few contacts she can be encouraged to verbalize some of her feelings of fear, rejection by and toward her husband, and possible guilt. A long-range goal that probably could not be accomplished while he is still hospitalized would be to meet jointly with both Mr. and Mrs. Raymond to help facilitate improved marital verbal communication. It would be necessary to engage a community resource in their home town to follow through with this. If there has been a long-standing pattern of dysfunctional marital communication, this may be an unrealistic goal. Another alternative would be to prepare Mrs. Raymond for more effective communication patterns with her husband so that she can achieve some of this on her own after discharge.

Current information regarding this couple is sketchy. We will attempt to get further information regarding the patient's past history, the patterns of marital interaction, and Mrs. Raymond's functioning as an individual person prior to the patient's illness. We will attempt to explore the nature of the sexual relationship, though this is not a priority goal.

We will work to establish a relationship with Mr. Raymond via frequent visits, verbalizing for him some of the feelings we believe he might be experiencing, and hoping that this might elicit a reaction. We will attempt to ascertain how Mr. Raymond has responded previously to crises in his life as one means of assessing the severity and appropriateness of his current reaction.

Referrals will be made for visiting nursing services and homemaker services to help Mrs. Raymond deal with some of the practical problems of caring for Mr. Raymond at home. She will be helped to use patient's Medicare coverage to obtain necessary special equipment.

3. A Detailed Treatment Plan (Worksheet Form)

A group was participating in training on the Analytical Thinking Model using the "Case of Mr. H." All the steps involving identification of feelings and behaviors had been worked through. When it came time to develop a treatment plan, the group listed four possible goals and then ranked them in order of priority. Each goal was then broken down into very specific objectives and techniques for achieving the objective. Notice how global, textbooklike goals ("develop trust," "help him deal with reality") are broken down into specific behaviors the worker can use to achieve the objective.

The notes that follow are based on the group discussion and include some comments regarding the thinking process of the group as the treatment objectives were identified and discussed. The notes are in the style that would be used in the worksheet phase of the steps in the Analytical Thinking Model. The treatment plan shown here would need to be rewritten and summarized if it were to become part of a formal entry in a case record. It took the group approximately two hours to develop the ideas presented here.

treatment goals

1. Establish a relationship with Mr. H.

2. Help him deal with the realities of the situation.

3. Help him become future oriented.

treatment goal one: establish a relationship with Mr. H.

This could be done through the following techniques and behaviors on the part of the social worker.

1. Develop trust:

   (a) Get close to Mr. H. Reach out and touch him if social worker feels comfortable with this.

   (b) Be warm and empathetic.

   (c) Talk about interesting, neutral things that are not heavily laden emotionally.

   (d) Be consistent and reliable. If you say you are going to do something, do it!

2. Bring up unacceptable feelings for Mr. H. The social worker can put them into words for him, which will make it easier for him to talk about his feelings.

3. Start where he is at. This is a typical textbook mandate in social work practice. How do we do this?

   (a) Ask Mr. H to tell us how he feels.

   (b) Sit quietly; permit silence. A pushy, overtalkative social worker will not be as effective in establishing a relationship with this patient who is quiet, meditative, and withdrawn.

4. Visit Mr. H regularly and often, even if only for a few minutes to pop into his room once or twice every day or so.

treatment goal two: help Mr. H deal with reality

We started immediately to talk about the treatment approach we would use to achieve this goal and then realized that we first needed to define what we meant by "reality." What are the realities in this man's life that he must be helped to deal with? We identified several:

1. Mr. H could die if he continues to neglect his disease process.

2. He can no longer support his family.

3. He will be nonambulatory for quite a while.

4. His wife is no longer visiting him at the hospital, indicating difficulties in their relationship somewhere.

5. His prognosis is that he will eventually become blind. There was considerable discussion as to whether or not we should help him deal with this reality or if we should tell him about it. It was agreed that to tell him now would only give him another unpleasant thing to deal with which would be overwhelming for him. Thus this will be delayed and not dealt with until sometime later.

Techniques for helping Mr. H deal with reality:

1. Give him factual education regarding diabetes and the care of his condition.

2. Let him see other amputees by having him go to the Rehabilitation Center for physical therapy training there.

3. If he seems to respond well to other patients with similar problems, then he could be prepared for entrance into a diabetic group.

4. Talk to him about reality and his feelings.

5. Contact Mrs. H and determine her feelings about client's situation.

6. Help Mr. H get financial assistance from all possible resources—social security, welfare programs, food stamps, VA.

7. Emphasize the other roles that he can have in his family in addition to supporting them financially: father, husband. Obviously he is having some difficulties at present dealing with the husband role and probably will have in the future; therefore, this may be a difficult area to deal with.

8. Get marital and family history.

During this discussion the question was raised, "Suppose we talk to the wife and she tells the social worker that she is planning to leave her husband—simply desert him for another man or to live independently. What would we do then?" We agreed this would be a most unpleasant reality for Mr. H to have to deal with. It generated considerable discussion as to whether or not he should be told about his wife's impending departure. Also, questions came up about the timing for telling him about his wife's leaving and the method for doing so. The social worker might be the one to tell him; the wife could be encouraged to visit the hospital and give him the news; the social worker could use techniques to help Mr. H reach this recognition and insight himself. We agreed that timing was crucial—just because the social worker knows that the wife is planning to leave does not mean that he has to rush in and immediately share this information with the patient. Perhaps it would only make his depression worse and set him back therapeutically and emotionally. Also, we know that when patients learn information themselves or gain insight on their own rather than being told by someone else, it is much more meaningful to them and usually much more growth producing. Reality is also that the wife probably would not tell him even if encouraged, because she already has discontinued her visits with Mr. H. Along with deciding how to handle this situation, it would be very important for the social worker to obtain detailed marital history. What has been the relationship between these two people? Maybe Mr. H would be relieved to see his wife leave.

treatment goal three: get Mr. H future oriented

We decided that this was definitely a long-range goal. Reality is that his future does look rather bleak at this point in time. Rehabilitation training or job retraining will definitely be long-range, and prospects for even being accepted in such a program appear rather dim at this point. Therefore, he will have enough to cope with thinking about the present realities without having to think about his increasing dependency, which will occur in future years.

treatment goal four: build Mr. H's family support systems

It was decided that this would be a worthwhile goal to add to the original three that were identified. It could be accomplished by:

1. Making a home visit to talk to Mrs. H. if she will not respond to the social worker's request to come to the hospital.

2. "Finding out where her head is at" by asking her why she has not visited her husband and also by talking with her about her goals.

3. Giving her factual education regarding Mr. H's disease process and how it is cared for.

EXAMPLES OF DIAGNOSTIC SUMMARIES

The following examples are taken from actual recordings done by social workers and students with various kinds of training and experience. Some are perfectly awful, contributing nothing to the record they appeared in, and are included here as examples of what *not* to do. Others are merely a restatement of facts, lacking the essential ingredient that might make them diagnostic—analysis. A few are highly analytical and contain specific treatment plans based on the diagnostic assessment. Many of the poor examples were written by persons who had never been exposed to the Analytical Thinking Model; unfortunately, they are rather typical of case record entries made by both BSW- and MSW-level students and practitioners. Almost all of the well-done summaries were prepared by persons who had received training in the Analytical Thinking Model and had gone through the step-by-step worksheet process, either individually or in a group discussion, before preparing the final diagnostic statement.* Some of these were written by the same students who had produced completely ineffective summaries just a short time before.

Grammar and spelling appear as recorded by the worker in these examples. The reality is that many social workers write poorly, and "real-life" examples must reflect how social workers write—not how they would write if their material were to be edited professionally. Identifying details have been altered.

EXAMPLE 1   Poorly written diagnostic summary, indicating worker's lack of understanding of how to do it

The following summary was written by a BA-level social worker who had had minimal training in how to do diagnostic summaries. Her degree was in a non–social science field. The entry was found in a case record under the heading "diagnostic summary."

This is the case of an old couple who due to their years and physical condition are not able to work nor to attend vocational classes. Their only close relative in the U.S. is their son Enrique who cannot provide in full for our client and his wife. They were advised to report any changes in their situation.

EXAMPLE 2   Three entries by a worker who has absolutely no understanding of the term "Worker's Impressions"

The following entries were made by an intake worker who had received some beginning training on how to use this heading but obviously hadn't yet grasped it. Difficulty with the English language may be contributing to his problems.

Nice person, educated, good character.

Is a nice person, great personality, anxious to find a job, she stated she has not found a job here. She will like to go to the north with son.

Is a nice person, great personality, she once studied English in order to work in her skill.

---

*This does not mean that others could not also produce meaningful summaries.

EXAMPLE 3 Poorly written paragraph containing
highly unprofessional remark

The following was written by a BA-level worker who was just starting to learn diagnostic thinking. His degree was not in social work. The entry was found in a case record under the heading of "worker's impression."

Mrs. A. is 60 years old and looks much older. She is about 4'10" tall and a very skinny person. She has long grey hair, has brown eyes and a very poor appearance. Although I am sorry to say it, to give an accurate description of this lady, one would have to imagine a witch from one of the horror movies.

EXAMPLE 4 Paragraph containing some diagnostic
statements that show analytical thinking in spite of
worker's difficulty with English

This worker held a BA-level degree, probably not in the social sciences. English is obviously not her native language. Yet her recording shows that she understands what analytical-diagnostic thinking involves, and she clearly differentiates between how she, as opposed to her client, views the needs and problem areas.

Client is a very young and pretty woman who is facing a very hard medical problem (cancer of the breasts—possibility of having to have both removed). She is under a big stress and takes the news of her sickness with a big severity. She spoke about that she suffers from cancer very serenely but without a doubt she is very depressed and sad. She wanted to be operated and is very worried about her possibility to recover her physical condition as soon as possible in order to continue working for her children.

EXAMPLE 5 Superficial but satisfactory diagnostic
statement showing that no social work services are
needed

The following was written by a BA-level practitioner who had received beginning training in diagnostic thinking.

This is a case of a divorcee age 59. Strengths in this case consist of excellent relationship she enjoys with her daughter which affords her security so vital in this age group. From client's remarks, this lady has the love, concern, and understanding of her daughter. Furthermore, this lady is aware of her constitutional limitations due to health but is not overwhelmed by them. She tolerates them and voices no futile laments. Our client is taking necessary steps through the clinic to hopefully ameliorate health problems. Weaknesses consist of her poor health and lack of English, which render her non-rehabilitative. Mrs. H. recognizes her need to be one of a medical and financial nature and both necessities are covered by our program.

EXAMPLE 6 Simple but satisfactory diagnostic
summary and service plan containing some analytical
thinking and recognition of "I don't know"

The following was written by a BA-level worker in a public welfare setting. The worker's degree was not in the social sciences.

I am uncertain at this point as to the actual potential of Mr. Jones toward a more permanent type of employment. The medical evaluation report indicates he is capable of attending special classes. I am not certain what this means. The medical people seem to feel that Mr. Jones is not capable of holding a job and indicate that he is doing all he can at the present time. I feel that more definitive information is indicated in terms of Mr. Jones' potential for employment of a more permanent nature.

service planning

The special review is scheduled for 12/79 at which time I will discuss with Mr. Jones his feelings regarding employment. It might be that if he were to engage in a more strenuous, demanding type of work situation, his mental condition would be adversely affected. I feel that Mr. Jones is the type of person who has to be doing something and who desires to be independent. However, in view of his psychiatric condition, he may be doing all he can at the present time. If so, and if further medical information indicates that he cannot be employed on a permanent basis, the case should be transferred to a basic service payments caseload.

EXAMPLE 7 Elementary but effective diagnostic
statement

The following was produced by a financial assistance worker holding a BA degree in psychology. It shows some understanding of the psychodynamics of human behavior and ability to think analytically.

Both client and his wife seem to be undergoing a great deal of despair and anxiety. We received the impression that this has been a very drastic change in every aspect, such as emotional, cultural, etc. It also contributes to their depression, their poor health condition which prevents them from becoming self-supporting. Therefore, they feel that they have to depend on their daughter and son-in-law. We received the impression that client's wife does not wish to be a burden to anyone and does not want to implement these obligations to their married daughter and son-in-law. They do wish, in the near future, to become independent, find their own apartment where they can live alone, as well as to become self-employed. Nevertheless, we have our doubts whether Mr. and Mrs. Hernandez will cooperate with rehabilitation plans in the near future if recommended by the doctor. This latter statement was based on client's wife's attitude as we feel that she is somewhat negative, pessimistic, and she is undergoing a tremendous amount of emotional stress and separation anxiety from her daughter. We feel that further rehabilitation plans would have to be based upon the doctor's recommendation. Mrs. Hernandez is under medication and we feel that she is extremely depressed and overly anxious regarding her present situation.

EXAMPLE 8 Brief but well-written diagnostic
statement and treatment plan

The following was written by an undergraduate student with no prior work experience. Her supervisor had helped her study the Analytical Thinking Model. The excerpt was written at the time a case was being closed.

It is my impression that Mrs. A. is a very anxious woman, worried about financial security and frustrated by ill health. These two factors climaxed when she was hospitalized and she reacted by becoming very depressed and dependent. She spent a lot of time explaining why her family is unable to help her and why she, with a heart condition and a daughter, needs help. Her anxiety over finances and her physical complaints seem to be interdependent; one aggravates the other, it appears. For this reason, readmission is a possibility. If the case is reopened, I feel casework objectives should include:

1. Helping the patient to develop a stronger self-concept, so that she would feel less need to worry about dependence upon family for financial recourse.

2. Examining the relationship between the patient and her daughter.
3. Discussing employment alternatives if she should face the reality of losing her job.

EXAMPLE 9 Diagnostic summary written by an undergradaute student

The following was written by an undergraduate student in her second field placement. She had previous experience in social work. It is quite analytical in that the worker includes her observations.

My experience with this client was that he did not verbalize his feelings to any meaningful degree. My impression is that he has probably never shared his feelings and has been relatively emotionally isolated as a result. He stated that he had known his wife for several years prior to their marriage and yet could not (or would not) offer any reasons which might account for her behavior. He stated that he had been a heavy drinker some years ago and had worked as a cook and construction worker. This type of life style does not facilitate the building of lasting relationships since many persons employed in these occupations are transients. It was difficult to learn a great deal about this person's intrapsychic processes because of his unwillingness to communicate; however, his reaction to his wife's behavior did not, in my opinion, seem appropriate to the situation and this could represent probable unconscious denial of anger. Another possibility is that he has a genuinely passive personality and his apparent acceptance of the situation with his wife represents feelings of being unable to exert any control over the events in his life.

EXAMPLE 10 Summary-style diagnostic statement and treatment plan showing in-depth diagnostic thinking

This example was written by an MSW with several years of postgraduate experience. The diagnostic statements were written as part of a discharge summary concerning a patient who was about to leave the hospital after an extended stay. There had been a long-term and intensive relationship with the social worker during this time.

Mr. F. was seen twice weekly by this worker in casework therapy. This is an extremely well-defended, withdrawn young man who relates poorly to all people. In the past seven years he has developed a fantasy self-concept which maintains a comfortable level of anxiety for him. He utilizes cliches to relieve anxiety and maintain emotional distance from other people.

Mr. F.'s entire view of the world revolves about TV and books. He attempts to maintain a pose of wisdom, defending his inadequacies by "putting down" others with sarcasm. Part of this young man is aware of his fantasies; however, to give this up would render him vulnerable and exposed to himself and to others.

Short-term goals to help Steve move toward people and social situations have been minimally achieved. He indicates he spends less time isolated at home. He has been involved with some social activities here at the hospital. Most recently, therapy has moved toward relating to others in a more appropriate manner. At this point in time, he views people as objects that are without real identity. He has no true identity of himself. We are into much resistance now as anxiety is coming into his conscious awareness.

recommendations

Steve F., an apparent simple schizophrenic, will be leaving the hospital soon. My concerns are that without outside professional help, he may move back into isolationism. This young man will need continued ongoing therapy for a number of years.

EXAMPLE 11 Well-written diagnostic summary based on the analytical thinking model

The following was produced by an undergraduate student with prior paid social work experience. She was in her second half of field placement. Her supervisor had been helping her learn the Analytical Thinking Model.

The patient was described by her sister and cousin as being "slow." She had led a very sheltered life with her family and has had little formal education, but whether she has any actual organic retardation is unknown. She is a very passive, dependent person, but her life situation has undoubtedly been a factor which has contributed to this. She is very childlike in her affect. She is open, friendly and at times easily frightened or upset. She is a widow, but evidently knows little about her economic situation or whether she receives Social Security benefits.

It is my impression that she will not be subject to the emotional stress that normally results from having had major surgery and intractable illness because she is unaware of the implications of her prognosis. (I was informed by her physician that she is terminally ill. Her exact prognosis in terms of time left to live is unknown.) It is my feeling that at this time, or unless she indicates a desire to know, no useful purpose would be served in relating this information to her.

Mrs. B.'s needs, aside from her physical care, will predominately be in the area of support and reassurance. Since she is such a dependent person, she has not developed the internal strengths which serve to counteract episodes of depression, frustration and emotional upset which she experiences.

pending treatment plans

Ongoing treatment should include continued supportive counseling with her and her family. Her physician has advised that Visiting Nurse Services are indicated on a daily basis for her during the first week after her discharge; therefore, discharge planning for this will be necessary. A continued effort to have the patient and her family contacted by a volunteer from the ABC club would be useful, and an investigation into patient's possible eligibility for Social Security benefits is also indicated.

EXAMPLE 12   Well-written treatment plan

The following is the treatment planning section of a diagnostic summary written in the middle of a second-year graduate student's last semester of school. He had been studying the Analytical Thinking Model for several months and also had prior paid social work experience.

---

plans and goals

Now that there has been ample sharing of information between medical and social service staff, along with our involving the family group, we expect that Patricia's manipulations will not be as successful as heretofore. Likewise, in a joint effort of the medical and social service staff, we have set very specific expectations of Patricia such as regular clinic appointments, her notifying the staff in the event she cannot come to clinic, and commitment on the part of her family to support a program of regular clinic attendance. Along with this I attempt to have weekly contact with Patricia, primarily by phone but also in the form of face-to-face interviews at two-week intervals. My casework method will involve clarification based upon reality orientation. We will continue to work toward Patricia's being more honest in her relationships and developing a capacity to deal appropriately with her anxieties and needs.

EXAMPLE 13   Diagnostic summary written by
first-year graduate student with no prior experience or
training in social work

The student author of the following example was completing the end of her first semester in field placement. She had not received any training on diagnostic thinking or treatment planning in the classroom at the time this was written. She had been given the Analytical Thinking Model to read as a self-instructional exercise before doing this, her first diagnostic summary. Her supervisor felt it was an unusually well-written summary for a beginning student but that it could be improved, primarily through more discussion of how the patient sees her problems and needs and more specifics regarding the past events that might be causing the guilt feelings.

Mrs. A. is experiencing and faced with a great deal of anxiety regarding the birth of her first baby and the new role of mother that she will be assuming. This anxiety is manifested in both fear and guilt which she has verbalized indirectly. Some of this fear regarding the infant's prolonged hospital stay in the intensive-care unit seems both legitimate and realistic. Less clear and possibly with more ramifications is a fear which appears to be instilled and reinforced by Mr. A. It seems that he initially and now his wife, believe that they may be endangered of losing custody of the infant. This is further intensified for Mrs. A. because associated with this she views a possible rejection by her husband. Coupled with this fear is guilt from both past and present events. It does not appear that Mrs. A. is or was able to verbalize these feelings in her relationships with significant others in the past such as immediate family or in the present with her spouse.

Significant others in her life have cast her into a dependent role, a role fostered and perpetuated by both Mrs. A. and others around her. This has undoubtedly led to her low self-concept. This role of dependency is being threatened by the arrival of the baby because someone will now be dependent on her. Mrs. A. is faced with a double bind because caring for the baby means loss of her accustomed role yet loss of the baby or a failure to assume the role of mother "adequately" (as defined by her husband) may result in loss of her role due to rejection by her husband.

social work treatment plan

Because fear of losing the baby seems paramount, Mrs. A. is resistant to help at this time. Hopefully by approaching her in a nonthreatening, nonjudgmental way she will agree to participate in joint interviews with her husband. When this occurs further information regarding Mrs. A.'s past history, both medically and socially, will be explored. It may be that medical help will be indicated for Mrs. A's petit mal seizures which are not under control. As a result her behavior is sometimes unpredictable.

In addition, Mrs. A. will be encouraged to ventilate her feelings of fear and guilt. Support and reassurance will be given along with providing insight and information in caring for the infant. This may be done with additional support from community resources when the infant is discharged.

It would be hoped that in addition Mr. A.'s feelings toward his wife and baby will be explored. Along with this, marital relationship and possible counseling to facilitate communications between the couple will be attempted. However, this will occur secondary to previously mentioned plans and may be extended to a community mental health center.

EXAMPLE 14   Well-done diagnostic summary and treatment plan by second-year graduate student

The author of this summary had prior social work experience and was halfway through her second year of field placement at the time this was written. She had been studying the Analytical Thinking Model and had received special training in this approach. Notice how clearly the worker interjects her own analysis, which the reader is free to accept or reject. There are also statements indicating areas that have not been explored or are unknown. The following material appeared as part of a detailed history, following the "social history outline." Plans are being made to discharge "Mrs. Smith" from the hospital. She has only a few days or weeks to live.

Mrs. Smith is chronologically a young woman; however, she appears to be 20 years older. Physicians and family members have told her of her diagnosis and prognosis. It is difficult to assess at this point just how much of this she was able to or wanted to comprehend. Mrs. Smith has been sick for most of her adult life. It seems to me that her procrastination as well as that of her husband in seeking medical attention is probably well founded as far as they are concerned. Medical science has not really had much to offer them and I suspect they feel the same way. Mrs. Smith's prolonged illness has made it necessary for her to be dependent on others, particularly in relationship to her husband, daughter and mother. The roles which each of them have had to adapt to will probably create severe stress which they will need to identify and work out when Mrs. Smith dies. The idea of a nursing home placement for Mrs. Smith was realistically discussed by Mrs. Adams (patient's daughter) and Mr. Smith, but I think they decided not to go through with it because: (1) her prognosis was measured in terms of days; (2) they genuinely felt they, as a family, could do a better job; and (3) it was culturally more acceptable to keep her at home.

I was not able to meet Mrs. Smith's mother before Mrs. Smith was discharged. I am unaware of how she feels toward her daughter, son-in-law or her granddaughter, or how she is coping with the new demands being placed on her.

Mr. Smith seems to be functioning on a submissive level and dependent on his daughter for major decisions. I suspect this role is not a new one for him. I feel that some degree of frustration, anger and perhaps guilt will probably surface if Mrs. Smith's illness prolongs itself more than expected. He tends to be excitable and loud, and I feel this pattern of behavior is due in a large part to his feelings of inadequacy and low self-esteem created by situations which he could not handle.

Mrs. Adams, on the other hand, has aggressively taken over the role her father "should have." Perhaps she had no choice. She is a mature young woman facing enormous responsibilities placed upon her without much hesitation. She is able to weigh those resources she has at hand and move them around to fit her needs. I am not aware of how her marriage and interfamily relationships function, but I feel that the pressure might at some time become more than she can deal with. It might become very important for her to have an outlet. This, however, does not have to be social work.

treatment plan

1. I will continue to see patient's daughter and attempt to get her to verbalize her feelings toward the role she seems to have taken up in terms of what this will do to her self-image as a woman, wife, mother, daughter and granddaughter. I will offer her emotional support so as to help her deal with any guilt or anxiety created by her circumstances.
2. With Mr. Smith, emotional support from other members within the family structure will be very important. He will probably need help in reevaluating his life goals and how to achieve them.
3. I will be making a home visit to see Mrs. Smith for the purpose of assessing the feelings and problems related to Mrs. Smith's care and how the family has managed since Mrs. Smith's discharge from the hospital.

EXAMPLE 15 Diagnostic summary written by a
beginning student applying the analytical thinking model

The following was written by a first-quarter undergraduate student who had received several hours of special training in the Analytical Thinking Model. It is fairly effective, in the sense that the student indicates beginning ability to do analytical thinking. She obviously hasn't yet achieved in-depth understanding of the psychodynamics of human behavior, but that will come with continued training and experience. This is a good diagnostic summary for a beginning student just learning to think analytically. The student's grammar and sentence structure leave much to be desired.

The client feels that she needs some kind of financial assistance. She feels that her husband isn't paying the bills and she has no one to depend on except herself. The friend that she can depend on she says is sick herself and can't get around. She says the same thing for her sister.

She seems to have more confidence in her first doctors than the doctors she has now. This may be due to the fact that the first physician said she had water on the foot instead of an ulcer.

I feel the client is indeed in need of financial assistance. She is due her Social Security providing that she is eligible to receive it. She also could use some more of an interaction with her physician, and possibly this will give her more confidence in them.

The client seem somewhat depressed. This could possibly be due to the fact that she is going to be operated on soon. She is also highly anxious to get the operation over with now that she has accepted it.

The client and her sister attempted to get financial assistance by applying for Social Security. She says it has been three weeks since her sister applied for Social Security and neither one has been contacted.

The client says also that she contacted the Public Welfare Department and they told her that her husband made too much money to be eligible.

As in reference to the client's changing of doctors, no attempts have been made to resolve this problem.

ideal treatment plan

(a) Get financial assistance immediately; (b) get information about time of surgery; (c) speed up the process of Social Security (if eligible) or public welfare.

realistic treatment plan

(a) Attempt to get financial assistance; (b) contact sister and see what has been done as in reference to applying for Social Security; (c) check with Social Security to see if client is eligible and if so what is the delay if any; (d) check to see if anything can be done to speed up process or a substitute to fill in until client receives assistance; (e) check possibly with husband to see if any bills are overdue, or about payment of bills; (f) contact doctors to find out whether or not surgery is being done. If so, when?

As in reference to the client's willingness and ability to carry out the treatment plans. There is not enough information to answer that statement. I don't know.

EXAMPLE 16   Four summaries on the same case

The following four diagnostic summaries were written by students participating in training in the Analytical Thinking Model. They were given a case summary and asked to write a diagnostic summary and treatment plan based on what they had read.

A.   This first example is the best in the group, produced by an undergraduate student who apparently has considerable understanding of the psychodynamics of human behavior, especially pertaining to physical illness. She also has some specific treatment approaches in mind. The case example presented a man who was told he needed to have his foot amputated. He was threatening to get up and walk out of the hospital against medical advice at the time the social worker was called to see him.

The patient is currently facing a critical situation; that is, the doctors have recommended further amputation to stop the spread of gangrene which is resulting from uncontrolled diabetes. The patient must decide whether or not to accept their recommendation and consent to surgery. As he sees it now, the problem is to find an "escape" from the hospital and a means of saving his foot. He is extremely fearful of further mutilation and the changes he foresees as a result of it. These changes include a change in body-image, loss of ability to work, loss of his role as breadwinner, and increased dependency. He has feelings of anger toward himself, his wife, and the medical staff. These are being expressed inwardly and outwardly as denial and an "urge to flee"; also, through ventilation, projection onto staff, and testing the limits of their tolerance of his behavior. He may also be feeling guilty or responsible for his own condition and believe that it would be better emotionally and financially for his family if he were to die rather than live the rest of his life as a "cripple" and a burden to them. A strong contributing factor in this belief is his realization that previous efforts to control his disease have failed and a feeling that nothing can help him now.

Client will probably continue to become angrier, more hostile, and verbal as he expresses his anxiety and ambivalence. His threats to leave against medical advice may continue but he is probably not capable of carrying them out.

short-term treatment plan

(First interview with Mr. Y. as he is threatening to leave the hospital) I would approach the patient, hoping to convey to him through a nonjudgmental attitude his own right to self-determination. In a totally private atmosphere I would encourage him to ventilate his feelings, express my empathy for him, discuss the advantages and disadvantages of all choices open to him, let him make his own decision of what to do, and support him in it. To bolster his self-image, I would reflect back to him his strengths as they appear in the interview and through what I know of his past history.

long-range treatment plan

(After the first contact) If patient elects surgery, I would try to help him accept his changed body-image and utilize his full potential for increased functioning. If he does not elect surgery, I would try to help him deal with the meaning and prospect of death in the near future.

B. This example was produced by a graduate student. Notice the repetition of facts and the superficial and limited analysis. The treatment plan is very generalized and straight from the textbook. Unfortunately, many MSW's produce diagnostic statements that aren't much better!

Mr. Y. is a 46-year-old man who is hospitalized with diagnosis of diabetes mellitus (uncontrolled) with diabetes neuropathy. There are complications which necessitate the amputation of patient's foot.

Having not met Mr. Y. but from reading his case history and generalizing I would assume that he is experiencing a great deal of anger, anxiety and fear. Some of these feelings have been expressed overtly to the nursing staff, especially the feeling of anger. However, there are so many things Mr. Y. must be feeling that I cannot pick up from his case history.

By the patient's refusing surgery, I would assume that it is because of fear—fear of what? I cannot say at this time. Patient's feelings will have to be explored.

treatment plan

Establish contacts with patient in an effort to establish some degree of rapport or atmosphere where patient will feel free to ventilate his feelings. Help patient gain insight into his feeling so that he can make realistic and effective decisions.

C. The third example was done by a student about to graduate with a BSW degree. She had had several field placements, but apparently was having real difficulty in understanding what a diagnostic summary is. Notice that the recording is mostly factual and contains little analysis. Observe the grammar and spelling.

Mr. Y. is a married 46-year-old black male. Mr. Y. diabetic condition started to occured approximately five years ago at the age of 41. During the past 3 years he has been hospitalized for various problems connected with his diabetic condition. Recently Mr. Y. was hospitalized and gangrene was discovered in 3 of his left toes, the affected toes were amputed. Before discharge from the hospital it was realized that Mr. Y. gangrenous condition has spread thru his entire foot, which now much be amputated. Mr. Y. refuses the surgery.

Mr. Y. has 5 children, four of the five are grown-up and out of the house. Up until a year ago Mr. Y. (student stopped writing here).

treatment plan

I would attempt to get some pertinent data and information and feelings from the patient.

D. The last example was also written by a graduate student who had never had formal training in the diagnostic thinking process. It is also largely a repetition of facts with limited analysis. The original handwritten version contained many crossouts and was barely legible, indicating that the student really struggled with the exercise and must have experienced considerable anxiety in writing his first diagnostic summary.

This is the fifth admission for this 46-year-old black male whose hospitalization was precipitated by diabetes mellitus. Prior to discharge it was discovered that the patient needed an amputation of his foot, which he refused. The reality of the situation is that if amputation is not done, the patient could die.

The patient has been physically active most of his life doing manual labor. The patient's anger and refusal to be treated can be seen by his refusal to consider the problem and appropriately deal with it.

short-term treatment plan

Prepare patient to agree to have the amputation.

long-term treatment plan

Accept the amputation, and adjusting to it in terms of employment and living situation.

EXAMPLE 17 Well-written diagnostic summary showing analysis and prognostic statements based on worker's analysis

Notice how the author of this summary not only analyzes the meaning of her client's behavior, but goes on to state what she predicts might happen as a result of the underlying feelings. This level of performance should be expected of an MSW-level casework student about to graduate. Notice also that the treatment plan has been broken up into short- and long-range goals. The plans seem appropriate and certainly present the areas the worker intends to deal with. However, they are not quite so specific as might be desired. The student had received training in the Analytical Thinking Model.

This patient has recently undergone a traumatic change in his life, and is exhibiting behaviors which indicate a severe depressed state. For instance, patient has terminated all communication with friends and relatives, sleeps a lot, and is uncooperative with any treatment plan. It is suspected that patient is experiencing guilt feelings for not having followed thru with treatment (prior to hospitalization) and for not being able to provide for his family. The feeling of guilt may be leading to patient's withdrawn state.

Patient also seems to be feeling anxiety due to his loss of independence and masculine role as provider for his family, both factors which patient's wife states are very important to him. This is exemplified by patient's reluctance to accept AFDC (welfare aid). Patient has made no attempt to regain these factors, which indicates a possible feeling of hopelessness.

Patient seems to have a very low self-concept, which may be due to loss of previously mentioned roles, and has terminated his primary source of support, his communication with his wife and family. It is suspected that wife has interpreted patient's unresponsive behavior as rejection, and therefore has discontinued her visits to him in the hospital.

Patient's wife states that patient does not express his feelings openly. With this in mind, patient may be turning his feelings inward and attempting to punish himself for his present situation. Thus, again, patient is denying help of any kind. Patient seems to have denied his diabetes prior to hospitalization by not following thru with treatment procedures. He may

174

now be feeling responsible for his condition, thus angry at himself and guilty toward others for his mistake.

Patient's family's feelings are unknown due to no involvement thus far with this social worker. However, it is reported that patient's 12-year-old son has recently begun to oversleep, which could be due to developing diabetes, or some reaction to present family situation. Patient's wife was quite demanding of hospital staff during her visits, possibly due to misplaced anger at herself or patient.

It is suspected that, if no intervention occurs, patient may become suicidal.

treatment plan

Short-range goals

1. To encourage pt. to express his feelings concerning his dependence, medical situation, and wife's discontinued visits.
2. To involve family in patient's care.
3. To encourage patient to cooperate with therapy.
4. To act as a referral source in meeting patient and family's concrete needs.
5. To help patient deal with the reality of his current situation.

Long-range

1. To facilitate the improvement of patient's self-image.
2. To facilitate more open communication between patient and wife in order to create a support for the patient.
3. To assist patient in planning for his future.

EXAMPLE 18   A field instructor writes a diagnostic summary to show a graduate student what one should look like

A second-year graduate student had been working with a field instructor on a very complex case situation. The student's attempts to produce a diagnostic summary were commendable but still left something to be desired. The field instructor decided to do one of her own, based on the facts known to her about the case through the student. This instructive technique should be used sparingly, as some students might become discouraged upon comparing what they produce with the efforts of their more experienced field instructor. Other might tend to copy the field instructor's approach blindly rather than try to develop their own.

Mr. Denton is a divorced middle-aged man and father of two adolescents. He has a terminal illness and his life expectancy is measured in terms of weeks. He has gone rather rapidly from an independent, self-supporting life style to that of virtually total dependence upon others for his basic physical care and life functions. He is in the process of working through his feelings regarding his impending death, his severance of his relationship with his children, and making peace with himself. He has verbalized sadness at the prospect of leaving his children, especially his daughter, who has been most dependent upon him, and has asked that she be kept in this geographical area so that he can visit with her until the time of his death. There are indications that perhaps he has not been the most effective father figure for his children. Undoubtedly, Mr. Denton must be experiencing some anxiety, guilt, and/or remorse about this, but he has thus far not verbalized these feelings.

Patient's son has been visiting him regularly and there has been some honest discussion regarding the future. Billy does not wish to become involved in planning for his younger sister and this probably is understandable in view of his particular situation. It appears he might be involved with some kind of substance abuse. While ideally we would like to maintain contact with him to assist in evaluating and dealing with this problem, this is probably unrealistic in view of the fact that Billy will reach the age of legal adulthood in a few weeks and is anxious to be out on his own. Thus he probably would not follow through with any social service involvement. The father's feelings regarding his son, his awareness of possible problem areas in his son's life, and his possible contribution to these problems, as well as his thoughts regarding Billy's future plans, are essentially unknown at this point.

Another social service agency is actively planning for the care of the daughter. She is not aware of her father's illness and prognosis but is reacting with considerable anxiety, which is showing up in decreased school performance and changes in eating and sleeping patterns.

Several neighbors and friends of the family have been extremely involved in this situation. One had offered to take the daughter into her home and then did not follow through with this plan. The patient's reaction to all of this and his feelings about these people planning for the care of his children remain unknown.

casework planning

1. At this point it may not be appropriate to delve into and activate Mr. Denton's feelings regarding his father role as he reviews his past life and the situation of his children. However, he undoubtedly must be struggling with this internally. We will wait for Mr. Denton to give us some clue that he has a need to talk about these feelings.

2. Mr. D. occasionally displays a sense of hopelessness, which is realistic in view of his prognosis and the physical discomfort he experiences continuously. Emotional support in terms of a caring person being present as much as possible should be of some help. We will encourage nursing staff to give him as much extra attention as possible, and will elicit the help of a mature volunteer to spend time with him.

3. Mr. Denton indicates many times a desire to communicate deeply with rather subtle verbal and nonverbal clues. We must be very attentive to these and not shy away from discussing these areas when he indicates a need to do so.

4. We are focusing on Mr. Denton while another community agency is concerned primarily with the planning for the two children. We will coordinate closely with this agency in terms of information exchange. It is important to involve Mr. Denton in this process as much as possible, at least keeping him informed of what is going on. He will soon reach a point where he will be physically unable to participate in any planning.

5. A financial assistance worker will look into possible financial benefits for the Dentons, including Social Security.

EXAMPLE 19 Advanced diagnostic statement written by undergraduate student nearing graduation

The author of this recording was in the middle of a block field placement and only weeks away from graduation. She had been working very intensively with a client thought to be "mildly depressed" at the time she acquired the case. This particular student demonstrated advanced skills and was able to move from information gathering to real counseling with her client.

Mrs. Smith's depressed mood and anxiousness to talk led me to assume she had something she really needed to get out. She is obviously very concerned about her weight problem, and seems to attribute this as the source of all her problems. However, it may be possible that she uses her weight as a defense relating to an actual fear of getting "back on her feet." It could be assumed that Mrs. Smith actually fears rejection by society or being seen as an inadequate woman as a result of her husband leaving her for another woman.

A major problem at the present, which I feel needs immediate attention, are the uncomfortable feelings Mrs. Smith is experiencing concerning her son being alone with her ex-husband. It is possible that some basic information or understanding regarding his emotional problem would be very beneficial in helping her deal with these feelings. She is constantly thinking about this and needs to overcome having nightmares about it.

On the positive side, Mrs. Smith has a strong ego, as she realized that she could not continue to live with this man, and actually forced him to move out even though she did love him. She recognizes that she is suffering feelings of guilt and depression, but does not see this as being "mentally ill." However, she does realize that professional counseling could help her deal with some of the stressful problems she has encountered.

treatment plan

I plan to continue to strengthen my relationship with Mrs. Smith and be supportive in helping her understand how mental health practitioners can be helpful. It is also important to determine if Mrs. Smith still has suicidal thoughts. I also plan to discuss with her such things as legal visitation rights of her husband, as well as the content of the dreams she has been having. I also plan to discuss Mrs. Smith's relationships with friends and family to determine if she is beginning to become involved in any social activity. I intend to visit her bi-weekly and as a main goal, encourage her to seek professional counseling.

Other than working with Mrs. Smith to help her become emotionally stable, I plan to continue with the concrete services mentioned in the Treatment Plan dated 12-4-73.

EXAMPLE 20 Diagnostic statement written by an advanced undergraduate student nearing graduation

This recording is based on contacts with an elderly woman whose case was about to be closed by the agency at the time it was assigned to the student. She was refusing some recommended medical treatment, and the general feeling was that "that's her right, so if she doesn't want the treatment, we should close the case." We decided to make one last attempt to get to know her as a total person and explore more deeply the cause of her feelings toward the recommended medical treatment. This advanced student quickly established a strong relationship with the client, and discovered, to everyone's surprise, that she was dying of a physical problem totally unrelated to the illness everyone knew about, which was not life threatening. One of the treatment goals quickly became that of helping the client verbalize her feelings about death. This was extremely difficult for the student, as it forced her to come to grips with her own uneasy feelings about death before she could handle the subject effectively with her client. Several intense interviews followed, and the diagnostic summary example included here reflects her assessment of those sessions. She had been studying the Analytical Thinking Model and was functioning at an unusually advanced level for an undergraduate student.

In my past contacts with Mrs. Snyder during the past month, I explored her awareness and knowledge of the extent of her cancer. She had gaps in her feelings about death. She indicated that she was not afraid of being dead, but went on to say that if anyone was ready to die, they shouldn't be afraid. Mrs. Snyder then admitted in subsequent interviews that she was not ready to die and was afraid. She has, however, started going back to church and plans to attend regularly. I feel this is indicative of her making a step to be reconciled to God.

Mrs. Snyder is open about expressing her fear of suffering and pain and has equated these directly with the process of dying. When we talked about her sister's death, she was able to express the fact she wouldn't want to be kept alive artificially on a machine and be made to suffer as she had suffered. She indicated that she had thought about suicide but wasn't able to cope with the fact she had thought about it. She said she "wouldn't do anything crazy by stop taking my medication or taking too much because I'm not in that much pain and besides it is wrong." She was reluctant to talk about these feelings with me, which is understandable, because she is not able to face them herself.

She seems to have some guilt feelings concerning the heart attack her sister had just before she entered the hospital. This had resulted in her death. It seems that Mrs. Snyder and her sister had an argument just before the heart attack. Mrs. Snyder seems to have resolved this, and states that the reason she feels her sister died was the fall she had while at the hospital. This belief, along with her fear of suffering and being in pain, has been manifested in her admitted fear of surgery and of the hospital. Mrs. Snyder has said that she trusts her doctor. I believe her greatest fear at this time is that of becoming dependent on someone, which would mean total helplessness on her part. She brought these fears out in such statements as hating to move from her house, but being afraid she would not be able to manage by herself if she were hospitalized, and wanting to get a new hearing aid even though she knows she is dying.

She has not revealed to me whether she does or does not drink. I have not confronted her with the fact I am aware of her past history of alcoholism.

treatment plan

1. Individual counseling. This will help Mrs. Snyder deal with her feelings about death and dying, her feelings of helplessness, and her fear of becoming totally dependent on someone. I will also discuss with her her past history of drinking and help her deal with her feelings and emotions about this.

2. Companionship services. I plan to explore Mrs. Snyder's feelings about having someone her own age come out to visit her regularly. If she is interested in this service, I hope to obtain it through the Senior Citizen's Center.

3. Medical services. Mrs. Snyder will need hospital, physician, and drug assistance. She is presently able to function in her home, but as her disease progresses, then possibly some type of homemaker or home health aid will be needed.

Time frame for completing the above plans: 6 months.

EXAMPLE 21 An MSW with ten years of post-MSW experience produces an advanced diagnostic statement showing in-depth casework involvement

The following diagnostic statement was written for case presentation in a small social work unit meeting.* The author is a highly skilled caseworker with ten years of post-MSW counseling experience. She had earned the respect of many colleagues for her keen skills and in-depth approach to helping her clients. The following diagnostic summary demonstrates advanced understanding of the psychodynamics of human behavior. The author clearly indicates her diagnostic impressions of what she observed. The role of the social worker in the treatment process comes through very clearly, and the patient's and her family's response to social work intervention is described and assessed. Goals are spelled out, and progress and lack of progress in achieving these goals are documented. Perhaps most significant is that this diagnostic statement is not merely an intellectual exercise—it represents hours of effective, intensive involvement on the part of the social worker as she provided treatment to this adolescent and her family. A newly graduated MSW student would not be expected to write a diagnostic summary with this degree of depth, nor would he be expected to provide the treatment it suggests took place. While an intellectually bright student might be able to produce impressive-sounding textbook analyses of complex presenting problems, few would be able to follow through effectively with the treatment plan. Thus this diagnostic statement illustrates the degree of skill expected of a mature professional who has been in social work practice for a number of years post-MSW. It illustrates an ideal that the beginning caseworker can strive for as a long term goal in his professional development.

This diagnostic statement concerns a sixteen-year-old adolescent girl with a history of several years of medical problems. At one point both she and her parents stopped medical treatment, against their physician's advice. Further physical problems developed and at least one physician reached out to the family to attempt to get them

*Identifying details have been altered to preserve confidentiality. A special section, "Questions and Issues for Consideration," has been included at the conclusion of the diagnostic summary. These reflect some of the issues the worker felt she had to deal with in providing services to this family.

back into treatment. They again refused, and traveled some distance with their teenager to obtain treatment through unorthodox, untrained persons. When the patient failed to improve, she was subsequently hospitalized. Even though she was treated very intensively, she got worse and was found to have metastatic cancer. She died at the hospital about three months after admission. The social worker had been asked to see the patient and her family soon after admission to help them deal with some of their feelings regarding the daughter's life-threatening illness.

background information

The patient was an only child who lived at home with her parents. Her parents were college educated and her father held a high-level business-management position with a small firm. When her state of health permitted, patient was a college student. Her mother, basically a homemaker, had a dance studio and taught occasionally at a local university.

assessment

Family dynamics were complex and characterized by neurotic interaction. Patient's father was insecure, domineering, and sought to enhance his low self-esteem by deprecating his wife. Her response was passive-aggressive behavior, with alternating spurts of submissiveness followed by outbursts of anger and hostility. There had been a long-standing rivalry between mother and patient for father's attention and affection. Patient was described by her mother as always being willful and egocentric, manipulative, and experiencing difficulty with peer relationships throughout her life. In early adolescence she presented with psychophysiological symptoms of internalized anger and hostility resulting in ulcerative colitis.

Parents were intellectually aware of patient's diagnosis and prognosis but initially in a stage of massive denial. Guilt and anxiety at forsaking traditional treatment methods made it too painful to face patient's obvious terminal (dying) condition. Father presented with grossly inappropriate affect (continuous masklike smiling) and was immobilized. He had been unable to function and perform on his job for many months and was at risk of losing it. Mother verbalized resentment, anger, rejection, and critical attitude toward patient. This was, in my personal experience, atypical behavior; most family members repress and deny negative feelings and idealize patients in this stage of disease process. I interpreted this as a reinforcement of the mother's denial. The understandable stresses precipitated increasingly hostile destructive marital interaction instead of serving as a cohesive force. More and more they displaced anger onto professional staff and onto each other.

Although patient was aware of her diagnosis, verbalized fears, and obviously wanted to talk of impending death, parents resorted to evasion, false reassurance, and game playing; for example, they brought brochures for her to select the stereo they would buy her when she was discharged.

social work intervention

Efforts to engage patient in a counseling relationship were negated by her physiological and psychological states, but more so by feelings of threat and resistance on the part of both parents, which they nonverbally communicated to their daughter. Indeed, this was so threatening to them that for a period of a week or ten days they withdrew from counseling with me, had an interview with another counselor, then elected to reestablish their relationship with me. I sought to have patient's need met by involving and consulting with patient's nurse around helping patient deal with her feelings. The nurse was a mature, sensitive person who had effectively coped with death in her own family as well as with patients.

Goals with parents were: (1) to enable them to work through feelings of guilt, ambivalence, and anger; (2) to gain acceptance of inevitability of death so they might deal with their own feelings and establish communication with patient; (3) to begin movement into the grief and mourning process; (4) to begin reassessment of the marital relationship and begin establishment of a new equilibrium between themselves.

The mother progressed in working through a lot of guilt, hostility, and ambivalence. As her denial broke down, she began to verbalize to me and then to the patient the positives in the mother-daughter relationship. She allowed herself to enter into a state of anticipatory grief and at the very end was able to communicate to patient her feelings of loss, and permit patient to express her feelings around her death.

The father remained highly defended. Denial and intellectualization remained his primary defense mechanisms. There were occasional appearances of overt depression, withdrawal into sleep, bargaining, seeking religious support (although he was not practicing any religion at all throughout his adult life). To the end he verbalized belief that "a miracle would occur" and never participated in the meaningful interchange between patient and her mother.

questions and issues for consideration

1. How do you feel about my electing to accept the parents rather than the patient as clients? What is your approach when the patient could benefit from counseling and family resists?
2. Would you feel comfortable having another professional work with the patient, with active communication and consultation between you?
3. Recognizing that all of us experience ambivalence in working with the terminal patient, especially in this age group, was my decision a "cop-out?" How do you handle your feelings?
4. Do you see my intervention in the marital relationship as appropriate? Why or why not?
5. How do you usually handle maladaptive defenses—in this case employed mostly by the father—what techniques do you use? What is involved in your decision regarding what to reinforce and when not to support?

CONFIDENTIALITY: PHYSICALLY SAFEGUARDING CASE RECORDS

CHAPTER **12**

Confidentiality used to be a simple topic. As long as social workers kept their mouths shut and "didn't blab about their clients," confidentiality was considered maintained. Unfortunately, the situation is much more complex today as federal legislation determines what must be recorded and how privacy must be maintained in certain settings, and as massive computerized data bank systems compile private information on hundreds of thousands of individuals. Many individuals and groups seek access to confidential records daily. Furthermore, as consumers become increasingly aware of their privacy rights, they press for the right of access to their files and bring suits against helping professionals when confidentiality is not maintained.

There are many ways in which confidentiality can be violated. This chapter will discuss only those guidelines and issues that concern social service case records.* There are two aspects to consider: (1) protecting information contained in records against unauthorized disclosures; and (2) using recording techniques that prevent potential confidentiality problems. The sections that follow will cover these points.

A DAY IN THE LIFE OF THE "HENRY SMITH" RECORD: A HORROR STORY†

9:00 A.M. All is peaceful. The "Henry Smith" (Henry for short) case record is resting quietly in a locked file cabinet in a back room. "Henry," the record, is age nine, having been known to the QRX Counseling Center for that period of time. He has been seen at periodic intervals by various social work staff. He is nice and fat—in fact, overweight—as he bulges at the seams of his manila folder with six inches worth of summaries, weekly progress notes, test results, reports of psychiatric consultations, forms, and identifying data. Henry—the client whose life this pile of papers documents—is being seen weekly by Carolyn Frank, MSW.

9:45 A.M. Carolyn pulls the record and carries it to her desk to leaf through it. In comes the secretary who borrows it, takes it to her desk, files some new pages, and removes several others for reproduction. Henry remains atop the clerk's desk while part of his innards are spirited off to the Xerox machine in another part of the building. Three copies are made and, ten minutes later, Henry is complete again as the originals are returned to the file.

Henry returns to worker Carolyn's desk. At 10:41 she discovers a page missing— the original of a court order giving custody of Henry's kids to his ex-wife! She dashes to the secretary in a mild state of panic, accusing her of all sorts of carelessness. And where has the missing page been? Soaking up the heat from the Xerox machine, where it was left after the last copy was made. The secretary runs to the reproduction room, hoping it's still there. It isn't. Fifteen minutes later she's tracked it down—

---

*For a much more detailed discussion of confidentiality see Suanna J. Wilson, *Confidentiality in Social Work: Issues and Principles* (New York: Free Press, 1978). It contains a bibliography of over 500 references, goes into greater detail about all of the subjects mentioned in this chapter, and discusses many issues pertaining to confidentiality that are not mentioned here. See especially the chapters concerning confidentiality of case records, consumer access to record materials, and privileged communication. This text also presents a detailed breakdown of the Federal Privacy Act of 1974. Many illustrations of court cases and actual incidents are provided.

†Perhaps not all the incidents described here have ever happened to the same case record in the same day; however, all actually have happened at one time or another.

181

somebody from another office in the building found it, read it, couldn't figure out who it belonged to, and left it in the care of the administrator in charge of duplicating until someone claimed it.

Henry remains on Carolyn's desk while she goes to lunch. Suddenly he feels another person's presence—someone is turning his pages. She has a plastic bag in one hand and a vacuum cleaner in the other—the maid! She's eagerly reading every page. Can't somebody stop her?

At 1:40 a student enters the room, shuffles through the papers on Carolyn's desk, and locates Henry. Off he goes to the student's desk. A piece of paper falls out on the way and drifts under a chair in the waiting room, but no one seems to notice. For the next hour, Henry is examined intensively by the student, who takes detailed notes. Two other students come and sit nearby, and Henry's ears burn as the most intimate details of his life are discussed. The talk continues, loudly, as two additional staff join them and they all leave together for a late lunch. Is there no such thing as privacy anymore?

3:00 P.M. Only two more hours to go—surely the rest of the day will be peaceful for Henry. But no, at precisely 3:07 a supervisor comes in and is delighted finally to have found Henry. Time for peer review. Off he goes to a conference room where he joins the company of fourteen other records being scrutinized by four staff. Finally, at 4:12, the session adjourns and Henry is returned by a volunteer worker to his position in the file cabinet.

Poor Henry. Today is the monthly board meeting, starting at 5 P.M. All is well until 5:39, when Carolyn brings Henry forth to illustrate some of the agency's internal problems in its service delivery system. The speed with which Henry is passed around the table from board member to board member leaves him feeling dizzy and disoriented. Twenty minutes later he is back in Carolyn's possession. At 6:45 everyone rises and Henry sighs with relief—"It's over! I can now go home and rest in my file cabinet."

Unfortunately, Carolyn has different ideas. Unbeknownst to her supervisor, Carolyn has fallen behind in some of her recording. So Henry, along with five other records, is stuffed into a satchel and transported by bus eight miles across town. On the way, a sweet-looking old lady peers over Carolyn's shoulder and reads everything Carolyn writes as she starts her recording on Henry while still on the bus. Carolyn doesn't even notice, and Henry has no way of warning her. As they exit at the bus stop, a sudden rain shower catches Carolyn without an umbrella, and the ink runs on several pages.

Henry finds himself entering a large, modern house where he and Carolyn are enthusiastically greeted by three children, two dogs, and one cat, accompanied by a hungry husband. Henry is deposited hastily on the dining room table while Carolyn heads for the kitchen to fix a late dinner. Meanwhile, the two-year-old son is restless. He has a nice new box of crayons to try out and can't find anything to draw on since Mama declared the wallpaper off limits. His roaming eye spots Henry. Wow! Six inches of paper! The child can barely reach Henry, but he manages to grab one corner of the manila folder and pull the whole thing onto the floor. Papers scatter all over and the youngster selects several pages for his art project. Carolyn becomes suspicious because the baby has been quiet for too long, and rushes in after three pages have been decorated with vivid colors. Carolyn administers a proper scolding, hastily reassembles Henry, and puts him on the coffee table. The crying youngster is hauled off to the kitchen with Mama and Henry is left in peace—but not for long.

The household's six-month-old puppy is teething—boy, could he use something to chew on. He spots Henry. Carolyn comes to Henry's rescue just as a big hunk is being torn out of several pages. As Carolyn returns to the kitchen once again, her fifteen-year-old daughter strolls in, anxiously awaiting her dinner. She's bored and hungry. Her eye falls on Henry and she soon discovers the most fascinating reading she's encountered in a long time! She quickly closes the folder as she hears Carolyn's footsteps approaching.

The next few hours are restful as the family eats dinner, collapses in front of the TV set, and ignores Henry. However, Carolyn is a night owl and at 11:30 P.M., when everyone else is in bed, she curls up on the sofa with coffee, danish, and Henry. Before her writing siege is over, raspberry filling has stuck several pages together and coffee stains mar pages 117 and 128, along with a signed "consent for release of information" form. At 1:53 A.M., Henry and his companions are retired for the night.

Early the next morning, Carolyn scurries to get ready for work. Henry is carried to the car, accompanied by the husband and three kids. Carolyn is the first to be deposited as the husband continues on to drop the kids off at school and drive an additional five miles across town to his job. Not until 10:17 A.M., when the student asks to see Henry again, does Carolyn realize she left all her case records in the car. Too late to do anything about it now. Poor Henry.

The following day there are no mishaps and Henry makes it to the office with Carolyn. Today is get-rid-of-the-excess-records day. The peer review results showed that the agency is keeping too many records too long—it's time to weed them out. A mandate is issued: all record materials over five years old shall be destroyed. Henry is literally torn asunder as pages 1–67 are removed and dumped into a big box along with hundreds of pages from other records. The flaps are closed on the box and a garbageman personally hauls it, and many other similar boxes, out to his truck to be moved to the incinerator. All goes well until they reach that place on Almond Street where the new sewer is being installed. The road is rough and, while the driver is navigating an unusually bad pothole, Henry's box falls from the rear of the truck. No one notices amidst the noise and confusion. As the box lands, the covers fly open and its contents spill into the street. Pages 5, 18, 53, and a court order declaring Henry mentally incompetent are blown over to the sidewalk outside the Buy-it-Here grocery store, where curious passersby pick them up, read them, and drop them carelessly to the ground. Finally, a distinguished-looking man with a briefcase gathers the lost pages and figures out that they belong to the QRX Counseling Center. The administrator is suitably horrified upon receiving the phone call that tells him what happened to Henry. His tone becomes sharp as he hastily arranges for a special maintenance crew to visit the area in an attempt to find the rest of Henry— and avert a major lawsuit.

Comments

An absurd story? Absolutely not! These kinds of abuse to case-record materials are happening daily in social work settings across the country. How many confidentiality violations were you able to spot? What should have been done differently? Were you able to identify with any parts of the story? Now that I have your attention and concern about the need to handle records in an appropriate manner to preserve confidentiality, we can continue with the rest of this chapter.

WHAT IS A CASE RECORD AND WHO HAS ACCESS?

The traditional case record contains various documents, usually kept in a manila folder, with some kind of binder or prong to hold everything together. Some files contain indexed dividers separating the various parts by topic or format (e.g., social histories versus forms or correspondence). In interdisciplinary settings, social work entries are often made on master charts or in files where various kinds of professionals do their recording. Thus one record might have entries by a psychiatrist, psychologist, physical therapist, social worker, medical doctor, nurse, or dietitian. These records are usually referred to as "charts" and are in special plastic or metal binders. There are always sectional divisions in the chart, and social work may or may not have its own individual section.

The contents of social work records (in noninterdisciplinary settings) typically consist of the following components. Not all would necessarily be found in any one record, and they will vary depending on the nature of the setting:

1. A face sheet containing identifying data (name, address, phone numbers, relatives, sources and amount of income, primary diagnosis or presenting problem, name of social worker, etc.).

2. Eligibility application forms (if applicable).

3. Various special summaries (e.g., intake report, transfer summary, etc.).

4. Regular, brief entries by the social worker (progress notes). These report on contacts with the client or document other case activity on a daily, weekly, or monthly basis, as required by the agency or setting.

5. Copies of pertinent correspondence and memos.

6. Copies of reports received from other agencies or disciplines.

7. Old material from previous case activity. This may be in the record or stored in a separate location (unless it is so old it has been discarded).

8. Computerized data forms or printouts (if applicable).

9. Special forms for specialized types of recording.

10. Miscellaneous forms (consent for release of information, medical forms, application for benefits from other agencies or programs, agreements re: fee schedules, income verification forms, etc.).

11. Other specialized material unique to the setting.

If a case record is defined as "something that documents/records social work activity with a specific consumer(s)," then we must realize that records don't have to be written. Tape recordings, video recordings, computerized data, and microfilms must be treated as "case records." One federal regulation has even gone so far as to define a record as being "any information whether recorded or not."* For purposes of this chapter, we shall assume that a record is something documented in a form that is visible or audible.

Who handles or has access to social service records in the average setting? Obviously the social worker and the secretary who does the typing or filing have a legitimate reason for seeing the material. But consider the following list of individuals who have routine access to all kinds of confidential record material in many agencies:

1. Social work supervisors and administrators.

2. Students.

3. Members of other disciplines who are part of the same agency or program.

4. Volunteers or their parent organizations.

5. Outside clerical staff (transcription pools and typing services).

6. Consumers of social work services ("clients").

7. Computer and data-processing personnel.

8. Outside researchers.

9. Consultants.

10. Agency attorneys or legal counsel.

11. Board members.

12. Persons conducting internal peer reviews.

13. External licensing and accountability authorities.

14. Parent organizations (if a social work agency is part of a larger network of agencies).

---

*Department of Health, Education, and Welfare, Public Health Service, "Confidentiality of Alcohol and Drug Abuse Patient Records—General Provisions," *Federal Register* 40, no. 127 (Tuesday, 7/1/75); part IV, p. 27804, sec. 2.11(o).

15. Third-party funding sources (such as Medicare, Blue Cross-Blue Shield, Medicaid, individuals/organizations supplying grant monies, etc.).

16. Researchers.

Thus agencies and settings where social workers practice must develop specific, written guidelines stating who can have access to records and under what conditions. The guidelines must clearly spell out the confidentiality regulations to be observed, and the agency must see that those individuals having access receive orientation and training on maintaining confidentiality of case-record materials. If an agency really means business about enforcing confidentiality requirements, it will make this obligation a part of the employee's job description and prescribe disciplinary action for offenders.

It is generally recognized that record materials can be shared *within an agency* without any violation of confidentiality. In reality, consumers are not being served by just their social worker—the setting employing that worker actually serves the client collectively. Thus, many people handle the case record. Even the Federal Privacy Act permits exchange of information among the agency staff. Even though all these people technically can review any record they wish, the trend today is to limit access to those individuals with a "need to know." In other words, the staff member or student must have a specific reason for seeing the record—he must need it or the information it contains in order to carry out his job. Curious staff are not allowed to read the records of family or friends, and secretaries are discouraged from reading everything they file out of sheer fascination.

PHYSICALLY SAFEGUARDING CASE RECORDS

Social workers like to get caught up in intellectualized discussions about the content of case records, to whom they should be released and how, and a host of other complexities. A basic first step is often overlooked. Records are usually something physical—a pile of papers, a reel of tape, or a video cassette. Certain precautions must be taken in everyday storage and handling to prevent unauthorized disclosures and high-risk carelessness:*

1.   Records should be kept under lock and key when not in use. When staff go home at the end of the workday, records should be locked in a desk, file cabinet, or special storage area.

2.   Records should not be left laying on top of the desk unattended for any length of time.

3.   Never take case records home! The "Horror Story" at the beginning of the chapter illustrates well the hazards involved. One administrator reported a ghastly incident to illustrate to a group of trainees why records should be kept at the office. He was taking some records home. He walked to his car and set the files on the roof while he got out his key and unlocked the door. It was only after he had driven some distance in a crowded urban neighborhood that he realized he had scattered pages of his records over several blocks.

4.   Try not to have a subject's entire case record on the desk when interviewing him. Its presence can make the client uneasy as he wonders, "What's written in there about me?" However, there are other hazards involved with leaving a case record exposed. One worker reported an incident in which a relative came to her office to learn the address of an AFDC mother so he could express his feelings of anger toward her. The worker got out the record to review the circumstances and kept it on her desk as she talked with the relative. During the interview she had to leave her office to take an outside phone call, and when she returned both relative and case record were gone. The record was never found.

*See the "Horror Story" at the beginning of this chapter for some good examples of carelessness!

185

5. There should be some kind of signout system so that staff can determine readily who has any given case record. Special forms can be completed and filed in place of the record to show that someone has checked it out on a certain date. When the record is returned to the file, the date is entered and the temporary form removed.

6. There should be careful monitoring of all Xerox copies of case-record materials. Many settings have their own reproduction equipment right in the main office, and improper copying could be done after hours by personnel with ulterior motives. This can be controlled in several ways. Staff could be required to obtain supervisory approval before copies are made; a form can be posted on the copy machine asking the user to describe the material being copied, the number of copies, and the purpose. Modern reproduction equipment can be ordered that is operated by a special "key" that must be plugged into the machine before it will operate. One individual can act as its custodian and see that it is kept under lock and key.

It seems hard to believe unauthorized copying can be a problem, yet it does happen. Most offenses simply cost the agency extra dollars as staff and students Xerox personal papers, or texts and journal articles for use in the classroom. However, confidentiality violations occur when case records are involved. Social workers are not the only offenders. Secretaries and others taking beginning social work courses at night have been known to Xerox pages of case records to take to class because they need "interesting" material to present. This may occur without anyone's knowledge, and the offender may not even see anything wrong with this activity.

7. Process recordings, tape recordings, and other verbatim material should be kept separate from the official, formal case record. These are used as teaching materials rather than documentation of daily case activity. They may contain so much explicit material they could prove troublesome for agency or client should they fall into the wrong hands. Thus, all the above precautions must be carefully observed. There must also be a system for erasing or destroying this material when it is no longer useful. In addition, other special precautions must be observed:*

(a) The client must give written permission for a tape (or audiovisual film) to be made.

(b) The client must give specific permission if the tape is to be used outside the agency in any way. He must be told who will see or hear it, and for what purpose, and be given the opportunity to refuse or to request that the tape be altered.

(c) The interviewer should give permission if a supervisor or other staff member wants to take the tape outside the agency.

(d) The client must be given the opportunity to request that his name and other identifying details be changed. This can be very difficult, especially with filmed material. A plan for preserving confidentiality regarding client identity would need to be worked out in advance of the filming, as the camera will need to film the entire interaction without showing any identifying features of the client.

8. All recorded materials must be considered as belonging to the agency. Students and staff should not be allowed to keep them when they leave the agency. Even process recordings must be returned to the supervisor and not be retained by the student. Paychecks for employees or final grades for students can be withheld, if necessary, until recorded material has been returned to the agency.

9. There must be a specific policy stating how long records will be kept before they are declared outdated, and then destroyed. Unfortunately, many settings have no such policy, and just keep accumulating records until they run out of space; only then do they go through their files and weed out the old material. Many governmental settings use centralized warehouses—individual settings or departments periodically

*See also Chapter 4.

send their records to these locations for long-term storage. For example, one Miami-based federal program sent its files to Atlanta, Georgia—over 600 miles away—for "indefinite storage." Another county program experienced a crisis when its local warehouse bulged at the seams with yellowing old records and could not accept any more. The various departments that relied on the warehouse for long-term storage were then left on their own to determine what to do with their old records, which were piling up at an unceasing rate.

It is not necessary to keep records forever. Social workers and pack rats have much in common when it comes to a tendency to hang onto every scrap of paper for life. Settings must determine the maximum length of time their records serve a useful purpose. This can be accomplished by answering several key questions:

(a) What period of time usually elapses between a case's being closed and reopened by the agency?

(b) How many staff actually *use* the old records, and how frequently are they used? Administrators tend to assume their use is much more frequent than it really is, and staff may exaggerate the frequency with which they refer to these records for fear of losing their security blanket.

(c) When old records are consulted, what are the reasons for referring to them?

(d) What kind of services are provided to most consumers? Are longitudinal records *really* necessary for effective service delivery?

(e) What risks are involved in keeping old record material around? For example, how frequently are records subpoenaed? When subpoena occurs, does it usually work to the client's/agency's best interest, or does the existence of a "subpoenable" record create problems? On the other hand, are the records from several years back necessary for the agency to protect itself or its clients in certain legal actions?

(f) How much clerical/social work time is expended in maintaining the old records—is it really worth it?

(g) How much physical space does the agency/setting have that provides *secure* (under lock and key) storage of old records?

(h) Do third-party payers and other funding sources require maintenance of old records?

(i) Do accountability, licensing, peer review, and other regulatory mechanisms require the existence of old records?

(j) Do local, state, or federal laws require that records be kept for a certain minimum period? If the agency is part of a larger agency network, does the parent body have record retention requirements that must be followed?

Many settings have examined these and other questions thoroughly, and decided to do away with virtually all old records. The biggest hurdle is usually that of weaning the social work staff from their dependency on the material. Once this has been accomplished, most administrators, staff, and clerical personnel hardly miss the old files, and find they can function quite effectively and efficiently without them.

10. There must be a secure method for destroying case records. Old case files cannot be dumped into the nearest wastebasket and carted off to the dump. All files must be rendered illegible and/or unidentifiable if outsiders must handle them to effect destruction. Pages can be torn or cut up into small pieces if only a few are involved. However, burning, shredding, and other larger-scale mechanical methods may have to be employed. If records must be taken some distance from the agency for destruction, they must be securely packaged and sealed in boxes so that no mishap can occur en route. Firms specializing in the destruction of sensitive record material can be found in large urban areas.

Audio and visual tapes need special attention. Since tape cassettes are reusable, magnetism is often employed to erase them. A secretary can perform this operation on her transcribing machine in small quantities, but an instantaneous process using special equipment must be utilized for larger quantities. Tapes should not be circulated for reuse until after they have been erased. This prevents the person who tapes from listening to whatever was recorded previously.

Physically safeguarding computerized data poses special problems. Most social work settings give this little thought. However, as the profession becomes more "progressive" and accumulates larger data bank systems, the security problems experienced by government and private industry will plague us as well.

Computerized data is usually a much briefer version of the complete case record. The kind of data recorded varies depending on purpose and the sophistication of the equipment. However, client-identifying data (name, address, age, and so on) are almost always included. Modern social service exchanges record contacts with various agencies and the nature of services provided. This information is then available to authorized users of the system. A few settings record their data by code, using identifying numbers instead of names, or a letter or numbering system to report various types of service provided. Other really large settings may use word-processing equipment that types data onto a screen and permanently records, on disks, everything that is typed into the machine. All this data can become massive in quantity, and yet is available with a few flicks of the finger to anyone who uses it. Thus confidentiality becomes a crucial issue.

The biggest problem with computerized data is security—keeping unauthorized users from gaining access. Full-time security guards are often employed to stand watch over the areas where the computer equipment is stored. However, some systems are keyed to give out information over the phone in response to an appropriate identification code. Such codes can leak out, rendering security guards useless. A few commonsense precautions must be taken to minimize illicit or unauthorized use of computerized data:

1. The client must know that personal data concerning him is being computerized.

2. His permission should be secured before information about him is fed into any data bank or computer.

3. The consumer must be aware of how the information is disseminated and have control over its use through an informed consent process.

4. The information must be maintained in a disguised manner to protect the identity of the individual.

5. The client must have full access to information pertaining to him that is stored in the system.

6. There must be a mechanism for allowing the consumer to correct, amend, or delete any data that is inaccurate or incomplete.

7. There must be a time- or purpose-limited definition of when the data is to be removed from the system so it does not remain there indefinitely after its original purpose has been accomplished.

8. Social work services should not be denied because a consumer refuses to permit identifying data to be fed into a computerized system.

9. There should be laws enacted specifically protecting the confidentiality of data bank information so that it is accorded the same, if not greater, protection than that provided for other forms of social service records.

CHAPTER 13

CONFIDENTIALITY: RELEASE OF INFORMATION FROM CASE RECORDS

Requests for confidential information in your case records will come from many sources. These individuals or programs can be quite insistent that they have a "need to know" or even a "right" to such confidential material. This information must never be released automatically—there must first be an evaluation to determine whether the information can be released, and in what manner. Agencies must provide policy and guidelines for staff and students that specify who can gain access to confidential record materials and under what conditions or circumstances.* The list of information seekers seems endless: internal agency staff, family or friends of the client, the client himself, the general public, other agencies or members of other disciplines, third-party payers (e.g., insurance companies), peer review, audit, and PSRO (professional standards review organizations), regulatory and licensing bodies, researchers, the news media, attorneys, the police, the courts, and so on. The response to each of these information seekers will vary somewhat, and the specialized techniques for handling each are too detailed to present here. However, there are a few basic principles that must be followed no matter who requests confidential information from social work records.

The client's permission must be obtained before information is disclosed in almost all situations.† Technically, the information recorded in a case record belongs to the client. His existence is what makes the data possible and most of what is recorded comes from the client directly or indirectly. Thus agency policies, federal laws, and court decisions repeatedly support the practice of allowing the client almost total control over the content of his record.

Therefore, the client is the one who must authorize all disclosures; his consent must be obtained before any information is released. Many settings have been doing this all along, but with abuses to the consumer's rights. It is not unusual for intake workers to have their new clients routinely sign a handful of blank consent forms "to make it easier for everyone." These forms authorize the agency to seek or release information about the client to almost everybody at any time under any circumstances. With the client's signature already obtained, the worker can fill in the blanks later when a need arises to disclose data. This system doesn't allow the client to maintain any meaningful control over the content of his case record. Thus many settings (and federal regulations) are requiring that the client's consent be "informed." "Informed consent" means the client knows what's going on when informa-

*For example, see *FSAA Position Paper on Confidentiality* (New York: Family Service Association of America, 1977). Several other national agencies have some type of policy governing confidentiality of records, while others have none. Small programs that are not part of a larger network are less apt to have any guidelines, while federally funded and administered programs coming under the jurisdiction of the Federal Privacy Act of 1974 have strict regulations calling for punishment by fine and/or imprisonment for violators. The NASW has come up with some guidelines pertaining to confidentiality; see, for example, "Policy on Information Utilization and Confidentiality" (Washington, D.C.: NASW, 1975). Unfortunately, they specifically address the problems of computerized data and do not offer specific or complete guidelines for agencies or practitioners in their daily practice.

†Common exceptions would be emergency situations when confidential information must be disclosed to save a person's life; when protection of minors is involved; exceptions to state statutes regarding the right of privileged communication; some incompetency and mental health proceedings; to prevent a crime from occurring (especially when someone is in danger); when required by law (i.e., release of information to the FBI in criminal investigations or reporting drug usage or gunshot wounds).

tion is released so he can determine intelligently if he wants it given out. Ten conditions must be met before consent can be considered "informed":

1. The consumer must be told that there is a desire or request to release certain data.

2. The consumer must understand exactly what information is to be disclosed. He cannot decide intelligently if he wants it revealed unless he knows exactly what material is in question.

3. In order for the consumer to know what is to be released, he should actually see the material and/or have it read to him and explained in terms he can understand.

4. The consumer must be told exactly to whom the information is being released—name, position, and affiliation.

5. The client must be told why the information is being requested and exactly how it will be used by the receiving party.

6. There must be a way for the consumer to correct or amend the information under discussion to assure its accuracy and completeness before it is released.

7. The consumer must understand whether or not the receiving party has the right to pass the information on to a third party. The consumer must have the right to specify that this not be done without his knowledge and written consent.

8. The consumer should be fully informed of any repercussions that might occur should he grant permission for the disclosure or not give permission.

9. The consumer should be advised that his consent for release of information is time limited and revocable. He should be advised how he can withdraw his consent and be given periodic opportunities for doing so.

10. The consumer's consent for release of information must be in writing on a "Consent for Release of Information" form.

The "Consent for Release of Information" form must be used properly. All of the above points should be discussed with the client before he signs the form to ensure that he is fully aware of his rights and is familiar with the material being disclosed. Copies of the consent form should be provided to the consumer, the agency or worker who secured his signature, and the party to whom the information is being disclosed. Consent forms cannot be filed away and forgotten. A new form must be signed whenever: (1) a disclosure of any kind is to be made; (2) there is a change in the party to whom the data is being released *or* additional information is sought by the same party; (3) a consent form on file expires; and (4) a previously signed consent form is revoked by the consumer and a new one is desired. There must be no blank spaces on the consent form when it is presented to the client for his signature, and it should be made available to him (or read to him) in his native language. The form itself should contain the following:

1. The agency/department/practitioner seeking the consumer's signature.

2. The date the form is signed.

3. The exact name, address, position, and related identifying data regarding the party to whom the disclosure will be made.

4. Description of the exact material to be released.

5. The purpose for the disclosure—why the receiving agency wants it and/or how the receiving party will be using the information.

6. Limitations imposed upon the receiving party as to how it may use the material, whether it can release it to third parties, and under what conditions, if any.

7. A statement indicating the period of time the signed consent form will be valid. An expiration date should be given that corresponds with the estimated time when the transfer of information will be completed.

8. A statement that conditions 1–10 (the discussion prior to requesting client's signature) have been reviewed.

9. A place for the client's signature.

10. An indication that carbon copies are going to the client, the agency file, and/or the party to whom information is being disclosed (or from whom it was requested).

Thus, releasing confidential information about clients is a formal process that cannot be conducted via an informal telephone call. The standard response to such inquiries should be, "I'm sorry, but we cannot release that information unless we have the client's written permission." In some situations it could violate the client's privacy rights even to admit that he is a client. The requesting party should then get a proper "Consent for Release of Information" form signed by the client, and submit it to you along with a formal request for the data. Make certain the other party's form is not a "blanket consent" that does not meet your requirements. If necessary, send the requesting party a copy of your release form to have the consumer sign.

Extra caution is needed when dealing with attorneys who ask for confidential information. They may phone or visit you in person. Their manner is usually very impressive and can send the nervous worker on a scramble to provide the information desired. Release of information to attorneys is no different from release to anyone else—the client's permission must be obtained. Lawyers know this. If they really want the data, they can go to court and get a subpoena ordering you to produce it. But this is a bother, costs money, and is time consuming. If a social worker can be caught off guard and information obtained through an informal contact, the attorney's job is much easier. This approach is unethical and frowned upon by conscientious attorneys; unfortunately, it sometimes works. The standard reply should be, as always, "I'm sorry, but I cannot release that information without my client's written consent." Even to admit that the individual is a client can be a violation of his confidentiality rights, so a better response might be, "I'm sorry, I cannot give you that information. If you will have Mr. Jones sign a consent form releasing the information you request, I'll check and see if he is known to our agency and talk with you further." Supervisory staff should be notified when an attorney seeks information, in case it should develop into a subpoena or court appearance.

SUBPOENAS

A subpoena is an impressive-looking paper sent to you by a messenger of the court. It tells you to bring yourself and/or your case records to a court appearance at a specific date, time, and place. It should state what information is needed, and give the name of the defendant (the person who is being accused or grieved against) and the plaintiff (the one bringing the charges or legal action). It spells out some rather frightening consequences for failure to comply with the subpoena. As a result, most social workers push aside normal duties in a frenzied effort to comply with the subpoena.

Subpoenas are not the fearsome documents most social workers think they are. They are important and cannot be ignored, but they can be challenged. It is not necessary to respond by automatically providing whatever data the subpoena requests. There are several ways to respond: (1) provide the data without question; (2) challenge the validity or relevancy of the subpoena or the information it requests; (3) contest it based on the right of privileged communication, other legal regulations, or precedences set by the courts through decisions rendered in similar situations. Obviously, the agency attorney must be involved, especially if a practitioner feels strongly that the information should not be produced. To contest the subpoena, it is necessary to appear in court or at a hearing at which the agency attorney will present his arguments for maintaining confidentiality. There have been cases in which the courts have ruled that the information need not be disclosed, and confidentiality was therefore maintained.* In many cases, however, the court has ruled that the information must be produced. This is a "court order." The agency/practitioner then has no choice but to comply under penalty of law, unless he chooses to appeal the ruling to a higher court.† Thus a subpoena is a serious attempt to obtain confidential information. In many instances it would be in the client's best interest to release the data requested, and disclosure occurs rather readily. However, the person who receives the subpoena must think "Should the information be released? Is this one of those situations where it should be contested?" before responding automatically.

THE RIGHT OF PRIVILEGED COMMUNICATION

Many social workers don't know what this is. Either they assume naively that all records must be confidential and therefore safe from the court, or they fail to realize that privileged communication statutes (laws) in their state make it legally possible for them to keep certain information from the courts in some situations.

Confidentiality as a concept is just that—a professional ethic that recognizes the sensitive nature of much of the information we gather and record about clients. The professional organization for social workers—the National Association of Social Workers—has issued some policy statements to this effect. However, all this provides no *legal* protection. The courts often ignore a helping profession's allegiance to the need to preserve confidentiality, and order the material disclosed in court based on various legal technicalities.

Privileged communication refers to the legal right of a client to forbid his social worker from disclosing confidential information in court. This is a right granted by state law. Psychiatrists, physicians, psychologists, accountants, clergymen, and various other professional groups have this coverage in some states. Social workers have only recently begun to press for the right of privileged communication, i.e., to have communications between them and their clients declared "privileged" so they don't have to be revealed in court if such is the client's wish. As of June 1979, fourteen states had granted this privileged communication coverage to social worker–client communications.‡ Practitioners and students practicing in these states must familiarize themselves with these laws. Privileged communication statutes vary from state to state, and the subject is a highly complex one. The statutes do not provide the absolute guarantee of confidentiality that many practitioners hope for; most contain many exceptions permitting or even requiring that confidential information be disclosed in certain circumstances.

Furthermore, in specific instances courts may overrule privileged communication statutes and order that the information be released due to a technicality in the law.** As a result, some authorities are beginning to question the value of privileged communication statutes for helping professionals and are arguing that the clamor to get this coverage is really a status game. They maintain that other approaches and legal arguments are actually much more effective in preventing disclosures.†† Thus, privileged communication statutes provide a very specific and often limited form of

---

*See Suanna J. Wilson, *Confidentiality in Social Work: Issues and Principles* (New York: Free Press, 1978), for case examples and further details.

†Several recent articles give helpful hints on how to respond to subpoenas. See Maurice Grossman, "The Psychiatrist and the Subpoena," *Bulletin of the American Academy of Psychiatry and Law* 1, no. 4 (December 1974): 245–53; Barton E. Bernstein, "The Social Worker as a Courtroom Witness," *Social Casework Journal* 56, no. 9 (November 1975): 521–25; and Barton E. Bernstein, "The Social Worker as an Expert Witness," *Social Casework* 7, no. 7 (July 1977): 412–17.

‡California, New York, Illinois, Maine, Michigan, Louisiana, Kansas, Kentucky, Arkansas, South Dakota, Colorado, Idaho, Delaware, Massachussetts. Virginia has attempted to obtain privileged communication for its social workers by regulation—incorporating a statement in its state law that it would be unethical for a social worker to disclose confidential information except under certain circumstances (the exceptions common to privileged communication statutes). However, since this is not an actual privileged communication statute, there is some question whether this regulation will hold up when tested in court.

**See Wilson, *Confidentiality in Social Work,* for a detailed discussion of these exceptions and examples of court cases involving social workers and other helping professionals.

††For example, see the writings of Ralph Slovenko in numerous psychiatric and legal journals.

protection, for a select group of licensed social workers practicing in a few states, against court-ordered disclosure of confidential case-record material.

FEDERAL PRIVACY ACT OF 1974*

This federal legislation came about as a result of increasing concern over the need to protect the privacy rights of citizens. At present† this law affects only federally funded/administered programs. However, hearings before the Federal Privacy Protection Study Commission during 1977 have produced recommendations that the provisions be extended to certain portions of the private sector as well, and bills already have been introduced in Congress to this effect.‡ Many social workers already practice or do their field placements in settings required to abide by Privacy Act regulations; the Social Security Administration (which includes SSI) and the Veterans Administration are two of the largest. As some version of these regulations may soon apply to other settings as well, a brief review of the major provisions of this act is included here. The requirements it sets forth require consumer access to records, prescribe guidelines for physically safeguarding records, regulate the release of information from consumer records, and affect how information is gathered and entered into the record.

The synopsis that follows is brief and covers only the highlights of the Federal Privacy Act. Persons practicing in settings coming under these regulations should consult supervisory and administrative staff for more detailed guidance and interpretations of the act.

1. Clients can find out what records are being maintained on them, and how they are used and disseminated by the agency.

2. Clients can prohibit these records that are to be used for a particular purpose from being used for any other purpose without giving written consent.

3. A client can have access to his record and bring with him a person of his choosing.

4. A client can have copies made of any or all of his records, though the agency may charge for this service.

5. A client can correct or amend his record as he feels necessary to render it complete and accurate.

6. There are some exceptions wherein the individual's written consent for release of information is not required:

    (a) When information is being released or exchanged among employees in the agency.

    (b) When data is being conveyed to researchers in disguised form.

    (c) When the information is being released to another governmental agency for law-enforcement activity.

    (d) In emergency situations to protect the health and safety of an individual. However, notice of the disclosure must be sent to the last known address of the individual.

    (e) When there is a court order.

---

*Public Law 93-579.

†November 1979.

‡See *Final Recommendations of the Privacy Protection Study Commission as Contained in the Final Report. A Summarized Version of Personal Privacy in an Information Society: The Report of the Privacy Protection Study Commission* (Washington: Government Printing Office, 1977). These recommendations should be acted upon during 1980 or 1981, and interested readers should watch the *Federal Register* for reports of forthcoming legislation or regulations. This massive 600-page report contains special sections of recommendations pertaining to governmental financial assistance programs, private employers (which would certainly include employers of social workers), medical records, and others.

(f) There are eleven other exceptions.

7. Agencies must keep the following information when they release data from their records:

(a) The date of the disclosure.

(b) The nature and purpose of the disclosure.

(c) The name and address of the person or agency to whom disclosure was made.

(d) This information must be kept for at least five years *or* the life of the record, whichever is longer.

(e) The above information must be available to the individual whose record is involved.

8. The agency keeps notes of all amendments or corrections made by the individual to his record. If information involved has been disclosed to someone prior to the addition of the corrections or amendments, the agency must inform all persons to whom the disclosure was made of the additions or corrections.

9. The client has the right to correct or amend his record, in which event:

(a) The agency must respond in writing within ten days after receiving written request for such change.

(b) The agency must either make the corrections or inform the individual that it refuses to honor the request. It must state the reason for the refusal, procedures for the individual to request a review of the agency's decision, and the name and address of the head of the agency.

10. If the individual disagrees with the agency's decision to refuse to amend or correct his record, the agency has thirty days from the date the individual requests a review of the decision to complete the review and make its decision.

11. When a disclosure is made regarding information in a record over which there has been a dispute, details surrounding the dispute, the individual's request, and agency's decision must be released along with the information itself.

12. Agencies must follow certain guidelines in gathering material for their records. The information must be relevant and necessary to agency purposes and must be collected as much as possible directly from the client himself.

13. The agency must set specific policies regarding the handling of records and safeguarding of confidentiality.

14. There are situations where an agency does not have to disclose records and information to the individual, such as:

(a) Information that would reveal the identity of a source that gave the data under promise of secrecy.

(b) If the information was gathered prior to a date specified in the Privacy Act.

THE EFFECT OF CONSUMER ACCESS ON SOCIAL WORK RECORDING

It used to be assumed in social work practice that the record was as confidential from the client as from everyone else. The record was considered the private property of the agency. However, the contemporary interpretation that the information in the record belongs to the client, along with increasing concern for consumer rights and implementation of the concept of "informed consent," mandate some form of client access. Furthermore, the Federal Privacy Act requires the right of consumer access to records; NASW guidelines recommend this practice; and it is being implemented by a growing number of social work settings. There are many arguments both for and against consumer access to social work records, and they will not be presented here.* Obviously, if clients don't see their records, there is little need to alter the recording practices our profession has been using for years. On the other hand, it appears that in the future social work consumers will have access to their records in most agencies. Thus let us assume that clients can see their records. How would this affect the way we record and maintain records?

How would your client react if he could read right now everything you've written about him in the past six months? What would he find in his record? There must be two main concerns: (1) will the recording affect the client adversely; and (2) what are the legal implications for the agency and client of recording certain data that is subsequently shared with the client?

Does the record contain unprofessional, judgmental remarks that insult the client's dignity as a human being? A reading of his record may tell him rather quickly how you really feel about him. Perhaps the record contains diagnostic information, written by you or obtained from other sources, that could be upsetting to the client. Maybe the entries contain material that really shouldn't be set down in a written record. If the record goes back a number of years, there may be unfortunate recording done by previous staff who weren't following the guidelines in use today. Must the client see that, too?

Such questions can provoke much anxiety. Old record material may have to be "cleaned up" before it is shared; however, federal law may prohibit this activity in some settings. If the Privacy Act concepts are followed, there can be no secret records. Old record material must either be shared or destroyed. If it's really poor, destruction may be the only answer. Similarly, confidential reports received from outside agencies before an open-record policy was inaugurated may have to be destroyed if they cannot be shared with the consumer without violating the confidentiality promised to the person or program who sent the material. Sensitive diagnostic material can be recorded in more general terms without giving every minute detail and impression; however, in some interdisciplinary settings, more detail may be required in order to fulfill some of the purposes of recording outlined in Chapter 2.

Perhaps the social work profession is putting the cart before the horse. We generate all kinds of information we feel the client shouldn't know about and then worry about how to keep it from him, how to record it, or how to share it without upsetting him. If we were more open with clients in our daily working relationships, there would be less concern over client reaction to seeing case records. The effective counselor will involve the client in the therapeutic process and inform him of what he's doing and why. Goals and ways of determining when the treatment goals have been accomplished are decided with the client. Diagnostic impressions are shared, at an appropriate time, to facilitate growth. Thus the consumer is a true participant, rather than a passive partner, in the social work treatment relationship. The case record that results from this kind of treatment process would contain little that is not already known to the client. If sensitive material must be recorded that has not yet been shared for some reason, the worker might interpret it verbally to the client during a conference rather than allow the client to see it himself. Another alternative would be to share the information with the client's representative (an attorney, doctor, or even another social worker) rather than with him directly. If the right of access exists and the client exercises his right frequently (which is rare), it may be necessary to delay recording certain data until it can be shared with the consumer therapeutically.

There is much fear that the client will disagree with what has been put in his record or become angry at what he reads. Again, a more open treatment relationship would help prevent such complications. However, consumers may take issue with diagnostic labels that they feel carry a negative connotation, and bring suit for libel or slander (or defamation of character) if sufficiently angry. Consumers have the right to bring suit over anything they like—no matter how absurd the charges. Social workers will

---

*See Wilson, *Confidentiality in Social Work.*

not be found guilty of defaming their clients through libel or slander unless the consumer can prove that the statements are false or malicious, and harm him in some way. Thus accurate, professionally stated diagnostic impressions are fully acceptable legally, even though your client may not like what he reads. However, the recorder should make certain that other recorded entries support his diagnosis in case he is called upon to defend his conclusions. If he has chosen to skimp on recording in an effort to avoid confidentiality and legal problems, he could easily find himself in worse trouble because the record lacks sufficient data for him to defend himself in court!

Consumer access to records makes it possible for the client to give fully informed consent when asked for permission to disclose material from his record. Otherwise, he can not know exactly what material is being released, and will have no opportunity to correct or amend it to ensure its accuracy before it is passed on to someone outside the agency. There has already been one lawsuit won by a client over this issue.* An individual who had been a patient in a state mental hospital asked to receive a copy of his most recent clinical summary prepared by hospital staff. When a lower court denied his request, he appealed, and a higher court ruled that "Where the legislature, in its wisdom, placed with the patient the right to designate a person and agency, named in the statute, who may have access to the record of his mental condition, it followed that, in order to properly exercise that right, the legislature clearly intended that the patient *have access to the record in order to determine whether and to whom he wished the report to be released*" (emphasis added).†

The ruling went on to state that "any ambiguity in statute as to whether report of his mental condition should be released to patient should be resolved in favor of the patient."‡ Thus a precedent has been set, and we can predict that more clients will use this argument, and be supported by the courts, in their efforts to gain access to their records and exercise control over disclosures from them.

Social work recording in records that are open to the consumer will certainly be written with less technical jargon. If the worker knows he's going to have to explain all the technical terms to his client, he will tend to write more clearly and thus make the sharing process easier for himself and his client. Records will become more accurate as clients challenge and question the data found in them, especially information that has been obtained third hand. Recorders will tend to use the client more as their primary source of information, rather than collecting information behind his back and worrying about how he might react to it.

The following recommendations regarding consumer access are proposed:

1. Consumers should have right of access to social work record materials.

2. The consumer who seeks access must realize that he may find some material upsetting, and should be prepared to assume some responsibility for the repercussions. Situations that constitute a valid complaint against the professional must be identified and differentiated from those recorded entries for which the professional cannot be held liable. These distinctions should be made known to the consumer and incorporated into any policies granting consumer access to confidential records.

3. There must be a process whereby certain information can be kept from the consumer when necessary. Student process recordings, preliminary or tentative diagnostic assessments, and similar data must sometimes be put into writing, especially by students, yet may not be "sharable."

4. If information is being kept from the consumer, he must be advised that this is occurring. The general nature of the material should be shared. If its existence should prove highly upsetting or anxiety provoking to the consumer to the point that his treatment is hampered, the material will have to be destroyed.

---

* *Sullivan* v. *State of Florida.* 352 Southern Reporter, 2d 1212 (Fla. District Court of Appeal, November 1977).
†Ibid.
‡Ibid.

5. When information is being shared with a consumer, the social worker who provided the services must be present to answer any questions, deal with anxieties, if any, and generally help the consumer digest what he is reading or hearing. If the social worker who delivered services and made the recording cannot be present personally, the responsibility should be delegated to another social worker who is qualified to provide similar treatment.

6. If there is concern regarding consumer reaction to selected material, a mechanism can be developed for sharing such information with the client's representative, rather than disclosing it to him directly. However, the types of information fitting this definition must be clearly specified in the policy, and preventive measures taken to ensure that all record material does not get assigned to this category.

7. The current trend toward doing away with all records should be reversed. Record-keeping practices must be altered rather than abolished. Entries in formal records should be made with the idea that "If they are written, they will be shared."

8. More open sharing with consumers of social work services regarding the treatment process and professional assessment must take place during the therapeutic process itself. This practice would decrease the secrecy of recordings, and client access would not be as threatening to the professional or the consumer.

9. Is it possible to provide effective and timely social work services if consumers are granted full access to our records? Is it possible to build in so many safeguards to protect "the poor, innocent, helpless, ignorant client" that he could quietly decompensate, in complete privacy, because a serious psychosocial or financial problem could not be tended to in a timely fashion? Instead of getting caught up in the issue of deciding "which is more important—consumer rights or the ability of a service delivery system to meet consumer needs," the social work profession needs to examine itself closely and make necessary internal changes so that both parties can be accommodated.

Perhaps the best guideline is this suggestion: pretend that your client is sitting beside you reading everything as you write in his record. Consider consciously what should and should not be documented, and figure out the most effective way of wording what has to be said. Be aware of things that might upset the consumer, but that must be recorded, and be prepared to deal with your client's reaction.

MATERIAL THAT DOESN'T BELONG IN BLACK AND WHITE

Regardless of the type of recording used, there are certain things that simply do not belong in black and white in any case record. Inappropriate entries could be used against the client if the record were subpoenaed. The agency or its staff could find themselves facing legal action and wishing that something that is in the record weren't there. The client may react adversely to inappropriate recording, should he gain access to his file. Thus the following kinds of information usually are not recorded in a case record.

Information regarding a client's political, religious, or other personal views does not belong in social work recording unless it has some direct and important bearing on the treatment process. Such bearing occurs rather rarely.

Intimate, personal details that have little or no relevance to the helping process should be omitted as well. Extreme details about a physical illness are usually not recorded. Obviously, social workers are not trained to diagnose or speculate regarding their client's physical ailments, but consider also the unfortunate reader who must wade through a lengthy description of a physical problem that may have been all right to listen to verbally but becomes offensive when expressed in writing. For example:

Mrs. Menton told me the doctor said she had maggots in her wound and she planned to go to the doctor this afternoon for minor surgery. She showed me her leg. The spot was horrible looking. I could see the maggots crawling around inside the wound, mixed with blood and pus. The smell was nauseating.

> Simply noting that the client had a wound with maggots would have been adequate—the explanatory details could have been omitted. A more palatable version of this entry might appear as follows:

Mrs. Menton told me the doctor said she had magots in her wound and she planned to go to the doctor this afternoon for minor surgery. The wound was most unpleasant to look at and there was also an offensive odor. It is surprising that Mrs. Menton would ignore this problem until it reached this stage.

> "Gossipy" information given the worker about other clients does not belong in a case record. It is not unusual for persons receiving the services of a large agency to know one another and occasionally to try to convince the worker that "I should get more money than that Mr. Smith down the street who just drinks up all his welfare check," or to explain helpfully that "You oughta see what goes on in Mrs. X's house!" The beginning worker or student often includes this kind of hearsay remark along with the more relevant material in his eagerness to achieve totally accurate and complete recording.
>
> Problems and frustrations in contacting and relating to social workers, agencies, and members of other disciplines do not belong in writing. The case record must not become a battleground for airing all the worker's frustrations as he experiences difficulties or personality clashes and delays in attempting to provide service to someone. The worker must also refrain from putting into writing his criticisms of the operation of his own agency's service delivery system. The case record is not the place to document these problems. They are more effectively handled by bringing them to the attention of supervisory or administrative staff so that proper evaluation and action can be taken. When staff and students enter such problems into case records, it is usually an indication that the practitioner became emotional over the incident and is using his recording as an inappropriate outlet.
>
> If a genuinely unpleasant incident has occurred, what is usually most important, and most appropriate to record, is the effect upon the consumer. Consider the following example:

Mrs. Franklin told me she had once again failed to receive her Social Security check and was afraid it had been sent to an incorrect address and gotten lost, as happened last month. I called the S.S. office and after ½ hour of dialing, finally got through the busy signal. Mr. Fuentes answered and explained it wasn't his case, and after getting the runaround between five different people, I asked to speak to the supervisor and told her that it was costing our agency a small fortune because I waste all of my time trying to get through their fouled-up bureaucratic system.

> This rather unpleasant experience could have been better said as:

Mrs. Franklin's Social Security check failed to come again this month. I had some difficulty getting through to the proper person in the Social Security office and finally had to speak to a supervisory person, Mrs. Henry. I can understand now why my client feels so helplessly dependent upon the system.

> Another example would be the following entry, written by a busy social worker assigned to the emergency room of a hospital:

Mr. Jones showed up again today in the ER. I had sent him to the XYZ Boarding Home yesterday and they had agreed to take him. Today they sent him back in with a note saying they feel he needs to be in a nursing home. I don't know how many times I've explained to them that this emergency room is <u>not</u> a hotel for people awaiting nursing home placement. I called Harry Bowden at the

Boarding Home and explained this once more and after some grumbling, he finally agreed to take Mr. Jones back until we could arrange for nursing home placement.

One wonders how Mr. Jones would feel if he were to exercise his right to see this medical record! A better way of describing this activity might have been:

Mr. Jones was sent to the XYZ Boarding Home on 3-18-73. On 3-19-73 the Home returned him to the ER, expressing their feeling that he needed to be in a nursing home. Following a contact with Mr. Bowden at the Boarding Home, arrangements were made for patient to return there until we can arrange placement elsewhere.

Finally, consider the following entry, which takes an internal staff member to task:

Jerry told me he had gone to the intake office and they had told him he could be seen only during the daytime. I explained that that just isn't true. Charlotte has told clients that before and just because she doesn't want to work nights doesn't mean the rest of us aren't willing to extend ourselves to serve our clients. I had to get the supervisor to join us before Jerry would believe me that we really could see him at night.

A proper entry might read:

Jerry was concerned whether or not he could be seen at night and after some discussion, this arrangement was worked out.

It would be hoped that this worker would share his other frustrations with his supervisor so that action could be taken to prevent recurrence of a similar incident in the future.

Details that might be misinterpreted or misused by others in the agency having formal or informal access to the case record should not be recorded. This precaution can be important in multidisciplinary settings where nonprofessionals as well as skilled practitioners may be handling the record.

Highly incriminating information that could be used against the client is usually omitted from social work recordings. If such records were to be subpoenaed by the court, this kind of information could prove quite damaging to the consumer. Criminal activity, drug abuse, fraudulent behaviors, and similar activities have to be examined and dealt with in some way, but do not necessarily have to be described in detail in a case record. Staff working in a criminal justice setting may focus their entire services on the fact that the client has broken a law. Effective protection of minors (i.e., child abuse) may require documentation of problematic or illegal actions. Settings involved with this kind of situation usually provide specialized recording guidelines. Their case records may or may not receive additional legal protection to prevent courts from securing access to documented incriminating activities.

Material that could be damaging to the client, should he exercise his right to read his record, is often omitted or altered.

Material that might be incriminating to the agency, should the client bring a suit for any reason, should not be recorded. For example, a consumer may tell a medical social worker that "Dr. Jones gave me the wrong medicine last night and that's why I got so sick," or "The nurse told me that the nurse's aide didn't notice that the oxygen had run out and that's how my child got brain-damaged." Such incidents must be brought to the attention of the appropriate physician or administrator, but should not necessarily be described in black and white in a client's record.

The fact that an incident report has been filed should not be mentioned in the formal record. Incident reports, usually submitted to administrative, legal, or risk-management personnel, document irregularities in treatment, usually in inpatient medical and psychiatric settings. These reports explain that the patient fell out of bed, received the wrong medication, and so on. The incident itself is usually mentioned in the formal record only as a thing that happened to the patient, because it might have ramifications for treatment. For example, if a patient sustained an injury from falling out of bed, he will need to be treated for this, and his medical record must reflect the diagnosis and treatment. However, the fact that his falling out of bed was an irregularity, the result of carelessness on the part of staff, or generated an incident report, is usually not recorded. This is the recommended policy of many settings, and seems designed to protect the institution more than the patient. The rationale for this approach is that if an attorney should subpoena the official record for a routine matter, he would not discover automatically that an incident report exists or an irregularity in treatment occurred. However, once the attorney discovers that this information exists, he can then specifically subpoena the incident report, which is filed in a location separate from the official chart. For better or for worse, this method of documentation also can prevent patients who gain access to their records from learning that there was an irregularity in their treatment. They would not ask to see copies of the incident reports if they did not know such reports existed.

A client may inform a social worker that he feels an irregularity has occurred in his treatment. He may be quite critical of the care he is receiving and very specific in voicing his concerns or complaints. Such statements can be recorded, but should be labeled clearly as coming from the client, e.g., "Mrs. Smith told me that. . . ." The worker may or may not agree with the client that an irregularity has occurred. If not, this opinion can certainly be included in the record as part of his or her professional assessment. However, if in agreement with the client, the worker's feelings and concerns should be expressed through proper administrative channels rather than through record entries.

Patients are sometimes admitted to inpatient facilities under aliases (AKA—also known as), or treated under false names as outpatients. This practice occurs most frequently with well-known individuals who could suffer considerable personal, financial, or career damage should it become known that they are receiving treatment from a psychiatric facility. Similarly, a famous person may need privacy and protection from the curious public while receiving routine medical treatment. On the other hand, some victims of crimes need protection so their attacker (who may even be a relative) cannot find them and attempt further harm. An individual having an abortion, an illigitimate child, or undergoing surgery for transsexual changes may need the protection of anonymity. Thus, staff making entries in such records must be extremely careful not to slip and refer to the person by his or her correct name. Some facilities take elaborate precautions to prevent even treatment staff from learning the true identity of the client. Unfortunately, this protection can contain dangerous loopholes if admitting, billing, and all nontreatment departments are not also notified of the special confidentiality requirements dictated by administration in behalf of a particular client.

If a staff member is being treated at the facility in which he or she is employed, treating personnel must ensure that only those professionals directly involved in treatment can gain access to the record. The employee's supervisor, professional colleagues (who might otherwise have access to any record they desire), and others should not have access to the employee's private data. If ironclad and written safeguards do not exist to guarantee this protection, it may be necessary to "sanitize" all material recorded in the treatment record, so that someone gaining access who has no business reading the record will not be able to learn intimate, personal, or highly sensitive information. The employee/client might be involved in reviewing and determining just what should go in his record if he or she is concerned about this type of confidentiality violation.

Some clients will reveal past or current criminal activity. This may or may not need to be documented in the record, depending on the circumstances. The worker must give conscious thought to this matter, and not just record the information automatically. It may be in the best interests of the client, the agency, and the worker not to record the controversial information. On the other hand, failure to do so could place the agency and the worker in a precarious legal position. This dilemma is too complex to discuss fully here, and workers encountering this situation are encouraged to research it further and consult their attorney.*

---

*See Wilson, *Confidentiality in Social Work*, pp. 115–24 for further discussion on issues the worker must consider when a client admits to past, current, or intended criminal activity.

Some settings may encourage social work staff to refrain from recording factual or diagnostic information that could not be supported in court. Phrases such as "allegedly," "seems to," "appears to be," "may be," or "client says" may be preferred to stating directly "this is the way it is." Diagnostic phrases that the treating professional is qualified to use based on his training are generally acceptable; however, the record should support the diagnostic labels that are being applied.

Finally, the fact that some bit of sensitive data has been omitted from the record should *not* be recorded. To mention in the record that certain data is missing is an open invitation to any reader to pursue the matter and find out what has been excluded. This would negate the entire purpose of omitting the data in the first place. However, this can leave the recorder in a quandary. He may fear supervisory criticism if his record appears incomplete, and want to defend himself by mentioning in the record that he has found it necessary to omit certain information. Situations of this kind should be brought to the supervisor's attention, especially if they deviate from the routine practice or experience of the setting. The worker can then defend himself, if necessary, through verbal discussions with his superior or through separate incident reports.

PRESERVING CONFIDENTIALITY OF MATERIAL BROUGHT FROM FIELD TO CLASSROOM

Most schools of social work ask their students to bring "live" case examples from their field placement experience into the classroom at various points during their training. Casework faculty may ask for diagnostic analyses of case dynamics, a social history, or illustration of a certain type of behavior or interviewing technique. Assignments may call for bringing process recordings, summaries, tape recordings, or other materials into the classroom. Unfortunately, many schools provide limited guidance on how to preserve the confidentiality of all this material that is being taken out of the agency setting. If fact, unbeknown to most students, some faculty who have had no direct client contact in years rely on student-produced case examples to give them live cases to work with in future classes, or to use as examples in papers they are authoring. Thus the material may receive a rather wide distribution over an extended period of time, and appropriate precautions must be taken to preserve confidentiality. The guidelines presented here should be followed along with any provided by the school. If the ideas presented here, the confidentiality requirements presented by the school, and those of the agency do not agree, select the ones that are *strictest* and follow them.

1. All names of clients, relatives, and significant others mentioned by name in a case record or recording must be altered. Fake names or incorrect initials can be used. If names are changed rather than simply erased or obliterated, a notation should appear clearly indicating that this has been done.

2. If the interview or case material concerns a highly unusual or much-publicized situation that could be identified easily even after the client's name has been changed, the nature of the primary diagnosis or presenting problem, proper nouns, and certain identifying information may also need alteration. True, this may affect the reality of the situation and make it more difficult for the student to present adequately what really happened, but if it comes to a choice between presenting accurate recordings in the classroom and preserving the privacy and confidentiality of the consumers served, the client's needs *must* take priority.

3. Material of a highly confidential or incriminating nature should not be taken into the classroom at all. If a student is not certain whether his recording fits into this category, he should consult his field instructor for guidance.

4. Process recordings are the property of the agency and should not be copied or retained by the student. They should be turned in to the student's field instructor

when their usefulness has ended or at the termination of field placement and should be stored separately from the official case record.

5. All material that students wish to take into the classroom should be reviewed first by the field instructor to ensure that proper measures have been taken to preserve confidentiality.

6. Tape- and videorecorded material cannot be adequately disguised to preserve confidentiality. Thus the client's permission must be secured before a student takes it into the classroom. Furthermore, certain technical steps should be taken to conceal identity even when the client has given permission for use of the material. If the recorded interview involves persons other than the primary client—family members, other students, or agency staff—it may be necessary to obtain their permission as well for the material to be taken into the classroom. Students should seek specific direction from their supervisor.

WHY HAVE CASE RECORDS AT ALL?

If the existence of social work recording and case records creates all these confidentiality problems, why not do away with records altogether? Chapters 1 and 2 have already presented some strong practical arguments in favor of case records. However, there are some legal ramifications as well. The agency may need its record to support a diagnostic label being challenged by the consumer as malicious or untrue. Child-abuse and custody cases, incompetency and guardianship, and other social-legal problems may require documentation, over a period of time, of the existence of certain behaviors, problems, or treatment approaches to bring about a desired action in the best interests of the client.

If a worker is challenging a subpoena and trying to convince the court that the confidential data it requests shouldn't be disclosed, he may need his previous record material to help him justify and substantiate his argument that certain material isn't relevant. Attorneys and judges are also wise to the game of "I don't keep records and don't remember anything about my client," and will question the effectiveness of any helping professional who claims he treats people, but can't remember anything about them. Thus, doing away with records may appear to be the answer to the novice practitioner or student who has not seriously studied and researched the nature of case records.

Since "no records" is obviously not the answer, we must concentrate instead on the way in which we gather data, the nature of our relationship with the people we serve (openness versus secrecy), and the way in which we maintain and safeguard records. If proper attention is given to these areas, social workers will be functioning on a preventive level, thus avoiding many of the supposed nightmares that advocates of doing away with all records seem to envision.

SELF-INSTRUCTIONAL EXERCISES

CHAPTER 14

EXERCISE 1 Rewriting a poorly written entry

In the following entry, made by a social worker in a case record, there are some real problems of grammar, spelling, and sentence structure. The setting is a residential treatment center for emotionally disturbed children. Your task:

1. Rewrite the worker's entry, using a summary style.

2. Do not follow any outlines. Make up suitable headings only if you feel they are needed.

3. Correct errors in grammar, spelling, and sentence structure.

4. Make the new entry clear, concise, and well organized.

The exercise should take no more than thirty to forty-five minutes.

4-18-77

The mother was seen in the office today by me again. It was a result of my calling her up yesterday that she showed up. Her dress was very simple, not what I espected at all. She seem ambivalent about coming to see me—didn't know what I was going to do I guess. Most of the time we talked about Charlie. He keeps running away from home. She can't understand this behavior. Last time the police aprehended him he was on the cornar of 20th and Bylor stret, about 8 miles from the center. Hitchiking was how he had to have got there the way Mrs. Milton figured it. I'm not so sure because with his low IQ (78) I guess he would have gotten a bus and just kept riding till he decide he want to get off. Then maybe from here somebody gave him a ride. With Mr. Milton working now things are much better at home for Mrs. M. Her other kids are having lots of prob-lems. Charlie went to the Dr. yesterday and the dr. told him he has coranary insuficency and she's real worried about him expecially seeing that he eats so poorly and just does'nt do like she asks him too and runs off and is gone for hours at a time so she just doesn't know where he's at or what he's doing or if he's alright or even when he'll come back home if at all. Anyway, she's real worried. About Charlie being in the high security area of our home was explained and Mrs. M. apreciate why the action was necessary. She's glad we have him controled now so she don't have to worry about him anymore. The fact she could visit him in one week when he's back in the regular building was all explained and she thought she'd come see him next tuesday. She's going to the welfare office then to see about her application and expects that'll relief her financial worries some. In the meanwhile, she's looking for a new place to live where it won't be so costley. Upon parting, we agreed she would come in to see me again next week so we could discuss her problems and situation some more, expecially since Charlie will be out of detention and she'll be able to visit him again.

EXERCISE 2 Writing an appropriate social history

You are a social worker in an interdisciplinary mental health clinic. A client has been seen at intake and subsequently evaluated by the psychologist and psychiatrist. You have also seen the patient several times and have met with the family once. Follow-ing is a list of key facts that have come to light thus far. They are numbered but are not presented in any particular order.

Your task is to write a social history, using the social history outline in Chapter 8, pp. 120–122. As this is a mental health rather than a medical setting, you will need to alter the headings and content of the suggested social history outline to fit the actual setting.

Use complete sentences. Develop your own diagnostic summary and treatment plan.

Dictate the finished product and have it transcribed if you are in field placement and have access to this equipment and clerical support to type your dictation.

An experienced worker with good writing skills should be able to complete this exercise in about thirty minutes to an hour. If you have never done this before, plan to spend at least one or two hours on the exercise. If the Analytical Thinking Model (pp. 144–146) is used to produce the diagnostic summary, this could take an additional one or two hours.

Facts

1. Identified patient: 14-year-old Tim Arango.

2. Referred by school guidance counselor because of Tim's acting-out behavior in school.

3. Mother is a housewife.

4. Tim failed 7th grade; is in 8th grade now.

5. Marriage—several separations, but the couple has always reunited.

6. Family income: $400 per week.

7. Tim's sister Julia was an unplanned baby.

8. The mother is one of 8 siblings and the only one who failed to go on to college.

9. Tim's brother Randall, age 12, gets all A's in school and is very athletic.

10. This is the second marriage for Mr. Arango. His first wife left him for another man a number of years ago.

11. Tim's problem behavior in school: skipping classes, coming late, gets into fights with other children, poor grades, talks back to the teachers, generally disrupts the classroom.

12. Psychiatric evaluation showed no abnormal findings and recommended family counseling for the children, especially Tim.

13. The family recently bought a sailboat. Payments are $122 monthly.

14. Mrs. A was pregnant with Tim before she got married at age 16 and quit high school.

15. Tim's siblings: one brother age 12; one sister age 4.

16. Mr. Arango encourages Tim's "manly" behavior. According to Mrs. A, the parents have fought consistently over how Tim should be disciplined.

17. Mrs. A is age 30.

18. Tim's behavior problem started 3 years ago.

19. This is a Latin American family.

20. Julia still wets the bed at night and is a "fussy eater," according to Mrs. Arango, but otherwise presents no unusual behavior.

21. Mrs. Arango would like to participate in some kind of marital counseling so that Mr. Arango will improve his behavior in the home.

22. Mr. Arango's mother died when he was age 4. He was raised by his father and grandfather. Mr. A's father died in 1970 following a long illness.

23. Monthly expenses: Mortgage $318; car payment #1 $129; furniture payments

$84; credit card payments total $112; TV payments $68; health and life insurance for the family $51; car payment #2 is $157; private school for the two younger children $400.

24. Psychological testing shows an IQ of 118 for Tim and some minor perceptual difficulties.

25. Randall had rheumatic fever with subsequent cardiac complications in 1971. He was virtually bedridden for 6 months, but now engages in normal activity, with some minor restrictions re: really strenuous contact sports.

26. Mr. Arango's mood is unpredictable; he vacillates between gentleness and rage.

27. You have been seeing Tim once weekly. You told Mrs. Arango you'd see her and Mr. Arango about twice a month.

28. Mr. Arango is a fine-finish carpenter and has been in the construction business for over 20 years. He is now a construction foreman.

29. You have seen Randall twice and Julia once so far.

30. Mrs. Arango had a hysterectomy two years ago.

31. Mrs. Arango says the family can't make it financially and are behind in several of their monthly payments.

32. Mrs. Arango never finished high school.

33. Mr. Arango is age 49.

34. The family lives in a four-bedroom house.

35. Tim refused to come to intake—Mrs. Arango came instead.

36. Mrs. Arango was raised in a family with an alcoholic father.

EXERCISE 3   Summary recording exercise

Pulling together a well-written summary is often not as easy as it looks. If one or two months have elapsed since the last summary, there may be many bits and pieces to be assembled. Notes from daily contacts may be scribbled on scraps of paper. There may be correspondence, reports from outside sources, and short record entries to be pulled together as well. All these notes must be sorted through before pen is put to paper.

Let us assume that you are sitting down to prepare a summary. You have gone through all your papers and have gathered a collection of material that you need to sort through and summarize. The following miscellaneous data are not presented in any particular order. You are a medical social worker and have been planning for your patient's discharge from the hospital. He is a paraplegic (paralyzed from the waist down) and confined to a wheelchair.

Your task is to:

1. Use the General Interim Summary outline in Chapter 8, pp. 122–124.

2. Organize the material according to the headings specified in this summary outline.

3. Use complete sentences.

4. Develop a diagnostic assessment and specific treatment plan based on the facts available (see Chapter 10 for suggestions). Do not repeat what is already known—*analyze*.*

---

*This could be done as a separate exercise if desired. The summary should be written first, however.

5. If your setting has dictaphones or tape recorders, dictate the final product.

The completed summary should be no more than two single-spaced typed pages. These guidelines are not rigid; however, remember that most people don't have time to read excessively long summaries. On the other hand, there is so much miscellaneous data to pull together in this particular case that it won't be possible to do it in a single page.

A worker with several years of experience who is also skilled in written communication could complete the summary in about thirty minutes or less by composing as he dictates. A worker with less experience might take an hour or so and would probably do a written draft or outline before dictating. If you've never done a summary before, you will need to write it all out in longhand exactly as you want the typed version to appear, and then read it into the dictaphone. Expect the exercise to take one to two hours, with an additional one to three hours if the Analytical Thinking Model is used to develop the diagnostic summary and treatment plan.

Hank Smith is the patient.

8-12-79 (scribbled note on back of telephone message)	861-2825. Mrs. Smith to call me back tomorrow re: wheelchair. Need extra wide.
7-11-79 (brief social work entry in case record)	Had contact with Social Security. They expect benefits of about $300 monthly to start in about 4 months. Pt. informed. He'll still have some unmet financial needs. Landlord threatening to raise rent to $210 monthly.
9-12-79 (record entry)	Learned today that pt. has 3 children from a prior marriage. Patient's ex-wife had just learned of his accident and has contacted me. She obviously has many positive feelings toward patient. Apparently patient initiated the divorce when a prolonged period of unemployment forced the family onto welfare and "he thought we'd be better off without him." She described pt. as being very difficult to live with, nontalkative except to "yell at me and the kids." She had wanted pt. to get counseling to improve their marriage, but pt. refused.
9-21-79 (entry in medical chart)	Mrs. Smith (patient's wife) requested that pt. be placed in a nursing home. She started work last week as a waitress in order to support her family. She feels patient cannot be left home alone and there is not enough money to hire someone to care for him while she's gone. Patient's mother is age 70 and willing to help out. Please advise if pt. could manage at home alone during daytime with visiting nursing services.
no date (note in worker's notebook)	Dr. says it'll be another 3 weeks before pt. goes home. Family to get catheter care training in one week. Nurse concerned they won't follow through. Wife to see me Monday.
8-6-79 (scribbled note)	Physical therapist and I finally made home visit. Volunteer service to build ramp at patient's home at no cost.
8-14-79 (note left in worker's box by social worker on weekend duty)	Saw Hank Smith today. Nurse very concerned—he's refusing to eat, talking back to nurses, threatening to leave the hospital against medical advice. Seems very depressed. Wouldn't talk much to me. Wife hasn't

visited in 3 days—he expressed fear of rejection and that "she's leaving me for another man." Told Hank you'd be up to see him Monday.

Jackie

8-15-79 (entry in medical record by social worker)	Pt. very depressed today. Questioning the value of life. I am requesting psychiatric evaluation for possible suicide potential due to patient's history of attempted suicide 3 years ago before becoming paraplegic (precipitated by loss of second child at birth).
8-22-79 (scribbled note)	Psych report back. "Normal situational response to paraplegia—no immediate suicide potential. Will follow pt."
8-24-79 (scribbled note)	Talked to Psych. He's prescribing antidepressant meds only—won't really be seeing pt. therapeutically. We agreed I'd handle that.
7-29-79 (telephone message left for worker)	Voc. Rehab. counselor called. Hank's case has been rejected as pt. refused services. Mr. Adams wants social worker to call him.
9-16-79 9-18-79 9-19-79 (scribbled note)	Tried to reach patient's wife. Sent telegram asking her to come see me. Dr. says pt. being discharged 9-26-79.
9-23-79 (entry in medical record)	Visiting nursing services are starting 9-29-79. No charge to pt. for first 20 visits.
9-15-79 (scribbled on back of phone message)	Call Miss Hinter, 228-6316. Soc. Security rejecting application. Medical reports showed pt. not permanently and totally disabled (!?).
9-2-79 (worker scribbled notes taken upon reviewing medical chart)	Temperature for past 3 days. Wt. loss of 10 lbs. in past 2 months. Nurse says pt. observed drinking heavily and intoxicated—how'd he get it? Wife very critical of medical care—giving floor staff hard time. Chronic bedsores.* Pt. concerned re: sexual functioning. (Can he?) Talk to dr.
9-6-79 (scribbled note)	Dr. says pt. can function sexually, but not have children. Pt. not necessarily impotent. Wife won't believe he can function—seems to be avoiding pt. Dr. says he explained to her what his sexual abilities and limitations are.
9-10-79 (entry in medical record by social worker)	Had conference with patient's wife today. Apparently their marriage of 4 years duration was strained even before his accident 6 months ago. She is just now able to discuss some of her ambivalent feelings toward patient. She had been thinking of taking the two kids and leaving him prior to his injury, but isn't so sure that's the right thing to do now. It appears she has not yet shared her feelings with patient; however, his depression may indicate he suspects all is not well.

*A condition that can develop when patients are bedridden for extended periods of time. The skin breaks down, causing a kind of ulcer to form on the back sides. If not aggressively treated, serious complications and even death can result.

	Discharge plans almost completed. Pt's mother moving in for a few days after patient's discharge to help out.
9-27-79 (telephone message)	Dr. Schmidt called. Wants to know when Hank Smith is going to be discharged to the nursing home. He needs the bed for another patient.
9-24-79 (entry in medical chart)	Pt. now aware that wife is working and now able to verbalize his feeling that she is considering leaving him. He knows of ex-wife's contact with me, but doesn't want to see her. Pt. talking of going to live with a friend on the other side of town. I'll explore further if this living arrangement would give him the care he needs.
7-3-79 (entry in medical chart)	Pt. rejected by Vocational Rehabilitation due to lack of motivation. They feel he may be a suitable candidate later on when depression lifts. They assure me age 43 is not too old to get into their program.
9-25-79 9-26-79 9-27-79	Called patient's friend—no answer. " " " " " "
9-30-79 (telephone message)	Dr. Vargas called re: Hank Smith. The Resthaven Nursing Home has a bed for him on Wednesday.
9-30-79 (entry by social worker in medical chart)	Pt. refuses to go to a nursing home and cannot be placed against his will. Frank discussion with pt. re: living arrangements post-discharge enabled him to express many feelings. Much anger was ventilated. Pt. agreed to go home till other arrangements can be worked out. Please complete referral forms for visiting nurse and also medical evaluation forms for S.S.I.
10-1-79 (entry in medical chart)	Still awaiting completed medical forms before pt. can be discharged.
10-3-79 (worker's note taken after reading dr.'s note in medical chart)	Pt. has developed pneumonia. Anticipate 2–3 weeks before he can be discharged.

EXERCISE 4 Letter-writing exercises

Social workers must be able to write clear, coherent letters to clients and others in connection with their day-to-day work. The following are some common situations necessitating a letter. Your task is to read each situation and to write a letter of some kind to take care of whatever needs to be done.

1. Miss Effon has been receiving SSI benefits for four months. Today she tells you that her check came but was only one-half the amount she thinks she should be getting ($188 as opposed to $366). You call the agency but "get the runaround" as you are referred from one person to another with no real answers. You decide to write a letter to the supervisor of Unit 18, who handles Miss Effon's check, in an attempt to get some action.

2. Your client has missed his appointment with you for two weeks in a row. You have not been able to contact him by phone. You'd like to arrange a home visit and decide to send a letter to him concerning this.

3. Your AFDC mother was known to the welfare department in another state. From what your client has told you, it sounds as if they might have had rather intensive involvement with her. They might have some helpful information in their records. Thus you decide to write them about the matter.*

4. You are leaving your present social work job at the XYZ Child Guidance Center because your husband is being transferred to another state. Your agency requires two weeks' notice of resignation in the form of a letter directed to the administrator.

5. You have decided to leave your present social work position at the ABC County Welfare Department. You have been very unhappy there and do not get along well with your supervisor. Your supervisor has also been quite critical of your performance and has rated you "unsatisfactory" in several areas. Thus you decide to leave before the situation gets any worse. The county requires two weeks' notice of resignation in the form of a letter directed to the administrator.

6. A social worker from an out-of-state agency has written asking you to send her a copy of your entire case record on the Brenda Healy case. Your supervisor says you cannot do that and asks you to write and tell her so. That's going to be difficult because you had already told the worker over the phone you felt certain you could send the record if she would request it in writing. What do you say now—"My supervisor says I can't?" Draft a letter that handles this situation tactfully and effectively.

7. The public school has threatened to expel a student unless he obtains professional counseling for his emotional problems. You have been seeing the youngster in treatment. The school principal asks for a letter from you to verify that the child has been in treatment.

8. You call the local welfare department to get some information about your client. You get the runaround and ask to speak to the supervisor. The following interaction occurs when someone picks up the receiver at the supervisor's extension:

(phone receiver is picked up—nothing is said)

You: Hello? Anybody there?

Response: Yeah, What'd 'ya want?

You: I was told this is the supervisor's office—Miss Jewel.

Response: Yes—what do you want? Oh Harry—put that over there. I'll be with you in just a second as soon as I get this caller off the phone.

You: Listen, I'm Henry Williams, social worker at the Brandon Clinic. I was referred to Miss Jewel because I'm trying...

Response (interrupting): Hurry up, will you—I gotta go.

You: May I speak to your supervisor please?

Response: He's not here—he's in a meeting.

You: What's his name? I'll...

Response: Sorry, I gotta go—call back later (hangs up).

You are incensed over the rude treatment you have received. You decide to draft a letter to the district manager to complain about it.

9. You are a medical social worker. The doctor has just informed you that your elderly patient is ready for discharge from the hospital tomorrow. You had thought that discharge would not be for several days yet and had been trying to reach the family, as they will have to give the patient some special care at home. You were going to write a letter asking them to contact you. Now there isn't time, so you decide to send a telegram instead.

*It is assumed that proper consent for release of information has been obtained on all situations that involve exchange of information.

EXERCISE 5 Memo-writing exercises

Memos are not really a form of social work recording per se. However, most social workers do have occasion to write memos in connection with their daily work, and these sometimes are placed in case records or administrative files in the office. Thus, this specialized style of writing should be mastered. Most settings use preprinted memo forms with the following headings:

```
                        MEMORANDUM
TO: (name and title of addressee)    DATE:
FROM: (your name and title)          SUBJECT: (a short phrase stating what the memo is
                                               about)
```

If preprinted forms aren't available, the headings can be typed in on plain paper. The name of the sender of the memo is almost always typed (unless the entire memo is handwritten). Since there is no place to put a signature, as in a letter, most people write their initials next to their typed name as a form of signature. If carbon copies are going to anyone, this is usually indicated by "cc:" at the end of the memo, followed by the names and titles of persons who get copies.

Complete each of the following exercises by writing a memo that takes care of the situation.

1.   You are new in the agency. Your supervisor asks you to draft a memo for other staff and students to tell them your working hours, areas of assignment, and main responsibilities. Use your imagination and come up with an appropriate memo.

2.   Think about a community resource you have worked with (or do research on one you're not familiar with). You decide that all staff and students in your setting should learn about the resource. Prepare a memo that explains what the resource is all about. Be sure to give enough information so that people can use the resource intelligently to its full potential.

3.   You have been working closely with the director of the Make-em-Well Mental Health Center. You're quite excited about their program and have asked the director to speak to your staff. Write a memo that announces this. Be sure to include all the information staff will need to make them feel like coming and enable them to get to the right place at the right time.

4.   You have drafted a new policy for the paperwork part of opening and closing cases in your agency. You would like other staff or students to tell you whether they think your ideas are any good. Draft a memo to them about this and make reference to the imaginary "attached revised policy."

5.   Think about your own in-service training needs. What kind of training would you like to receive, along with other staff or students, that would help you become more familiar with your agency, its program, or its consumers? Is there some training you would like to have to help improve your social work skills? Write a memo to the appropriate person in your setting and express your needs. Write clearly, concisely, and to the point. If necessary, inquire as to who would be the logical person in your setting to receive and take action on this kind of memo.

6.   Go back to 5 above. If you have handwritten the memo, give it to your school or agency secretary and have her type it as if it were "for real." Proofread it carefully so that it meets with your approval.

7.   You and your supervisor are supposed to meet every Wednesday at 2 P.M. For the past three weeks the supervisor has had to cancel the meeting for one reason or another. Efforts to reschedule the session have been unsuccessful and you just can't seem to pin the supervisor down to a definite time. A number of things are building

up that you need to talk about and obtain guidance on, and you're feeling rather frustrated and annoyed. Write a memo to the supervisor that reviews the problem and asks for an appointment. Think about whether you also want to include something about how you feel as a result of the problem.

8.   On Tuesday, July 20, you walk into the secretarial area in your office. Several persons are sitting in the adjacent lobby, waiting to be seen. As you enter the office you overhear two secretaries "badmouthing" a client who has just left. They are using four-letter words, mentioning the client's name quite audibly, and generally acting very unprofessional. You don't say anything to them because, after all, you are not their supervisor. But you do glance over at the waiting area and notice one of the clients get up and leave. Later his worker tells you that the man didn't wait for his appointment, and he can't figure out what happened. You mention the incident to your supervisor because you feel uncomfortable about it, but at the same time you don't want to cause trouble for anyone. Much to your surprise, the supervisor asks you to write her a memo describing what happened. She explains that there have been other complaints about these secretaries engaging in this kind of behavior, but she needs something in writing before she can take any kind of action. She urges you very strongly to write this memo. DO IT!

EXERCISE 6   Analyses of process recordings

The following exercises are based on several of the process recording examples in Chapter 6.

1.   Reread carefully process recording Example 8. Prepare a summary of the content of the interview and also include your diagnostic impressions. The summary should be in the form of a brief entry to be put in a social service record.

2.   Reread process recording Example 5. List all the differences you can find between the two recordings of this same interview.

3.   Reread process recording Example 1. This involves a twenty-two-year-old man who got into a fight, received knife wounds, and was subsequently hospitalized. The social work student is seeing him in the hospital to find out more about his life style so as to help prevent similar incidents in the future, if possible. Apply the Analytical Thinking Model to the information contained in the process recording. *Analyze* the meaning of the client's comments, behavior, and responses to the worker.

4.   Reread process recording Example 10. Label each counseling or interviewing technique that you can identify. Have your supervisor do the same thing, and compare your findings.

5.   Reread process recording Example 14. What alternate kinds of response could the worker have given that might have enabled the client to open up and talk more about his situation? At what point in the interview could the worker have interjected some techniques to prevent the client from merely sloughing him off as being "unhelpful"?

6.   Review the checklist of characteristics of beginning versus more advanced interviewing skills. Analyze process recordings 1, 2, 7, 8, 9, 14, 15, and 19. See also Exercise 10 in this chapter. Take each characteristic point by point and decide which level fits the interview you are analyzing. Ask your supervisor to do the same, and compare your qualitative and quantitative assessments of the recordings. You may wish to apply the rating scale method recommended in Chapter 6.

EXERCISE 7   Confidentiality violations survey

Purchase a small, inconspicuous notebook that you can carry around in your wallet, purse, or pocket. For one week jot down every violation of confidentiality of record materials that you observe. Watch closely for subtle violations (e.g., records left lying on a desk at night). Review Chapters 12 and 13 for possible violations. If your agency or setting is typical, you should be able to come up with several incidents over a five-day period of observation.

After you have observed and made note of the violations, share them first with your supervisor or other administrative-level person. If you are a student, share your observations with your field instructor first, but also share them with an agency supervisor. What recommendations can you make that would help remedy the situation and prevent further violations from occurring?*

EXERCISE 8 Experiencing the absence of records and recording

This exercise† will require special supervisory permission.

During a period of two calendar weeks, pretend that there are *no social service records of any kind* in the setting where you work or are in field placement. Do not consult any existing files or records *of any kind,* including master card files and other indexes containing client-identifying data. Do not write down *any* notes on any of your interviews, phone calls, or other social work activities except the name, address, or phone number of someone you have to contact. Fill out any forms that must be completed in order to provide a service (e.g., eligibility forms, consent forms) but *do not retain a copy.* (You may want to give the required copy to your supervisor to keep or distribute—just so long as you don't see it or refer back to it in any way). Do not keep any personal handwritten notes of any kind. Even if you are absent from work unexpectedly during the two-week experimental period, do not resort to records or recording of any kind. You will then be experiencing the world of no records and no recording.

Do the following:

1. Keep track of the number of clients you are able to see per day for the 2 weeks prior to the start of this exercise.

2. Keep track of the number of clients you see per day while doing the "no recording" exercise.

3. Keep a notebook with you at all times and jot down two things: (a) whenever you wish you had a record to turn to or wish you could take notes—describe the situation that made you feel this way; (b) whenever you are glad you didn't have to do any recording—make note of any complications or benefits that occur as a result.

4. Your supervisor should also be making note of whenever he or she wishes records existed as he works with you during this two week period.

5. How is the absence of records affecting your ability to provide effective services to your clients?

6. At the end of the two weeks, consider: would you want to continue having no records? Why or why not? If so, how could the agency go about doing away with existing records and converting to the no-record system? If not, would you have any suggestions for improving on the agency's existing recording and record-keeping practice as a result of your experiment?

*The material in your notebook should be destroyed once this exercise has been completed. Do not take the material into the classroom unless you have obtained specific permission to do so from your field instructor. Also, if it is to be taken outside the agency, you *MUST* disguise or alter it so that it could not be used against the agency in any legal actions. If you want to take the data out of the agency, you must be fully aware of the possible negative repercussions for you, the agency, and its clients, and should discuss this matter with your supervisor before taking any action.

†Supervisors or field instructors may need to alter the exercise somewhat in order to adapt it to the particular setting and its requirements.

7. Consider the possibility of somehow sharing with or presenting the results of your findings to an agency administrator, or perhaps even writing a paper on the experience and submitting it for publication.

8. Write the author of this text (c/o the publisher) and share your findings.

9. Go back and reread Chapter 1. Did you experience any of these problems?

EXERCISE 9 Dictating versus handwriting/typing: an efficiency study

The following research exercise* could be carried out in settings that do not use dictaphones to record social work activity and where there is a significant volume of material that has to be typed. The experiment could also be done in a setting where staff do use dictaphones.

1. Borrow a tape recorder or dictaphone from someone, if necessary. The small cassette tape recorders that many people own would be satisfactory.

2. Decide on a period of time during which you will conduct your research (e.g., one week, two weeks).

3. During this time period, continue submitting your work to the secretary for typing in the usual manner. However, *in addition*, dictate the same material into your tape recorder or dictaphone.

4. Keep track of the time you spend preparing material to be typed in the usual manner versus the time spent dictating it.

5. Ask the typist to make note of how much time she spends typing the material in the usual manner. Find out what her salary is and convert it to an hourly rate. This will enable you to make a very rough estimate of how much it costs per hour, per page, or per line to have material typed in the usual way.

6. Determine what a social worker at your level (or your anticipated degree level) makes in your setting. Convert it to an hourly rate. The difference between the time it takes to prepare reports and recording in the usual way versus the time it takes you to dictate the same material can be converted to dollars and cents. This will be the savings (or increased expense) that would result if you converted to a dictaphone. Multiply this figure by the number of workers on staff to determine the estimated savings for an entire department or agency.

7. Check around and find out what typing services charge to type dictated material. Compare the rates with what it costs for the agency to get material typed in the usual manner.

8. Obtain the cost of dictating equipment and several transcriber units. This would be a one-time expense that then becomes a capital equipment asset for the agency.

9. Determine estimated savings (or increased expense) in dollars and cents and in time if your setting were to convert to the use of dictaphone instead of its present method of recording. If these figures are organized and presented in a clear, dynamic manner, your research could help change your setting's method of recording.

Examine your results carefully and decide which recording method is most efficient/cheapest for you and the agency. Remember that this study omits many variables and less obvious factors such as overhead expenses, varying amounts of time

*This exercise may need to be altered to fit the unique requirements and working conditions of various settings in which social workers practice. The individual in private practice who is employing a secretary to perform typing services may also want to experiment with some version of this exercise.

taken by workers to prepare reports, and depreciation and repair of equipment. Thus your figures will be very rough estimates only. You will need to tighten up the research methodology if more accurate figures are desired.

EXERCISE 10   Pretending to be a supervisor

The magic wand is waved and you are now a field instructor. You have asked an undergraduate student who is just starting her first field placement to do a process recording for you. You told her to use two columns—one for dialogue and one for her feelings. A third column is reserved for your comments.

Your student hands in a process recording on an interview with Crystal Parker. What comments would you make in the "supervisory comments" column as her field instructor? Be very specific, commenting on case dynamics that the student may have missed and interviewing techniques that were used, and giving suggestions for improving the interaction. You might also want to comment on the process recording itself—whether the student did it according to the instructions given (see Chapter 5).

A second process recording, on Sara Smith, was produced by a different undergraduate student conducting his very first interview in field placement. What supervisory comments would you make?

You might also want to evaluate these two process recordings by using the checklist of characteristics of beginning versus more advanced interviewing skills and applying the rating scale suggested in Chapter 5.

A. The Crystal Parker Interview

SUPERVISORY COMMENTS	INTERVIEW CONTENT	GUT-LEVEL FEELINGS
	I entered the ward to find a 6-bed room. Crystal was asleep when I entered, but awakened easily when the sound of my voice inquired for her. I introduced myself and mentioned that the Dr. asked me to come see her. I noted that Crystal was a black female who appeared older than her 13 years. She spoke quietly and seemed at ease with my questions. We were cramped for space and positioning my chair by the bedside to be able to talk in a quieter voice was necessary for she could hardly be heard. I asked if she would consider any of the questions too personal and wanted privacy, then she and I could find a more secluded place. She said she was feeling "fine" and that we could talk there. I made inquiry about the baby and how she had slept. She did not display any marked facial emotional response. She did not smile, frown, or move her body in any particular way. She was not rigid in position as she did use her hands to move about the bedsheets but	I was curious and elated at this assignment. I was disappointed that my visit to the floor yesterday was timed when babies were there and that I was denied entry. An emergency doctor's appointment delayed the interview until today.

I felt confident because I had the guidelines of "Casework with Teenage Mothers" to work from.

I was received well by the staff and felt assured.

The time passed so quickly. I enjoyed the |

did not use them to punctuate her statements. We were soon interrupted by the Dr. asking her an abrupt question: "Do you want to go home today?" When she got assurance she could, she answered "yes" and then he asked if she had had a bowel movement yet. She answered "No" and he said very quickly, "Then you cannot go home until you do." He did not stay to explain but left and I tried to answer her question. I heard him mention her 3 lacerations and his inquiry earlier about how she felt "down there" so I asked her if she knew what a laceration was. She said she did not and I made a simple explanation about the fact of lacerations opening up and the possibility of constipation causing this discomfort. It helped that I had asked at the desk before entering the room about what this "3° laceration" notation meant on the cover of her chart. At the time I asked it was so that in talking with patient about discharge planning, I would be able to gauge the kind of personal care and possible special care needed in planning.

The arrival of the breakfast trays seemed to call for a termination of the interview and I excused myself for "coffee" and told patient I would see her "soon."

talking, was not restrained as I had been before when the patient's condition made me apprehensive about pain and want to rush the interview.

Annoyed at interruption.

I noted that pt. did not react to the news with questions. She needed to be questioned about her understanding. I made note of this and the already noted lack of physical clues to her reactions and decided that I must ask explicit questions.

See the Doctor later for confirmation of information and helpful opinions.

I did not want to end the conversation. I was thirsty for coffee but would rather have continued the interview.

B. The Sara Smith Interview

SUPERVISORY COMMENTS	INTERVIEW CONTENT	GUT-LEVEL FEELINGS
	I walked into the hospital room—seeing a black woman, appearing half-asleep lying in the first bed. The other patient wasn't visible behind the curtain, but three women were sitting at the foot of that bed visiting. I addressed myself to the former. •	I surprised myself by not really being nervous about this first contact with a patient—or any "client" really.
	W: Hello, are you Sara Smith?	
	Pt: Yes, I am.	

W: I'm Jim Brown, from the social service dept. Do you mind if I sit down?

Pt: No, not at all.

She spoke without really raising her head from her pillow— seemed pretty tired. The way she nodded her head and spoke led me to feel that she knew why I had come.

W: Your doctor sent me a note with regard to the possibility of getting some financial aid for you while you are unable to work, so I thought I'd come over to see you about it.

Pt: Yes, I do need some help—I don't have any money now.

She seemed to be looking rather inquiringly at me— which I didn't find strange considering her to be a 47-year-old black woman and myself a 21-year-old white, long-haired male.

W: Has the doctor told you when you will be leaving the hospital yet?

Pt: Yes, I'm supposed to get out today if everything's all right—but I haven't seen him today 'cause they had me down at the shower when he came 'round this morning. Hope he comes back this afternoon.

I felt rather warm toward her here because I got good feelings from her and understood how she might find me strange in this setting. I noted that she was obese as was said in the chart, but not to an extreme amount.

W: Has he told you if you'll be able to do your same work after you recuperate upon leaving here?

Pt: He says I can't do nothing too strenuous, but I told him my maid work was pretty light so I think I can do that again.

Feeling of relief that I got there when I did— before she left.

W: Well, that's good news. Did he say how long it will be before you will be able to start work?

Pt: Jus' said a long time...

I couldn't tell here if she was upset by this or if time just didn't matter much to her anymore.

W: Was he any more specific than that— like if it would be a month or two or what?

Pt: A long time—that's all I know.

I didn't want to press but I needed more info. It proved unsuccess- ful but figured after talking with the doctor I'd find out anyway.

This sort of confused me—not knowing what "a long time" might be to her, but I decided to take that up with the doctor. She was still lying in the same position on her left side as when I came in.

W: I was wondering if you have an apartment on the first floor or not—that would help you out some once you get home.

Pt: Yes, it's on the ground.

W: Do you have some friends or relatives nearby who might be able to give you some help if you need it until you can get back to work?

Pt: Oh yes, I've got some friends around who will look in on me. My mother just got here from _____, so she'll be here too but she's an invalid—got diabetes like me too.

Might be an emotional help, but may be an added "physical" problem.

W: Do you have any other relatives— such as sisters or brothers?

I knew the answer to this already but didn't know if I should just come out with it, so decided to let her bring it out herself, especially about her one sister's death from heart trouble.

Pt: I got one sister lives in _____ (same place as the mother). Had another one, but she died last year. She had same thing I got now almost.

I thought that this thought (the sister's death) might be an extremely sensitive point, but she didn't change her expression or show that she had added anxiety because of that point. I felt good that although it bothers her, she is not preoccupied with the thought.

W: I'm sorry to hear about that. Have you been living by yourself, or with someone else at your apartment?

Pt: I'm all alone now. My husband walked out on me—let's see—about nine months ago. Haven't heard from him since—just walked out and left me.

W: That must be really hard on you—had you been married a long time?

Really hit me hard—really able to relate and feel, on an emotional, personal level, but felt I shouldn't show all the distress I felt.

Pt: Not really, about four years come April. Just walked out and left me by myself.

I could see the pain in her face, which she seemed to be trying to hide.

W: Did you have any children?

Pt: No, I don't have any.

W: It must be pretty hard making it all by yourself.

Pt: Yes, real hard. My married name is Holcomb—I'm glad I never changed it here though—I been coming here for a long time and just kept the same name.

This was confusing me at first but I thought about it for a moment and under-stood what she was saying to me.

W: Have you been living alone ever since then?

Pt: Well, for a while this woman lived with me but now she left.

W: Was she helping pay the rent when she was there?

Pt: Yes, she helped out some, but now I just pay.

W: Were you working on your own, or through an agency or something like that?

I'm really wondering how she's making it—with only income as a

218

Pt: I just was working for a family on my own. A friend of mine knew they wanted somebody and told me, so I went.

W: I think that the welfare dept. may be able to help you out with some money until you can get back to work. Will you be able to get the same job back when you're able?

Pt: I don't know, might have to go looking again.

W: Well, we might be able to get you some help with that too possibly. I'll see what can be done.

(pause)

W: Have they been treating you pretty good here?

Pt: Oh yes. Everybody is so nice. Everybody's been real good to me. They really care.

W: Yes, I can understand that. When I was in the hospital in April they were pretty good to me too, but it's just not the same as being at home.

Pt: That's for sure.

W: Well, I tell you what I'll do. I'll get the welfare referral form filled out for you, so we can get you that help as soon as possible, Okay?

Pt: Yes, that will be fine. Thank you so much.

W: You're welcome. Oh—before I leave I'll check with the nurse for you to see if she knows for sure if you're leaving today or not. I'll stop back in a couple minutes to let you know what she says. See you then.

domestic to support herself.

By this point she was seeming to be a little more confident in me and what I could do for her, so I thought it a good opportunity to try to build a little to the relationship. She has now lifted her head up to me, resting it on her hand, and her expression seems happier.

For the first time in the interview she seemed very happy, smiling and laughing some. I knew that the trust was now there and that when I left she feels good and believe it was going to be done for her. This made me feel really good (her comment "that's for sure"). I didn't dwell on it because I didn't want to get sidetracked; but it seemed to bring us a little closer together.

Pt: Okay, goodbye.

W: She's not sure about your discharge either. She didn't have a chance to talk to the doctor yet. Anyway, I'll get going on that referral for you right now. I'll probably be back to see you again before you leave. Goodbye and have a good day.

Pt: Goodbye and thank you.

Upon leaving her spirits seemed much better and during the last words we had she had shifted her position and was almost sitting up. It turned out that the nurse did not know for sure either so I went back and told her.

Knew I must have forgotten a couple things I should have asked, but had a good feeling about Ms. Smith, and our interview.

That was the end of the interview. Upon finding out about how to fill out the referral form, I stopped in later to get her final permission to do so—filled it out, and gave it to the doctor, who was right there. Plan to check to see if she gets it and is doing all right at home.

EXERCISE 11 Applying the Analytical Thinking Model

The following examples have been used in training groups of social workers and students from a wide variety of settings and with diverse kinds of professional training and experience. The specifics of the case situation or the setting in which the situation occurs are not very important. What is pertinent is that these are typical case situations requiring diagnostic summaries and treatment plans. The emphasis should be on learning the process of thinking analytically and developing treatment plans. Some of the exercises ask you, "What should this counselor do?" This seemingly simple question cannot be answered effectively until after the steps in the Analytical Thinking Model have been worked through.

These exercises can also be used in a group situation with an instructor distributing the case example and the group going through the ATM steps together (see Chapter 10).

Several other self-instructional exercises in this Chapter also suggest or lend themselves to application of the ATM as an exercise (see, for example, Exercises 2, 3, and 10).

General Instructions for Completing the ATM Exercises

1. Study the Analytical Thinking Model presented in Chapter 10.

2. Go through each step in the outline

3. If the summary contains terms you are not familiar with, look them up before beginning the exercise. It is not possible to analyze something effectively when you don't know what it means.

4. Write out each step on a worksheet. Expect the process to take at least two hours the first time you do it.

5. When all the steps have been completed, go back and write a summary-style diagnostic summary and treatment plan that might be included in a case record.

You might want to experiment with writing a diagnostic summary and treatment plan before studying the ATM, and then setting it aside to compare with your efforts after applying the ATM.

Be very specific at all times—avoid generalities and jargon that attempt to cover up the fact that you don't really know what you're talking about or aren't really sure how to go about doing what you propose.

Don't get discouraged if the exercises prove to be difficult. Many MSW's with postgraduate experience have stumbled over them and discovered there is room for improvement in their diagnostic treatment skills as a result of studying the ATM.

GO!

A. Sandra I.: A "Divine Healing" Experience Causes a Young Adult To Discontinue Life-sustaining Medical Treatment

background

Sandra, age twenty-two, has advanced kidney disease. She has been receiving dialysis* three times weekly for the past three years. Prior to that time, she suffered gradual kidney failure, which did not become noticeable until she had lost most of her kidney functioning. At first it was hoped that diet and medication would prevent the need for dialysis; however, her condition continued to deteriorate. Two years ago a kidney transplant was attempted. Sandra's twenty-four-year-old brother donated one of his kidneys. Sandra was able to be off dialysis for several months with her new kidney. Unfortunately, her body rejected the donor kidney and it had to be removed. Last year she received another kidney transplant, this time from someone who had just died and had willed his kidneys for medical use. This transplant also failed and it is felt that she would not be a good candidate for any further transplants. Thus Sandra remains on dialysis.

Sandra finished high school and had started one year of college before her medical problems forced her to drop out of school. She now lives at home with her parents, two younger siblings, a grandparent, and the twenty-four-year-old brother, who works and contributes toward the household expenses. The family has a very moderate level of income and Sandra was the first in her family to attend college. Her father works as a salesclerk in a local store; her mother has never worked outside the home. The entire family is extremely religious, a factor that dictates the moral standards in the home and is felt to be responsible for the family's close-knit relationship. Sandra has talked many times of her religious faith as being an important source of strength throughout her illness. It has appeared to be a positive factor in her situation.

Sandra has attempted one or two jobs since developing the kidney disease; both were abruptly ended with the onset of further medical complications. Her original career goal was to become a nurse, but Sandra now questions if she will ever be able to achieve this.

current problem

Sandra missed her dialysis on Wednesday. This is most unusual. When you call her, Sandra reports, very excitedly, that she and her family have been to a tent

---

*Patients are connected to an artificial kidney machine for four to six hours. As the blood passes through the machine, it is cleansed of toxic impurities and waste matter—a task normally performed by the kidneys. Most dialysis patients would die or suffer severe complications if they did not receive dialysis on a regular basis. However, many dialysis patients can live somewhat normal lives except for their regular sessions on the machine.

revival meeting and that she has been miraculously healed. She goes on to describe how some of her usual symptoms have gone away—she even missed dialysis yesterday and is suffering no ill effects. She expresses gratitude for all everyone has done for her and states that she will not be returning to the hospital since she no longer needs dialysis. You are very concerned as you know that in a matter of days or weeks she will develop toxic uremia and die without medical attention. You beg her to return for dialysis, but to no avail.

You contact the parents, hoping they can talk some sense into Sandra. However, you find them fully supportive of Sandra's decision and thankful for the healing that has occurred.

your task

You feel helpless, frustrated, and angry. Use the Analytical Thinking Model to help you decide what to do and what approach to take in developing a realistic service plan to deal with this crisis.

B. The Y Family: A Totally Chaotic Interview Situation

introduction

The following incident, with some modifications, actually took place during a home visit by a social work student. The family had been receiving services from the agency due to possible child abuse or neglect. The family consists of Mrs. Y, age twenty-eight, Mr. Y, age forty, a daughter age six, a son age four, a daughter age two, and a baby age six months. Everyone except Mr. Y was at home during the worker's visit.

The Analytical Thinking Model can be used to analyze a case situation retroactively and plan for subsequent contacts. However, this thinking approach can also be applied "on-the-spot" as things happen while meeting with the client. Pretend that you are actually experiencing the following incident. Try to use the ATM simultaneously with your reading of the situation. What would you say and do *as the incident is happening?* What implications does your analysis have in planning for future contacts and social service goals?

the situation (as reported by the worker)

When I entered Mrs. Y's home, I encountered instant chaos. Mrs. Y and the three children greeted me at the door. The four-year-old and the six-year-old grabbed me around the legs in a bear hug. Mrs. Y was obviously in the middle of preparing dinner and continued working in the kitchen as we talked while I sat at the kitchen table. The house was old, cluttered, and in need of a good cleaning, though not what I would call "filthy." It seemed that every room in the house opened off the kitchen, as the four-year-old ran in and out of the room through four different doors, screaming at the top of his lungs. This continued throughout the interview. He seemed hyperactive. Mrs. Y hollered at him to "shut up," but with no apparent effect on his behavior. The six-year-old sat over in the corner during the hour I was there and barely said a word, but obviously took everything in.

All this was going on while I tried to discuss finances, the husband's employment, and other things with Mrs. Y. As we were talking, I noticed the two-year-old go into a closet and shut the door. She stayed there for several minutes, and emerged dragging a potty chair behind her. She pulled it out into the center of the room and sat down on it as if to use it (it was dirty from previous usings). However, she changed her mind and instead got up and walked over to the kitchen counter and proceeded to pull a whole bowlful of food over onto the floor. Mrs. Y jumped, screamed at her not to do that, and went to work cleaning up the mess. The little girl flew into a temper tantrum, ignoring her mother. She picked her potty chair up and literally threw it across the room. Then she went over to the kitchen counter, climbed up and grabbed a handful of scrambled eggs, and dumped them onto the floor. Mrs. Y shrugged her shoulders and did nothing. The two-year-old then picked the eggs up off the floor, tossed them into her potty chair, then proceeded to pick them out of the potty chair and eat them. All the while this was going on, the four-year-old continued running from room to room and Mrs. Y continued fixing dinner—and didn't seem nearly as disturbed (or nauseated!) as I was by all this chaos.

C. Helen Smith: An Obese Woman Who Won't Follow Her Special Diet

background

Mrs. Smith is a 54-year-old white female with a long medical history. She has received outpatient care for a number of years, and has had several hospitalizations within the past two years. Certain physical problems appear more or less chronic: hypertension, persistent fluid retention in the lower extremities in spite of low-sodium, low-calorie diet prescriptions; various dermatological problems that clear up but then return; anemia; and varicose veins. There are some irregularities in pulmonary function and Mrs. Smith's obesity is potentially life threatening.

Mrs. Smith reports that she has been overweight most of her life. She is 5'4" and on last hospital admission four months ago weighed 268 pounds. She has been on many diets, ranging from sensible low-calorie plans prescribed by her physician to the diet pill regime through local "obesity clinics." Mrs. Smith has been advised over and over of her need to lose weight by just about every nurse and physician who has had contact with her. She's been fully informed of the life-threatening implications and says she sincerely does try to follow her low-calorie diet. Yet she continues to present physical symptoms that clearly indicate she is not doing this successfully.

Socially, Mrs. Smith is somewhat alone. She has been divorced for many years. Her children are grown and living in other parts of the country and she has limited contact with them. She lives alone in a small apartment and receives financial assistance due to her inability to work combined with her lack of skills. She has been rejected by Vocational Rehabilitation as not being a suitable candidate for vocational rehabilitation in view of her age and physical condition. Mrs. Smith spends most of her time visiting with her neighbors, doing some knitting, and maintains that she really eats very little because she simply cannot afford it.

the problem

You have been following Mrs. Smith for some time. You are becoming quite concerned about her apparent denial of the seriousness of her weight problem and her continuing refusal to comply fully with medical recommendations. What kind of counseling approach should you take?

D. Mrs. R: A Complainant Suspects Possible Child Abuse or Neglect

clients

- Mrs. R, age twenty-eight
- Daughter, age eight
- Son, age six
- Daughter, age three
- Daughter, age three months

background

The following information summarizes the data found in the case record from point of opening to the present:

Mrs. R became known to the agency two years ago when a complaint was received from her mother-in-law describing the client as staying up all night and leaving the children without adequate supervision or in the care of her eighty-year-old, feeble grandparent. The initial home visit found client and children occupying a two-bedroom, run-down shack on the outskirts of the city. The two oldest children were home even though it was a school day; the house was very messy, with dirty dishes, papers, and soiled linens strewn all over; the three-year-old was observed wearing only diapers even though it was a chilly day; and the three-month-old baby badly needed a change of diapers.

During the two years the case has been open, Mr. R has been in and out of the home and Mrs. R has been toying with the idea of a divorce, but never seems to follow through. Several additional complaints have come in alleging child neglect, and complaining of at least one loud, drunken fight between Mr. and Mrs. R. Mrs. R told a social worker that this fight never occurred, believing the complainant to be her mother-in-law "who can't stand me and will do anything to try to discredit me."

The worker has helped with concrete needs including relocation to better housing, getting homemaker services, providing various types of financial assistance, transportation, and arranging doctors' appointments. The oldest son has seizures and occasionally must be rushed to the doctor. Mrs. R says he misses his father and has gotten somewhat "emotional" since he left the home "for good" nine months ago. However, neighbors report that he still visits the home, though Mrs. R denies this. The six-year-old has a very irregular school attendance, with Mrs. R offering explanation of frequent colds. The three-year-old appears healthy and normal, but did, according to Mrs. R, fall out of a lower tree limb approximately two months ago and fractured her arm. The baby is a fussy eater and requires a special formula, thus incurring extra expense for Mrs. R.

During the past two years, housekeeping standards have improved somewhat, but the place may be clean at one home visit and then relapse to less desirable conditions at subsequent visits. Mrs. R always promises to do better, expresses a strong desire to keep the children, and tries to be "the best mother I can under the circumstances." Workers have noted some progress but have also recorded, on six visits in the past year, the presence of various men in the home when they come to the door. Mrs. R always introduces them as neighbors, relatives, or friends. Furthermore, Mrs. R sometimes does not follow through with appointments made for her by the worker, and rather aggressive provision of concrete services has been necessary at times (such as taking her and the children to the doctor) in order to ensure follow-through. Other than these problems, Mrs. R does seem to be sincerely trying to better her situation.

current problem

A complaint has been received from a neighbor who reports that the eight-year-old son was at her home and told her that they sometimes do not have enough to eat and that Mrs. R occasionally shuts them all in the back bedroom for several hours at a time. The neighbor also complained that the kids sometimes, but not always, look dirty and poorly clothed.

worker's task

A complete reassessment of this case is now due. What action or service planning would you recommend if you were the worker? Be very specific.

E. Mrs. Q: An Unscrupulous Businessman Takes Unfair Advantage of a Young Mother During a Time of Emotional Distress

clients

• Mrs. Q, age twenty-five

• Son, age three

• Son, age one year, three months

background

Mrs. Q lives in a rural area of the state. She spent her youth as a migrant worker and attended public school only a few days each year. As a result, she is illiterate. Mrs. Q was married briefly as a teenager. The first husband left her for another woman and she had the marriage annulled. Her marriage to Mr. Q took place two years ago. They had lived together for some time before legalizing their relationship. Both children are from this union and are in good health.

Mrs. Q met Mr. Q while he was working on a construction job near a field where she was picking tomatoes. He had finished high school, completed his apprentice-ship, and was a full-fleged union member, making good construction wages. He was twenty-eight when they met. Mr. Q had been married at age twenty-two, divorced at twenty-seven, and still made monthly child-support payments to his former wife. Thus, while his income was high, it left Mr. and Mrs. Q with a rather modest life style.

Two years ago they bought a home on the edge of a small rural town. It was old and run down, but the low monthly payment of $125 appealed to them. Mr. Q started major renovations at minimum cost because of his carpentry skills. The Q's were financially independent and just reaching the point where they could begin putting some money into savings.

current situation

One year ago Mr. Q committed suicide. Mrs. Q was aware that he had had some emotional problems, but had no idea he would react so severely to the loss of his job. Savings were depleted within two months of his layoff and Mr. Q just couldn't face life any longer and shot himself. Mrs. Q was left with a small life insurance policy. This money soon ran out, and six months ago she applied for AFDC. Because of her emotional and many other needs, the case is receiving special services. Mrs. Q has managed to remain in the home and can just barely keep up the payments with her foodstamps and financial assistance. She is considering a return to school to learn to read and write so she can equip herself for some type of employment.

presenting problem

Several of your clients have told you lately about a man who approached them to do roofing jobs on their houses. He has tried to get them to sign contracts to have this work done at what appears to be an outrageous price. On your next routine visit to Mrs. Q's house, you discover that this roofer has been to visit and convinced her that her roof needed repair. Mrs. Q tells you that she signed a contract with this man eight months ago. She agreed to pay $10,000 for the work, with the roofer holding a second mortgage on the house. The monthly payments are $115 and Mrs. Q is now three months behind. With tears of desperation, she tells you that the roofing company has started foreclosure proceedings and plans to take away her house. Mrs. Q says she was very upset over her husband's death when this man started coming around, pressuring her to have the work done. She states she didn't really listen to what he was saying, and signed the contract just to get him off her back. She was too embarrassed to admit she couldn't read it. The work on the roof was done, but now Mrs. Q can't pay, and it appears she may lose her home.

your task

This case presents a very concrete problem for the worker to handle. However, because of the client's background, it is necessary to understand her present and past emotional state and personal needs in order to determine exactly how the present problem should be handled and to understand what Mrs. Q is and is not capable of doing in her own behalf. Apply the Analytical Thinking Model to arrive at a service plan that recognizes Mrs. Q's total personal needs as well as presenting a plan for dealing with her present financial-legal problem.

F. Mr. and Mrs. K: A Family Is Affected by the Father's Sudden Illness

setting

A general medical hospital

Mr. K, age 45, was admitted to the hospital on 2-11-75. His diagnosis was "CVA with right hemiplegia and global aphasia."* On 4-1-75 a referral was made to social service by a nurse on the floor. The reason for referral was, "Patient to be discharged in 1-2 weeks and needs financial assistance."

A review of the medical chart and interviews with Mr. and Mrs. K revealed the following information:

*CVA: Cerebral Vascular Accident (stroke).

Mr. and Mrs. K have been married for thirteen years. Mrs. K. is age 31—fourteen years younger than her husband. This is the first marriage for both. Mr. K had dropped out of high school in the tenth grade and went to work on construction at a low-level job. Mrs. K married immediately after high school and has never worked outside the home. They have three boys ages twelve, ten, and one. The ten-year-old has had poorly controlled grand mal epileptic seizures since birth and has been attending a special school. The other two children are in good health.

Mrs. K's mother (who lives nearby) was very much opposed to the marriage, primarily because of the age differential and the fact that she had hoped her daughter would go to college. She has had little to do with the family since then except occasional visits with the grandchildren on holidays.

The K's are a family who apparently "pulled themselves up by their bootstraps," having started their married life with almost nothing. Mr. K. eventually worked his way up to where he was earning $250 weekly operating heavy machinery on high-rise construction sites. They had a fairly new car, recently purchased new furniture, and several years ago bought a house with mortgage payments of $190. However, with the problems with the ten-year-old child, their expenses have been so high that they have not been able to accumulate significant savings. This precipitated the referral to social service when Mrs. K told a nurse on the floor that they were advised by the bank that they would need to make some mortgage payments soon or foreclosure proceedings would begin. Their other payments are also behind and Mrs. K has recently had to turn to her mother for direct financial assistance for food and essential expenses since their savings ran out the beginning of March.

Mr. K will be discharged home in a wheelchair. Even though he's been receiving daily physical therapy, the return of function has been minimal as the brain damage has been rather extensive. Because of the global aphasia, it has not been possible to determine exactly how much he is able to think, feel, and respond to his environment. He makes unintelligible noises and attempts to gesture. He still lacks control of urination and wears a catheter, that must be cleaned daily. He can feed himself and assist in dressing and basic toiletry activities with his left hand, though he was right-handed prior to the CVA.

The social worker must now analyze the information gathered in order to formulate a diagnostic assessment of the case dynamics and develop an appropriate treatment plan.

G. Tommy: A Twelve-Year-Old Is Referred to the School Social Worker for Counseling

You are a school social worker. One of the teachers has just asked you to see Tommy, a seventh-grader. The teacher gives you the following background information:

Tommy's sixth-grade teacher described him as a "quietly hostile" youngster who sat in the back row saying little and sometimes refusing to pay attention or participate in classroom activities and discussions. He was felt to be a loner, having few friends. His grades were barely passing.

His behavior in the seventh grade started out in a similar pattern. Tommy rarely participated in class and answered in monosyllables when addressed by the teacher. However, it is now February, and there have been some noticeable changes in his behavior. He has been observed hanging around with a group of tough older boys who are known to be using marijuana. Tommy now disrupts class periodically by talking or getting into arguments with other children. He seems bright, but is barely passing. Two days ago a small change purse turned up missing from the teacher's desk and all indications point to Tommy as the culprit. This prompted the referral to the social worker.

Tommy's parents have been to the school several times to meet with the teacher; most recently his mother came alone. Tommy's father has criticized the teacher's judgment sharply, feeling that Tommy is not responsible for his poor grades—she is. On one occasion he became quite angry and loud when the teacher refused to give

Tommy a passing grade in math. Tommy's parents have just recently separated and an older brother has also left the home to attend college. His mother has taken a job outside the home to support the family. She says she wants to help Tommy, but seems unsure what to do, commenting on her other children, who are bright, well behaved, and who have always gotten C's or better in school.

Your first interview with Tommy is very brief. He spends the entire session slouched in a chair, looking at the floor. All questions are answered with a yes, no, or shrug of the shoulders. Tommy doesn't understand why he needs to see you and expresses fear that the other children "will think I'm some kind of weirdo having to see a social worker." He ends the interview prematurely by getting up and walking out, announcing that you'd be better off seeing other kids who really need your help and stating that he will not see you again.

What should you do now?

H. Mr. and Mrs. Anders: An Elderly Husband Refuses To Place His Dying Wife in a Nursing Home

background

Mr. and Mrs. Anders are in their eighties. In 7-77, Mrs. A, who has a history of poor health, was hospitalized with complaints of severe pain, some mental confusion, and weight loss. She was found to have metastatic cancer. After several weeks of hospitalization, trying to at least get her stabilized, she became ready for discharge. The physician recommended nursing-home placement.

Mrs. Anders is on a catheter and requires tube feeding. She is not alert mentally and is for all practical purposes comatose. She is completely bedridden. Her skin is breaking down and decubiti prevention is nearly impossible. She requires full nursing care. As Mr. Anders is himself an elderly, rather frail man, it is not felt he could possibly care for his wife at home. Thus, nursing-home placement seems the obvious and most humane plan for all concerned.

the problem

Mr. Anders absolutely refuses nursing-home placement. He and his wife have been together for almost sixty years, and he refuses to "desert" her now. He insists on taking her home, where he will care for her in their one-bedroom apartment. He feels this is what his wife would want and he won't consider any other options. He seems fully alert mentally, though very unrealistic in his plans. It is obvious Mrs. Anders's death will be hastened by this plan, and her condition could deteriorate in a most unpleasant manner. The physicians and floor staff feel that Mr. Anders couldn't even lift his wife and they realize a certain amount of physical strength and exertion will be required to provide the physical care needed.

the counselor's dilemma

You have been asked to see Mr. Anders and try to talk some sense into him. You're prepared to offer him at least outpatient nursing services if he won't accept anything else, but you've been warned already by floor staff that he "won't allow any strangers into the house—I will provide personally all the care my wife needs."

What approach should the counselor take?

I. Steve Hunt: A Problem Employee Forces the Supervisor To Make a Difficult Decision (Large Systems)

There is no real "Steve Hunt." Bits and pieces have been taken from various situations to arrive at this fictitious case. It is not intended to represent any past or present employee or supervisee in any setting. Even though it is not based on an actual employee situation, it does illustrate a typical problem that can arise when there is a decline in a supervisee's performance.

instructions

1. Read the case example.

2. Write a *brief* paragraph telling what you would do if you were this person's

supervisor. Be *very* specific. If you respond with "I would consult with my supervisor," go on to say what you would do if you were your supervisor—don't cop out!

3. Now go back and apply the Analytical Thinking Model for large systems. Go through all the steps described in Chapter 10. Do this in writing. It will take you several hours if done properly.

4. Write a brief statement telling what you would do with this problem situation. Be very specific.

5. Compare your statement in step 4 with your initial decision in step 2, before you applied the ATM.

background prior to present employment

Mr. Hunt is seventy-one years old and has his Masters degree in Social Work from the University of Oshkin. This employee finished high school, spent several years in the service, then worked several more years before going on to college under the GI Bill while in his middle twenties. He received his BA degree in English at the age of thirty. Following this he taught in public schools for ten years and then spent several more years in an unsuccessful small business. It was during this time that Mr. Hunt realized that he really wanted, and had a strong need, to work with people in a helping relationship, and thus sought employment in the local public welfare department. After several years there, he obtained a stipend from his agency to attend graduate school and subsequently obtained his MSW at the age of forty-eight. He continued working in the public welfare department as a supervisor for four years until he completed his commitment to them. He then spent the next four to five years in a family service type of agency and then a brief period in a public health department where he was rather unhappy, as he found the work was not what he thought it would be. Eighteen years ago he began working for another branch of the setting where he is now employed. Twelve years ago he transferred, with retirement and seniority benefits intact, to his present setting. It is a large, multidisciplinary environment. Mr. Hunt is employed as a mental health caseworker.

his present employment situation

Mr. Hunt has been in social service here for twelve years. There are no mandatory retirement requirements. He has been a loyal, steady worker—not highly creative, not especially eager to move upward administratively—just reliable and consistently acceptable (average) in his performance. A few years ago he was assigned some supervisory responsibilities when a vacancy occurred in the department, but Mr. Hunt soon chose to return to direct services, where he has since remained. He has supervised several undergraduate and graduate students, however, and currently has one under his supervision.

Mr. Hunt's relationships with co-workers and his supervisors have been generally satisfactory. He is usually pleasant. However, as he is considerably older than the majority of social service staff (including his supervisor), it has been felt that he sometimes feels somewhat out of step and out of touch with the eager new crop of recent graduates that have joined the department in the past two to three years.

presenting problem

Mr. Hunt will complete his twenty years' employment eighteen months from now. He has verbalized rather strongly his intention to retire at that time and collect full benefits. He does not want to retire earlier, as these benefits would be substantially reduced.

Mr. Hunt has been married for many years. His wife is not well and medical expenses have been high. They have two grown children. One is married and living in a distant state. The second suffers from a birth defect resulting in limited ambulation, poor coordination, moderate mental retardation, and a visual handicap. This forty-year-old son lives at home with the Hunts and has required considerable care over the years. Mrs. Hunt has never worked outside the home. Mr. and Mrs. Hunt are buying their home; their mortgage will be paid off during the same year Mr. Hunt plans to retire. He figures if he can keep working until then, he'll be able to make it on his retirement income.

During the past year, there has been a marked change in Mr. Hunt's performance. He has always used an "average" amount of sick leave, but during the past year was absent for over thirty days with various physical problems of his own. His work has slowed down considerably, to the point that he is not able to handle an average workload at present. He is slow to adapt to changes and the supervisor has been having to repeat instructions to him numerous times. Sometimes he seems to be staring off into space, and it seems that his concentration span is lessening. His rate of careless errors on reports, forms, and dictation has reached an unacceptable level in recent weeks. Mr. Hunt has been wearing a hearing aid for several months now but it appears that it does not or cannot completely correct his increasing hearing deficit, which sometimes causes problems in communication. He is also developing a noticeable tremor of his hands. The supervisor concluded some time ago that Mr. Hunt is suffering from the typical problems of advancing age, which are affecting his functioning both mentally and physically. His graduate student, who has been with him for four months and has three more to go in placement, is not handling the situation very maturely and is loudly, and sometimes unprofessionally, critical and disrespectful of her supervisor.

Mr. Hunt's supervisor has been meeting regularly with him during the past year to discuss his changed performance. Mr. Hunt always promises to do better and makes a really sincere effort. His performance does improve for a time, but then slips back into the problematic pattern. He is not usually defensive, but when the supervisor attempts to comment that perhaps he should take advantage of his eighteen years of faithful service to the agency and go ahead and retire now, he becomes quite upset and emphasizes his plan to continue working until he can retire with full benefits in one and one-half years. In fact, the last time the supervisor made this suggestion, Mr. Hunt became quite angry and made it known that his brother is a practicing attorney in the area and that he has a close friend who is a congressman and "you aren't going to force *me* to retire!"

The supervisor is fully aware of Mr. Hunt's home situation and fully empathizes with his need to continue working, but at the same time, the department is suffering from his declining performance and there is little indication that he will be able to get back up to his previous level. His Annual Performance Evaluation is due in four months.

What should this supervisor do?

SELECTED READINGS

The following is not intended to be a complete listing of all readings on the subject areas given, but rather a representative sample of classics that endure with time, and recent material that reflects current trends and issues in social work practice today.

ACCOUNTABILITY, AUDIT, AND PEER REVIEW*

American Hospital Association, Society for Hospital Social Work Directors. *Development of Professional Standards Review for Hospital Social Work.* Chicago: Society for Hospital Social Work Directors, 1977.

Berkman, Barbara, and Rehr, Helen. "Social Work Undertakes Its Own Audit." *Social Work in Health Care* 3, no. 3 (Spring 1978):273–86.

Bonney, Norman L., and Streicher, Lawrence H. "Time-Cost Data in Agency Administration: Efficiency Controls in Family and Children's Service." *Social Work* 15, no. 4 (October 1970):23–31.

Chommie, Peter W., and Hudson, Joe. "Evaluation of Outcome and Process." *Social Work* 19, no. 6 (November 1974):682–87.

Ferguson, Kris, et al. "Initiation of a Quality Assurance Program for Social Work Practice in a Teaching Hospital." *Social Work in Health Care* 2, no. 2 (Winter 1976–77):205–18.

Fischer, Joel. "Is Casework Effective? A Review." *Social Work Journal* 18, no. 1 (January 1973):5–21.

Goldman, Milton. "An Agency Conducts a Time and Cost Study." *Social Casework* 45, no. 7 (July 1964):393–97.

Haselkorn, Florence. "Accountability in Clinical Practice." *Social Casework* 59, no. 6 (June 1978):330–36.

Hill, John G. "Cost Analysis in Social Work Service." In Norman Polansky, ed., *Social Work Research.* Chicago: University of Chicago Press, 1960, pp. 223–46.

Jaffe, Helen. "Recording as the Key to Peer Review." *Proceedings of the Tenth Annual Meeting of the Society for Hospital Social Work Directors*, American Hospital Association, September 24–26, 1975, Kansas City, Missouri, sec. 2.

Kiresuk, Thomas J., and Sherman, Robert E. "Goal Attainment Scaling: A General Method for Evaluating Comprehensive Community Mental Health Programs." *Journal of Community Mental Health* 4 (December 1968):443–53.

Loftus, Geoffrey R., and Levy, Rona L. "Statistical Evaluation of Clinical Effectiveness." *Social Work* 22, no. 6 (November 1977):504–505.

Newman, Edward, and Turem, Jerry. "The Crisis of Accountability." *Social Work* 19, no. 1 (January 1974):5–16.

Rosenberg, Marvin L., and Brody, Ralph. "The Threat or Challenge of Accountability." *Social Work* 19, no. 3 (May 1974):344–50.

Waldron, John. "A Communication Skills Assessment Rating Scale." In Milton M. Berger, ed., *Videotape Techniques in Psychiatric Training and Treatment.* Rev. ed. New York: Brunner/Mazel, 1978, pp. 85–90.

Wood, Katherine M. "Casework Effectiveness: A New Look at the Research Evidence." *Social Work* 23, no. 6 (November 1978):437–59.

CASEWORK/INTERVIEWING TEXTS

Banaka, William H. *Training in Depth Interviewing.* New York: Harper & Row, 1971.

Benjamin, Alfred. *The Helping Interview.* 2d ed. Boston: Houghton Mifflin, 1974.

Biestek, Felix. *The Casework Relationship.* Chicago: Loyola University Press, 1957.

Bird, Brian. *Talking with Patients.* 2d ed. Philadelphia: Lippincott, 1973.

Briar, Scott, and Miller, Henry. *Problems and Issues in Social Casework.* New York: Columbia University Press, 1971.

Brammer, Lawrence M. *The Helping Relationship: Process and Skills.* Englewood Cliffs, N.J.: Prentice-Hall, 1973.

*Articles listed here concern social work recording or interviewing/casework skills in some manner. Accountability, audit and peer review references that are almost exclusively administrative in orientation are not included here.

Combs, Arthur W.; Avila, Donald; and Purkey, William. *Helping Relationships: Basic Concepts for the Helping Profession*. Boston: Allyn and Bacon, 1971.

Cormier, William A., and Cormier, Sherilyn L. *Interviewing Strategies for Helpers: A Guide to Assessment, Treatment and Evaluation*. Monterey, Calif.: Brooks/Cole, 1979.

Davison, Evelyn H. *Social Casework*. 2d ed. Baltimore: Williams and Wilkins, 1970.

Delaney, Daniel J., and Eisenberg, Sheldon. *The Counseling Process*. Chicago: Rand McNally, 1972.

Dyer, Wayne W., and Vriend, John. *Counseling Techniques that Work*. New York: Funk and Wagnalls, 1977.

Edinburg, Golda M; Zinberg, Norman E.; and Kelman, Wendy. *Clinical Interviewing and Counseling: Principles and Techniques*. New York: Appleton-Century-Crofts, 1975.

Fischer, Joel, ed. *Interpersonal Helping: Emerging Approaches for Social Work Practice*. Springfield, Ill.: Charles C. Thomas, 1973.

Garrett, Annette. *Interviewing: Its Principles and Methods*. 2d ed. New York: Family Service Association of America, 1972.

Golan, Naomi. *Treatment in Crisis Situations*. New York: Free Press, 1978.

Hamilton, Gordon. *Theory and Practice of Social Case Work*. 2d ed. New York: Columbia University Press, 1951.

Hollis, Florence. *Casework: A Psychosocial Therapy*. 2d ed. New York: Random House, 1972.

Johnson, Dorothy E., and Vestermark, Mary J. *Barriers and Hazards in Counseling*. Boston: Houghton Mifflin, 1970.

Kadushin, Alfred. *The Social Work Interview*. New York: Columbia University Press, 1972.

Keith-Lucas, Alan. *Giving and Taking Help*. Chapel Hill: University of North Carolina Press, 1972.

MacKinnon, Roger A., and Michels, Robert. *The Psychiatric Interview in Clinical Practice*. Philadelphia: Saunders, 1971.

Parad, Howard J., ed. *Crisis Intervention: Selected Readings*. New York: Family Service Association of America, 1965.

Perlman, Helen Harris. *Relationship: The Heart of Helping People*. Chicago: University of Chicago Press, 1979.

Perlman, Helen Harris. *Social Casework: A Problem-Solving Process*. Chicago: University of Chicago Press, 1957.

Reid, William J., and Epstein, Laura. *Task-Centered Casework*. New York: Columbia University Press, 1972.

Roberts, Robert W., and Nee, Robert H., eds. *Theories and Practice of Social Casework*. Chicago: University of Chicago Press, 1970.

Sackheim, Gertrude. *The Practice of Clinical Casework*. New York: Behavioral Publications, 1974.

Schubert, Margaret. *Interviewing in Social Work Practice: An Introduction*. New York: Council on Social Work Education, 1971.

Turner, Francis J., ed. *Differential Diagnosis and Treatment*. 2d ed. New York: Free Press, 1976.

Turner, Francis J. *Social Work Treatment: Interlocking Theoretical Approaches*. New York: Free Press, 1974.

Younghusband, Eileen. *Casework with Families and Children*. Chicago: University of Chicago Press, 1965.

CODED AND STATISTICAL RECORDING

American Hospital Association, Society for Hospital Social Work Directors. *A Reporting System for Hospital Social Work*. Chicago: AHA, 1978.

Berkman, B.; Rehr, H.; and Rosenberg, G. *Classification of Problems and Outcomes in Hospital Social Work Services*. New York: Mount Sinai Department of Social Work Services, 1977.

Gay, Eleanor. "Collecting Data by Case Recording." *Social Work* 3, no. 1 (January 1958):76–80.

Hollis, Florence. "Explorations in the Development of a Typology of Casework Treatment." *Social Casework* 48, no. 6 (June 1967):335–41.

Hollis, Florence. "The Coding and Application of a Typology of Casework Treatment." *Social Casework* 48, no. 8 (October 1967):489–97.

Reid, William J. "Developments in the Use of Organized Data." *Social Work* 19, no. 5 (September 1974):585–93.

Seaberg, James R. "Case Recording by Code." *Social Work* 10, no. 4 (October 1965):92–98.

Seaberg, James R. "Systematized Recording: A Follow-up." *Social Work* 15, no. 4 (October 1970):32–41.

Simmons, John C. "A Reporting System for Hospital Social Service Departments." *Health and Social Work* 3, no. 4 (November 1978):100–112.

Vasey, Ivan T. "Developing a Data Storage and Retrieval System." *Social Casework* 49, no. 7 (July 1968):414–17.

COMPUTERIZED DATA

Abels, Paul. "Can Computers Do Social Work?" *Social Work* 17, no. 5 (September 1972):5–11.

American Psychiatric Association, Task Force on Automation and Data Processing. "Automation and Data Processing in Psychiatry." Washington, D.C.: APA, 1971.

Boyd, Lawrence H., Jr.; Hylton, John H.; and Price, Steven V. "Computers in Social Work Practice: A Review." *Social Work* 23, no. 5 (September 1978):368–71.

Curran, W. J., and Bank, Rheta. *Safeguarding Psychiatric Privacy: Computer Systems and Their Uses.* New York: Wiley, 1975.

Erikson, K. T., and Gilbertson, D. E. "Case Records in the Mental Hospital." In S. Wheeler, ed., *On Record: Files and Dossiers in American Life.* New Brunswick, N.J.: Transaction, 1976, pp. 389–412.

Fuller, Theron K. "Computer Utility in Social Work." *Social Casework* 51, no. 10 (December 1970):606–611.

Gabriel, E. R., Chairman. Joint Task Group on Confidentiality of Computerized Medical Records. "Ethical Guidelines for Data Centers Handling Medical Records." Adopted by the House of Delegates of the Medical Society of the State of New York, March 1975; adopted by Board of Directors, Society for Computer Medicine, November 1975, and also adopted by the National Association of Blue Shield Plans.

Gobert, J. J. "Accommodating Patient Rights and Computerized Mental Health Systems." *North Carolina Law Review* 54 (January 1976):153–87.

Godwin, William F., and Booade, Katherine Anne. "Privacy and the New Technology." *Personnel and Guidance Journal* 50, no. 4 (December 1971):298–304.

Guthrie, D., et al. "Data Bases and the Privacy Rights of the Mentally Retarded: Report of the AAMD Task Force on Data Base Confidentiality." *Mental Retardation* 14, no. 5 (1976):3–7.

Harrison, Annette. "The Problem of Privacy in the Computer Age: An Annotated Bibliography." Santa Monica, Calif.: Rand Corporation, December 1967.

Hill, Gareth S. "Ethical Practices in the Computerization of Client Data: Implications for Social Work Practice and Record Keeping." Washington, D.C.: National Association of Social Workers (early 1970s).

Kedward, H. B., et al. "Computers and Psychiatric Data Recording: Rationale and Problems of Confidentiality." *Comprehensive Psychiatry* 14, no. 2 (March–April 1973):133–37.

Kelley, V. R., and Weston, H. B. "Civil Liberties Guidelines for Computerized Management Information Systems of Mental Health Facilities." *American Journal of Orthopsychiatry* 44, no. 2 (1974):279.

Kelley, Verne R., and Weston, Hanna B. "Computers, Costs, and Civil Liberties." *Social Work* 20, no. 1 (January 1975):15–19.

Luce, Gay. "The Computer as Psychiatric Aid and Research Tool." *Mental Health Program Reports No. 2.* Washington, D.C.: Department of Health, Education, and Welfare, February, 1968.

Mair, W. C. "Computer Abuse in Hospitals." *Hospital Progress* 58, no. 3 (1977):61–63.

Miller, A. R. *The Assault on Privacy: Computers, Databanks, and Dossiers.* Ann Arbor: University of Michigan Press, 1971.

National Association of Social Workers. "Policy on Information Utilization and Confidentiality." Policy adopted at the NASW 1975 Delegate Assembly, May 30–June 3, 1975, Washington, D.C.

Noble, John H., Jr. "Protecting the Public's Privacy in Computerized Health and Welfare Information Systems." *Social Work* 16, no. 1 (January 1971): 35–41.

Pascoe, J. "MIB: It Has 12 Million Americans at Its Fingertips." *Prism* 2 (1974):28.

Rand Corporation. "A Bibliography of Selected Rand Publications: Privacy in the Computer Age." Santa Monica, Calif.: The Rand Corporation, August 1976. SB-1047.

Spitzer, R. L., and Endicott, J. "Automation of Psychiatric Case Records: Will It Help the Clinician?" *Clinical and Basic Research* 31, no. 11 (1970):45–46.

Stern, L. C. "Medical Information Bureau: The Life Insurer's Databank." *Rutgers Journal of Computers and Law* 4, no. 1 (1974):1–41.

Westin, A. F., and Baker, M. A. *Databanks in a Free Society: Computers, Record-Keeping and Privacy.* New York: Quadrangle/New York Times Book Co., 1972.

Wilson, Dolores Y. P. "Computerization of Welfare Recipients: Implications for the Individual and the Right to Privacy." *Rutgers Journal of Computers and Law* 4, no. 1 (1974):163–208.

CONFIDENTIALITY—FEDERAL REGULATIONS (AND ARTICLES DISCUSSING THEM)

"A Chapter of Legislative History: Safeguarding the Disclosure of Public Assistance Records: The Legislative History of the 'Jenner Amendment'—Section 618, 1951." *Social Service Review* 26 (June 1952):229–34.

Computer Security Guidelines for Implementing the Privacy Act of 1974. FIPS Publication 41. Washington, D.C.: National Bureau of Standards, 1975.

"Confidentiality of Alcohol and Drug Abuse Patient Records—General Provisions." Department of Health, Education, and Welfare, Public Health Service. *Federal Register* 40, no. 127 (July 1, 1975),pt. IV.

Family Educational Rights and Privacy Act of 1974. Amends Public Law 93-568, effective November 19, 1974 ("The Buckley Amendment").

"Federal Privacy Act: Disclosure of Medical Reports in Social Security Disability Claims." *Journal of Kansas Medical Society* 76, no. 11 (November 1975):282.

Federal Privacy Act of 1974. Public Law 93-579. December 31, 1974.

Freedom of Information Act. Title 5, United States Code, Section 552, 1966.

Helms, D. J. "A Guide to the New Federal Rules Governing the Confidentiality of Alcohol and Drug Abuse Patient Records." *Contemporary Drug Problems* 4, no. 3 (1975):259–83.

Lewis, D. C. "Health and Privacy—The Confidentiality of Drug Treatment Records." *Contemporary Drug Problems* 4, no. 3 (1975):285–95.

Lewis, D. C. "Privacy Rights and Record Confidentiality in Drug and Alcohol Abuse Treatment Programs." *Journal of Psychedelic Drugs* 8, no. 4 (1976):324–26.

Moss, D. "Confidentiality of Alcohol and Drug Abuse Patient Records." *Medical Record News* 47, no. 3 (1976):61–64.

National Bureau of Standards. *Computer Security Guidelines for Implementing the Privacy Act of 1974.* FIPS Publication 41. Washington, D.C.: National Bureau of Standards, 1975.

Oda, D. S., and Quick, M. J. "School Health Records and the New Accessibility Law." *Journal of School Health* 47, no. 4 (1977):212–16.

"Privacy of Medical Information Act." Bill S. 865, reported in the *Congressional Record*, Proceedings and Debates of the 96th Congress, First Session, Vol. 125, no. 43. Washington, D.C.: April 4, 1979. This bill is under consideration and would amend the Federal Privacy Act of 1974, basically extending its concept to medical records maintained by private and federal facilities that receive various forms of federal funds.

Privacy Protection Study Commission. "Final Recommendations of the Privacy Protection Study Commission as Contained in the Final Report." Washington, D.C.: Privacy Protection Study Commission (no date). This is a summarized version of *Personal Privacy in an Information Society.*

Privacy Protection Study Commission. *Personal Privacy in an Information Society.* Washington, D.C.: Government Printing Office, 1977.

"Privacy Rights of Parents and Students," Part II. Department of Health, Education, and Welfare, Office of the Secretary. Final Rule on Education Records. *Federal Register* (June 17, 1976), pp. 24662–24675.

Sacks, Herbert S. "Checks and Balances Stymie Title XX Confidentiality Threats." *Connecticut Medicine* 40, no. 7 (1976):471–73.

Sacks, Herbert S. "Editorials: PSRO and the Privacy Act: Progress in Confidentiality Guarantees." *Connecticut Medicine* 39, no. 11 (November 1975):702–703.

Sacks, Herbert S. "Strategies and Remedies for Confidentiality Deficits in Title XX and Title IV D Legislation." *Connecticut Medicine* 40, no. 2 (1976):140–42.

Sacks, Herbert S. "Title XX: A Major Threat to Privacy and a Setback for Informed Consent." *Connecticut Medicine* 39, no. 12 (1975):785–87.

Stromberg, R. E. "Medical Legal Forum: When May a Hospital Release Alcohol or Drug Abuse Treatment Records?" *Hospital Forum* (California) 18, no. 9 (December 1975):20.

U.S. Department of Health, Education, and Welfare. "Records, Computers and the Rights of Citizens." Report No. (OS)73-94. Washington, D.C.: Government Printing Office, 1973.

Weissman, J. C., and Berns, B. R. "Patient Confidentiality and the Criminal Justice System: A Critical Examination of the New Federal Confidentiality Regulations." *Contemporary Drug Problems* 5, no. 4 (1976):531–52.

Zdeb, M. J. "A Student Right of Privacy: The Developing School Records Controversy." *Loyola University of Chicago Law Journal* 6, no. 2 (1975):430–45.

CONFIDENTIALITY—GENERAL ISSUES

Aldrich, Robert F. *Health Records and Confidentiality: An Annotated Bibliography with Abstracts.* Washington, D.C.: National Commission on Confidentiality of Health Records, 1977. A revised version will soon be available and can be obtained at 1211 Connecticut Ave., NW, Washington, D.C. 20036.

American Medical Record Association: *Confidentiality of Patient Health Information: A Position Statement of the American Medical Record Association.* Chicago: American Medical Record Association, no date. The statement was adopted by the AMRA Executive Board in December 1977. Copies may be obtained from them at 875 N. Michigan Avenue, Suite 1850, Chicago, Illinois 60611.

American Orthopsychiatric Association. "Position Statement on Confidentiality of Health Records." June 1975.

Annas, G. J. "Legal Aspects of Medical Confidentiality in the Occupational Setting." *Journal of Occupational Medicine* 18, no. 8 (1976):537–40.

Arnold, Selma. "Confidential Communication and the Social Worker." *Social Work* 15, no. 1 (January 1970):61–67.

Bernstein, Barton E. "The Social Worker as a Courtroom Witness." *Social Casework* 56, no. 9 (November 1975):521–25.

Bernstein, Barton E. "The Social Worker as an Expert Witness." *Social Casework* 58, no. 7 (July 1977):412–17.

Campbell, B. C. "Confidentiality of Health Records in Emergency Medical Services Systems." *Medical Record News* 46, no. 3 (1975):16–20.

Carroll, James D., and Knerr, Charles R. "Bibliography." Unpublished, mimeographed listing of several hundred references pertaining to confidentiality and research. Obtained from the authors at the University of Texas at Arlington, 1977.

Confidentiality of Health and Social Service Records: Where Law, Ethics and Clinical Issues Meet. Proceedings of the Second Midwest Regional Conference, December 1976. Chicago: University of Illinois at Chicago Circle, 1976.

Family Service Association. *The Lawyer and the Social Worker: Guides to Cooperation.* New York: Family Service Association of America, February 1959.

Foster, L. M. "Do You Want to Share Your Therapy Tapes with the Court?" *Professional Psychology* 5 (1974):369–73.

Grossman, Maurice. "Confidentiality in Medical Practice." *Annual Review of Medicine* 28 (1977):43–55.

Grossman, Maurice. "The Psychiatrist and the Subpoena." *Bulletin of the American Academy of Psychiatry and Law* 1, no. 4 (December 1973):245–53.

Harrison, A. "The Problem of Privacy in the Computer Age: An Annotated Bibliography," December 1967. Santa Monica, Calif.: Rand Corporation, Publication No. RM-5495-PR/RC.

Hayt, E., and Hayt, J. *Legal Aspects of Medical Records.* Berwy, Illinois: Physicians' Record Committee, 1964.

Hofmann, Adele D. "Confidentiality and the Health Care Records of Children and Youth." *Psychiatric Opinion* 12, no. 1 (January 1975):20–28.

Hofmann, Adele D. "Is Confidentiality in Health Care Records a Pediatric Concern?" *Pediatrics* 57 (1976):170–72.

Hofmann, Adele D.; Becker, R. D.; and Gabriel, H. Paul. "Consent and Confidentiality." In *The Hospitalized Adolescent: A Guide to Managing the Ill and Injured Youth.* New York: Free Press, 1976, pp. 211–32.

Hunt, K., and Turn, R. "Privacy and Security in Databank Systems: An Annotated Bibliography, 1970–1973." Santa Monica, Calif.: Rand Corporation, Publication No. R-1361-NSF, March 1974.

Kelley, Verne R., and Weston, Hanna B. "Civil Liberties in Mental Health Facilities." *Social Work* 19, no. 1 (January 1974):48–54.

Levine, Richard Steven. "Access to 'Confidential' Welfare Records in the Course of Child Protection Proceedings." *Journal of Family Law* 14, no. 4 (1975):535–46.

Levine, Richard Steven. "Child Protection Records: Issues of Confidentiality." *Social Work* 21, no. 4 (July 1976): 323–26.

McCormick, Mary J. "Privacy: A New American Dilemma." *Social Casework* 59, no. 4 (April 1978):211–20.

National Association of Social Workers. "Model Licensing Act for Social Workers." Washington, D.C.: NASW, 1973.

National Commission on Confidentiality of Health Records. *Rx Confidentially.* Newsletter published quarterly by the commission. It reports on conferences, publications, government activities, and other items of interest to people concerned with confidentiality of health records.

"News of the Societies: National Federation of Societies for Clinical Social Work: Ethical Standards of Clinical Social Workers." *Clinical Social Work Journal* 2, no. 4 (Winter 1974):312–15.

Noll, J. O. "The Psychotherapist and Informed Consent." *American Journal of Psychiatry* 133, no. 12 (1976):1451–53.

Noll, J. O., and Hanlong, M. J. "Patient Privacy and Confidentiality at Mental Health Centers." *American Journal of Psychiatry* 133, no. 11 (1976):1286–89.

Nye, Sandra G. "Model Law on Confidentiality of Health and Social Service Information." Appendix B in *Confidentiality of Health and Social Service Records: Where Law, Ethics and Clinical Issues Meet,* Proceedings of the Second Midwest Regional Conference. Chicago: University of Illinois at Chicago Circle, December 1976, pp. 260–82.

Reynolds, Mildred M. "Threats to Confidentiality." *Social Work* 21, no. 2 (March 1976):108–113.

Riscalla, L. M. "Records—A Legal Responsibility." *Journal of Rehabilitation* 40, no. 1 (1974):12–14.

Rosen, C. E. "Why Clients Relinquish Their Rights to Privacy Under Sign-away Pressures." *Professional Psychology* 8, no. 1 (1977):17–24.

Sacks, Herbert S. "Politics, Privacy and the Parent Locator Service: The Physician's Responsibility." *Connecticut Medicine* 40, no. 1 (1976):61–63.

Spingarn, Natalie Davis. *Confidentiality: Report of the Conference on Confidentiality of Health Records, Key Biscayne, Florida, November 6–9, 1974.* Washington, D.C.: American Psychiatric Association, 1975.

Springer, Eric W. "Professional Standards Review Organizations: Some Problems of Confidentiality." *Utah Law Review* 1975 (Summer 1975):361–80.

Volkman v. Miller, 383 N.Y.S. 2d 95 Supreme Court, May 13, 1976.

"Widespread Theft of Medical Records Found by Denver Grand Jury." *Hospitals* 50, no. 15 (1976):22–23.

Wilson, Suanna J. *Confidentiality in Social Work: Issues and Principles.* New York: Free Press, 1978. Contains a bibliography of over 500 references pertaining to many aspects of confidentiality covering various disciplines, but including nearly everything written on confidentiality and privileged communication in the social work literature from the early 1900s through 1975. The above listing does contain a number of newer references (1976–1979) that are not in the *Confidentiality* bibliography.

CONSUMER ACCESS TO RECORDS

Abel, Charles M., and Johnson, H. Wayne. "Clients' Access to Records: Policy and Attitudes." *Social Work* 23, no. 1 (January 1978):42–46.

"Adult Adoptee's Constitutional Right to Know His Origins." *South California Law Review* 48 (May 1975):1196–1220.

Auerbach, Melissa, and Bogue, Ted. *Getting Yours: A Consumer's Guide to Obtaining Your Medical Record.* Washington, D.C.: Health Research Group, 1978. Copies may be obtained by contacting them at 2000 P Street, N.W., 20036.

Baran, Annette; Pannor, Reuben; and Sorosky, Arthur D. "Adoptive Parents and the Sealed Record Controversy." *Social Casework* 55, no. 9 (November 1974):531–36.

Brodsky, Stanley L. "Shared Results and Open Files with the Client." *Professional Psychology,* Fall 1972, pp. 362–64.

Chaiklin, Harris. "Honesty in Casework Treatment." *The Social Welfare Forum, 1973.* NCSW, Atlantic City, May 27–31, 1973. New York: Columbia University Press, 1974, pp. 266–74.

"Discovery Rights of the Adoptee—Privacy Rights of the Natural Parent: A Constitutional Dilemma." *University of South Florida Law Review* 4 (Spring 1975):65–83.

Gordon, Richard E., and Barnard, George W. "Why a Patient Should Never Get a Copy of His Psychiatric Report." *Consultant* 14, no. 12 (December 1974):110–11.

Kaiser, Barbara L. "Patients' Rights of Access to Their Own Medical Records: The Need for New Law." *Buffalo Law Review* 24 (Winter 1975):317–30.

Memel, S. L. "Medical Records and the Patient's Right to Access." *Hospital Medical Staff* 5, no. 7 (1976):13–18.

Sorosky, Arthur D.; Baran, Annette; and Pannor, Reuban. *The Adoption Triangle: The Effects of the Sealed Record on Adoptees, Birth Parents and Adoptive Parents.* Garden City, N.Y.: Anchor Press, 1978.

DIAGNOSTIC ASSESSMENT

Freeman, Edith H.; Kalis, Betty L.; and Harris, M. Robert. "Assessing Patient Characteristics from Psychotherapy Interviews." In *Crisis Intervention: Selected Readings*, Howard J. Parad, ed. New York: Family Service Association of America, 1965, p. 349.

Freeman, Henry. "Applying Family Diagnosis in Practice." In Eileen Younghusband, ed., *Casework with Families and Children.* Chicago: University of Chicago Press, 1965, p. 165.

Freeman, Henry; Hildebrand, Catherine; and Ayre, Donald A. "A Classification System that Prescribes Treatment." *Social Casework Journal* 46, no. 7 (July 1965):423.

Ganter, Grace, and Polansky, Norman A. "Predicting a Child's Accessibility to Individual Treatment from Diagnostic Groups." *Social Work Journal* 9, no. 3 (July 1964):56.

Gomberg, M. Robert. "Family Diagnosis: Trends in Theory and Practice." In Eileen Younghusband, ed., *Casework with Families and Children.* Chicago: University of Chicago Press, 1965, p. 39.

Kadushin, Alfred. "Diagnosis and Evaluation for (Almost) All Occasions." *Social Work Journal* 8, no. 1 (January 1963):12–19.

Mullen, Edward J. "The Relation Between Diagnosis and Treatment in Casework." *Social Casework Journal* 50, no. 4 (April 1969):218.

Parad, Howard J., and Caplan, Gerald. "A Framework for Studying Families in Crisis." In Howard J. Parad, ed., *Crisis Intervention: Selected Readings.* New York: Family Service Association of America, 1965.

Perlman, Helen Harris. "Diagnosis: The Thinking in Problem-Solving." Chap. 11 in *Social Casework: A Problem-Solving Process.* Chicago: University of Chicago Press, 1957, pp. 164–82.

Perlman, Helen Harris. "Family Diagnosis in Cases of Illness and Disability." In *Family Centered Social Work in Illness and Disability: A Preventive Approach*, Monograph 4. New York: NASW, 1961, p. 7.

Phillips, Davis Campbell. "Of Plums and Thistles: The Search for Diagnosis." *Social Work* 5, no. 1 (January 1960):84–90.

Roberts, Robert W., and Nee, Robert H., eds. "Assessment of the Client in His Situation." In *Theories and Practice of Social Casework.* Chicago: University of Chicago Press, 1970, pp. 49–57.

Scherz, Frances H. "Exploring the Use of Family Interviews in Diagnosis." *Social Casework Journal* 45, no. 4 (April 1964):209.

Siporin, Max. "Deviant Behavior Theory in Social Work: Diagnosis and Treatment." *Social Work Journal* 10, no. 3 (July 1965):59.

Witte, Ernest F. "Social and Cultural Factors in Casework Diagnosis." *Social Work Journal* 4, no. 3 (July 1959):15.

MINORITY CONCERNS

Aguilar, Ignacio. "Initial Contacts with Mexican-American Families." In Francis J. Turner, ed., *Differential Diagnosis and Treatment in Social Work.* 2d ed. New York: Free Press, 1976, p. 512.

Baird, Keith E. "Semantics and Afro-American Liberations." *Social Casework* 51, no. 5 (May 1970):265.

Beasley, Lou M. "A Beginning Attempt to Eradicate Racist Attitudes." *Social Casework* 53, no. 1 (January 1972):9.

Berlin, Sharon B. "Better Work with Women Clients." *Social Work* 21, no. 6 (November 1976):492–97.

Burgest, David R. "Racism in Everyday Speech and Social Work Jargon." *Social Work* 18, no. 4 (July 1973):20.

Carter, James H., and Haizlip, Thomas M. "Race and Its Relevance to Transference." *American Journal of Orthopsychiatry* 42, no. 1 (January 1972):865.

Cooper, Shirley. "A Look at the Effect of Racism on Clinical Work." *Social Casework* 54, no. 2 (February 1973):76.

Brown, Caree Rozen, and Hellinger, Marilyn Levitt. "Therapists' Attitudes Toward Women." *Social Work* 20, no. 4 (July 1975):266.

Cormican, John D. "Linguistic Issues in Interviewing." *Social Casework* 59, no. 3 (March 1978):145–51.

Davenport, Judith, and Reims, Nancy. "Theoretical Orientation and Attitudes Toward Women." *Social Work* 23, no. 4 (July 1978): 306–310.

Delgado, Melvin. "Puerto Rican Spiritualism and the Social Work Professions." *Social Casework* 58, no. 8 (October 1977):451–58.

Fischer, Joel, et al. "Are Social Workers Sexists?" *Social Work* 21, no. 6 (November 1976):428–33.

Ghali, Sonia Badillo. "Culture Sensitivity and the Puerto Rican Client." *Social Casework* 58, no. 8 (October 1977):459–68.

Gitterman, Alex, and Schaeffer, Alice. "The White Professional and the Black Client." In Francis J. Turner, ed., *Differential Diagnosis and Treatment in Social Work*. 2d ed. New York: Free Press, 1976, p. 526. (Note: This article can also be found in *Social Casework* 53, no. 5 [May 1972]:280.)

Gochros, Jean S. "Recognition and Use of Anger in Negro Clients." *Social Work* 11, no. 1 (January 1966):28.

Hallowitz, David. "Counseling and Treatment of the Poor Black Family." *Social Casework* 56, no. 8 (October 1975):451.

Kadushin, Alfred. "The Racial Factor in the Interview." *Social Work* 17, no. 3 (May 1972):88–99.

Knutson, Andie L. "Cultural Beliefs on Life and Death." In Orville G. Brim, Jr., et al., eds., *The Dying Patient*. New York: Russell Sage Foundation, 1970, p. 42.

"La Causa Chicana." Special issue of *Social Casework* devoted to Chicanos (Mexicans). 52, no. 5 (May 1971).

Lewis, Ronald G., and Ho, Man Keung. "Social Work with Native Americans." *Social Work* 20, no. 5 (September 1975):379.

Medina, Celia, and Reyes, Maria R. "Dilemmas of Chicana Counselors." *Social Work* 21, no. 6 (November 1976):515–18.

Mizio, Emelicia. "White Worker—Minority Client." *Social Work* 17, no. 3 (May 1972):82–86.

Morales, Armando. "Institutional Racism in Mental Health and Criminal Justice." *Social Casework* 59, no. 7 (July 1978):387–95.

Perlmutter, Felice Davidson, and Alexander, Leslie B. "Racism and Sexism in Social Work Practice: An Empirical View." *Administration in Social Work* 1, no. 4 (Winter 1977):433–42.

Petro, Olive, and French, Betty. "The Black Client's View of Himself." *Social Casework* 53, no. 8 (October 1972):466.

Pierce, Chester M. "Psychiatric Problems of the Black Minority." In Gerald Caplan, ed., *American Handbook of Psychiatry*. 2d ed., vol 2. New York: Basic Books, 1974, chap. 33.

Red Horse, John G., and Lewis, Ronald. "Family Behavior of Urban American Indians." *Social Casework* 59, no. 2 (February 1978):67–72.

Reiner, Beatrice Simcox. "The Real World of the Teenage Negro Mother." *Child Welfare* 47, no. 7 (July 1968):391–96.

Scanzoni, John H. *The Black Family in Modern Society*. Boston: Allyn & Bacon, 1971.

Shannon, Barbara E. "Implications of White Racism for Social Work Practice." *Social Casework* 51, no. 5 (May 1970):270.

Siegel, Jerome M. "A Brief Review of the Effects of Race in Clinical Service Interactions." *American Journal of Orthopsychiatry* 44, no. 4 (July 1974):555.

Sotomayor, Marta. "Language, Culture, and Ethnicity in Developing Self-Concept." *Social Casework* 58, no. 4 (April 1977):195–203.

Stempler, Benjamin L. "Effects of Aversive Racism on White Social Work Students." *Social Casework* 56, no. 8 (October 1975):460.

Stevens, Barbara. "The Psychotherapist and Women's Liberation." In Francis J. Turner, ed., *Differential Diagnosis and Treatment in Social Work*. 2d ed. New York: Free Press, 1976, p. 132.

Thomas, Susan Amelia. "Theory and Practice in Feminist Therapy." *Social Work* 22, no. 6 (November 1977):447–54.

Young, Whitney M., Jr. "Tell It Like It Is." *Social Casework* 49, no. 4 (April 1968):207.

Zietz, Dorothy, and Erlich, John L. "Sexism in Social Agencies: Practitioners' Perspectives." *Social Work* 21, no. 6 (November 1976):434–49.

MISCELLANEOUS

Dyer, Wayne W., and Vriend, John. "Analyzing a Counseling Interview: The Tape-of-a-Tape Continuous Feedback Approach to Trainee Supervision." In Wayne W. Dyer and John Vriend, *Counseling Techniques that Work*. New York: Funk & Wagnalls, 1977, pp. 104–24.

Gottlieb, Werner, and Stanley, Joe H. "Mutual Goals and Goal-Setting in Casework." *Social Casework* 48 (October 1967):471–77.

Kadushin, Alfred. "Interview Observation as a Teaching Device." *Social Casework* 38, no. 7 (July 1956):334–41.

National Association of Social Workers. "Code of Ethics of the NASW." Washington, D.C.: NASW, adopted by the Delegate Assembly of NASW, October 13, 1960, and amended April 11, 1967.

Seabury, Brett A. "The Contract: Uses, Abuses, and Limitations." *Social Work* 21, no. 1 (January 1976):16.

Wilson, Suanna J. *Field Instruction: Techniques for Supervisors*. New York: Free Press, 1980.

PRIVILEGED COMMUNICATION

Bernstein, Barton E. "Privileged Communications to the Social Worker." *Social Work* 23, no. 4 (July 1977):259–63.

"Confidential and Privileged Communications: Guidelines for Lawyers and Social Workers." In *Law and Social Work: Statements Prepared by the National Conference of Lawyers and Social Workers*. Washington, D.C.: National Association of Social Workers, 1973.

"Court Upholds Confidentiality of Social Work Communications." *Hospitals* 48 (February 16, 1974):116.

Diamond, Bernard L. "Psychiatric Prediction of Dangerousness." *University of Pennsylvania Law Review* 123 (December 1974):439–52.

Foster, H. H., Jr. "An Overview of Confidentiality and Privilege." *Bulletin of the American Academy of Psychiatry and Law* 4, no. 3 (1976):393–401.

Glassman, Michael. "Recent Cases—Privileged Communication—Psychiatry: Psychotherapist Has a Duty to Warn an Endangered Victim Whose Peril Was Disclosed by Communications between the Psychotherapist and Patient." *University of Cincinnati Law Review* 44 (1975):368–75.

Grossman, Maurice. "The Psychiatrist and the Subpoena." *Bulletin of the American Academy of Psychiatry and Law* 1, no. 4 (December 1973):245–53.

"Group Therapy and Privileged Communication." *Indiana Law Journal* 43 (1967):93–105.

Gurevitz, H. "Tarasoff—Protective Privilege Versus Public Peril." *American Journal of Psychiatry* 124, no. 3 (1977):289–92.

"NOTE: The Social Worker-Client Relationship and Privileged Communications." *Washington University Law Quarterly* 1965 (1965):362–95.

Nye, Sandra G. "Model Law on Confidentiality of Health and Social Service Information." In *Confidentiality of Health and Social Service Records: Where Law, Ethics and Clinical Issues Meet*. Chicago: University of Illinois at Chicago Circle, December 1976, pp. 260–82.

Nye, Sandra G. "Privilege." In *Confidentiality of Health and Social Service Records: Where Law, Ethics and Clinical Issues Meet*. Chicago: University of Illinois at Chicago Circle, December 1976, pp. 80–99.

Plank, Robert. "Our Underprivileged Communications." *Social Casework* 46, no. 7 (July 1965):430–34.

Reynolds, Mildred. "Privacy and Privilege: Patients', Professionals' and the Public's Rights." *Clinical Social Work Journal* 5, no. 1 (1977):29–42.

Roth, L. H., and Meisel, A. "Dangerousness, Confidentiality, and the Duty to Warn." *American Journal of Psychiatry* 134, no. 5 (1977):508–511.

Sadoff, Robert L. "Informed Consent, Confidentiality and Privilege in Psychiatry: Practical Applications." *Bulletin of the American Academy of Psychiatry and Law* 2, no. 2 (June 1974):101–106.

Slovenko, Ralph. "Psychiatrist-Patient Testimonial Privilege: A Picture of Misguided Hope." *Catholic University Law Review* 23 (1974):649–73.

Slovenko, Ralph. "Psychiatry and a Second Look at Medical Privilege." *Wayne Law Review* 6, no. 2 (Spring 1960):175–207.

Slovenko, Ralph. *Psychiatry and Law.* Boston: Little, Brown, 1973.

Slovenko, Ralph. "Psychotherapy and Confidentiality." *Cleveland State Law Review* 24 (1975):375–96.

Slovenko, Ralph, and Usdin, Gene L. "Privileged Communication and Right of Privacy in Diagnosis and Therapy." *Current Psychiatric Therapies.* Vol. 3. New York: Grune & Stratton, 1963, pp. 177–319.

Slovenko, Ralph, and Usdin, Gene L. *Psychotherapy, Confidentiality and Privileged Communication.* Springfield, Ill.: Charles C. Thomas, 1966.

Stone, A. A. "The Tarasoff Decisions: Suing Psychotherapists to Safeguard Society." *Harvard Law Review* 90, no. 2 (1976):358–78.

Tarasoff v. Regents of the University of Calif., 13 Ca. 3d 177 (1974).

"Tarasoff v. Regents of University of California: The Psychotherapist's Peril." *University of Pittsburgh Law Review* 37 (Fall 1975):155–68.

PROBLEM-ORIENTED RECORDING

Abrams, Kathleen Shea; Neville, Robert; and Becker, Marjorie C. "Problem-Oriented Recording of Psychosocial Problems." *Archives of Physical Medicine and Rehabilitation* 54 (July 1973):316–19.

Biagi, Ettore. "The Social Work Stake in Problem-Oriented Recording." *Social Work in Health Care* 3, no. 2 (Winter 1977):211–22.

Burrill, George. "The Problem-Oriented Log in Social Casework." *Social Work Journal* 21, no. 1 (January 1976):67.

Finestein, Alvain R. "The Problems of the Problem Oriented Medical Record." *Annals of Internal Medicine* 78, no. 5 (May 1973):751–62.

Gilandas, Alex John. "The Problem-Oriented Record in a Psychiatric Hospital." *Journal of Hospital and Community Psychiatry* 23, no. 11 (November 1972):336–39.

Grant, Richard L., and Maletzky, Barry M. "Application of the Weed System to Psychiatric Records." *Psychiatry in Medicine* 3 (1972):119–29.

Hartman, Barbara L., and Wickey, Jane M. "The Person-Oriented Record in Treatment." *Social Work* 23, no. 4 (July 1978):296–99.

Houghton, Lisbeth. "Problem-Oriented Medical Recording: A Challenge to Improved Patient Care." *Proceedings of the Tenth Annual Meeting of the Society for Hospital Social Work Directors*, American Hospital Association, September 24–26, 1975, Kansas City, Missouri, sec. 3.

Johnson, Harriette C. "Integrating the Problem-Oriented Record with a Systems Approach to Case Assessment." *Journal of Education for Social Work* 14, no. 3 (Fall 1978):71–77.

Kane, Rosalie A. "Look to the Record." *Social Work* 19, no. 4 (July 1974):412–19.

Lesser, Richard, and Marino-Nigut, Leslie. "Problem-Oriented Recording and Management by Objectives: Two Tools of Accountability." *Proceedings of the Tenth Annual Meeting of the Society for Hospital Social Work Directors*, American Hospital Association, September 24–26, 1975, Kansas City, Missouri, sec. 3.

Martens, Wilma M., and Holmstrup, Elizabeth. "Problem-Oriented Recording." *Social Casework* 55, no. 9 (November 1974):554–61.

Mazur, Walter P., *The Problem-Oriented System in the Psychiatric Hospital: A Complete Manual for Mental Health Professionals.* Garden Grove, Calif.: Trainex Corporation, 1974.

Ryback, Ralph S. *The Problem-Oriented Record in Psychiatry and Mental Health Care.* New York: Grune & Stratton, 1974.

Ryback, Ralph S., and Gardner, Johanna S. "Problem Formation: The Problem-Oriented Record." *American Journal of Psychiatry* 130 (March 1973):312–16.

Spitzer, Kurt, and Welsh, Bettey. "A Problem-Focused Model of Practice." *Social Casework* 50, no. 6 (June 1969):323–29.

Veterans Administration, Social Work Service. *Documenting Quality Social Services Utilizing the P.O.M.R. System.* Washington, D.C.: VA, June 1976. Unpublished proposal that was not implemented.

Weed, Lawrence L. *Medical Records, Medical Education and Patient Care.* Cleveland: Case Western Reserve University Press, 1969.

PSYCHODYNAMICS OF HUMAN BEHAVIOR (BASIC TEXTS)

Ackerman, Nathan W. *The Psychodynamics of Family Life.* New York: Basic Books, 1968.

American Handbook of Psychiatry. 2d ed. New York: Basic Books, 1974, 1975. This comes in six volumes:

Volume 1: *The Foundations of Psychiatry*, ed. Silvano Arieti.

Volume 2: *Child and Adolescent Psychiatry*, ed. Gerald Caplan.

Volume 3: *Adult Clinical Psychiatry*, ed. Silvano Arieti and Eugene Brody.

Volume 4: *Organic Disorders and Psychosomatic Medicine*, ed. Morton F. Reiser.

Volume 5: *Treatment*, ed. Daniel X. Freedman and Jarl E. Dyrud.

Volume 6: *New Psychiatric Frontiers*, ed. David A. Hamburg and H. Keith H. Brodie.

Cameron, Norman. *Personality Development and Psychopathology: A Dynamic Approach.* Boston: Houghton Mifflin, 1963.

Coleman, James C. *Abnormal Psychology and Modern Life.* 5th ed. Glenview, Ill.: Scott, Foresman, 1976.

Erikson, Erik. *Childhood and Society.* New York: Norton, 1963. See esp. the chapter on "Eight Ages of Man," pp. 247–74, which discusses life-cycle stages.

Erikson, Erik. *Psychological Issues, Vol. I, No. I, Monograph I: Identity and the Life Cycle.* New York: International Universities Press, 1959.

Fraiberg, Selma H. *The Magic Years.* New York: Scribner, 1959.

Freud, Ana. *The Writings of Ana Freud, vol. 6, 1965: Normality and Pathology in Childhood—Assessments of Development.* New York: International Universities Press, 1965.

Goldenson, Robert M., ed.; Dunham, Jerome R.; and Dunham, Charlie S., associate eds. *Disability and Rehabilitation Handbook.* New York: McGraw-Hill, 1978.

Group for the Advancement of Psychiatry. *Normal Adolescence.* New York: GAP, 1968.

Hall, Calvin S., and Lindzey, Gardner. *Theories of Personality.* New York: Wiley, 1957.

Kolb, Lawrence C. *Modern Clinical Psychiatry.* 9th ed. Philadelphia: Saunders, 1977.

Mussen, Paul; Conger, John; and Kagan, Jerome. *Child Development and Personality.* New York: Harper & Row, 1963.

Reichel, William, ed. *Clinical Aspects of Aging.* Baltimore: Williams & Wilkins, 1978.

Rowe, Clarence J. *An Outline of Psychiatry.* 6th ed. Dubuque, Iowa: Brown, 1975.

Saul, Leon J. *Emotional Maturity: The Development and Dynamics of Personality and Its Disorders.* 3d ed. Philadelphia: Lippincott, 1971.

Schneiders, Alexander. *Personality Development and Adjustment in Adolescence.* Milwaukee: Bruce, 1960.

Stone, L. Joseph, and Church, Joseph. *Childhood and Adolescence.* New York: Random House, 1966.

RECORDING—GENERAL CONCEPTS

American Hospital Association, Society for Hospital Social Work Directors. *Documentation by Social Workers in Medical Records.* Chicago: AHA, 1978.

Benjamin, Alfred. "Recording the Interview." In *The Helping Interview.* Boston: Houghton Mifflin, 1969, pp. 56–61.

Chea, Mary Wong. "Research on Recording." *Social Casework* 53, no. 3 (March 1972):177.

Davison, Evelyn H. "Case Recording and Reports." In *Social Casework.* 2d ed. Baltimore: Williams & Wilkins, 1970, pp. 94–103.

Dwyer, Margaret, and Urbanowski, Martha. "Student Process Recording: A Plea for Structure." *Social Casework* 46, no. 5 (May 1965):283.

Dyer, Wayne W., and Vriend, John. "Personal Masterpiece Construction: Log-Keeping Guidelines for Counseling Group Members." In *Counseling Techniques that Work.* New York: Funk & Wagnalls, 1977, pp. 266–68.

Dyer, Wayne W., and Vriend, John. "Using a Log to Increase Counselor Skills." In *Counseling Techniques that Work.* New York: Funk & Wagnalls, 1977, pp. 56–93.

Hamilton, Gordon. *Principles of Social Case Recording.* New York: Columbia University Press, 1946 (reprinted in 1973).

Hutter, A. Helen. "Practical Applications of Recording Social Work Activities in a Medical Setting." *Proceedings of the Tenth Annual Meeting of the Society for Hospital Social Work Directors*, American Hospital Association, September 24–26, 1975, Kansas City, Missouri, sec. 2.

Kadushin, Alfred. "Recording." In *The Social Work Interview.* New York: Columbia University Press, 1972, pp. 214–16.

Kogan, Leonard S., and Brown, Benjamin H. "A Two-Year Study of Case Record Uses." *Social Casework* 35, no. 6 (June 1954):252–57.

Lusby, Sarah T., and Rudney, Bernice D. "One Agency's Solution to the Recording Problem." *Social Casework* 54, no. 10 (December 1973):586–90.

Pinkus, Helen. "Recording in Social Work." In *Encyclopedia of Social Work*. Washington, D.C.: NASW, 1977, pp. 1161–68.

Schubert, Margaret. "Recording." In *Interviewing in Social Work Practice: An Introduction*. New York: Council on Social Work Education, 1971, pp. 48–52.

Tuzil, Teresa Jordan. "Writing: A Problem-Solving Process." *Social Work* 23, no. 1 (January 1978):67–69.

Urbanowski, Martha L. "Recording to Measure Effectiveness." *Social Casework* 55, no. 9 (November 1974):546.

Wilke, Charlotte. "A Study of Distortions in Recording Interviews." *Social Work Journal* 8, no. 3 (July 1963):31–36.

Williams, Carter C., and Wien, Janet. "The Casework Letter." *Social Work* 3, no. 1 (January 1958):55–61.

VIDEOTAPING

Berger, Milton M., ed. *Videotape Techniques in Psychiatric Training and Treatment*. Rev. ed. New York: Brunner/Mazel, 1978.

Blackey, Eileen. "The Use of Audio Visual Aids in Training." *Family* 31, no. 9 (November 1950):366–71.

Dyer, Wayne W., and Vriend, John. "Guidelines for Analysis of Group Counseling Tapes." In *Counseling Techniques That Work*. New York: Funk & Wagnalls, 1977, pp. 269–72.

Fields, David Noah. "Legal Implications and Complications—Model Forms for Signed Releases." In Milton M. Berger, ed., *Videotape Techniques in Psychiatric Training and Treatment*. Rev. ed. New York: Brunner/Mazel, 1978, pp. 303–314.

Gruenberg, Peter; Liston, Edward H., Jr.; and Wayne, George J. "Intensive Supervision of Psychotherapy with Videotape Recording." In Milton M. Berger, ed., *Videotape Techniques in Psychiatric Training and Treatment*. Rev. ed. New York: Brunner/Mazel, 1978, pp. 121–25.

Meltzer, Rae. "School and Agency Cooperation in Using Videotape in Social Work Education." *Journal of Education for Social Work* 13, no. 1 (Winter 1977):90–95.

Oswald, Ida, and Wilson, Suzanne. *This Bag Is Not a Toy: A Handbook for the Use of Video Recording in Education for the Professions*. New York: Council on Social Work Education, 1971.

Rhim, Bonnie C. "The Use of Videotapes in Social Work Agencies." *Social Casework* 57, no. 10 (December 1976):644–50.

Rosenbaum, Max. "The Issues of Privacy and Privileged Communication." In Milton M. Berger, ed., *Videotape Techniques in Psychiatric Training and Treatment*. Rev. ed. New York: Brunner/Mazel, 1978, pp. 315–26.